CAMRA'S
101

BEER DAYS OUT

TIM HAMPSON

CAMRA
BOOKS

Picture Acknowledgements

With thanks to all the pubs and breweries who allowed us to use their images. Specific thanks go to:

p3 Cath Harries; p4 (t) Welcome to Yorkshire; (b) Smudge 9000 (Flickr); p6 (t) Welcome to Yorkshire; (b) Kim Adams; p18-19 exfordy (Flickr); p23 & 24 Smudge 9000 (Flickr); p28 (t) exfordy (Flickr); (b) Robert Wicks; p28 Karen Roe (Flickr); p30 & 31 Cath Harries; p35 Jim Holden / Alamy; p33 Ascot Racecourse/RPM; p34 & 35 Katie Hunt; p36 Hayley Wincott (Flickr); p37 Reading Tom (Flickr); p39 (b) Mike Cattell (Flickr); p40 Charles D P Miller (Flickr); p41 iJammin (Flickr); p42-43 Katie Hunt; p46 Cath Harries; p48 Katie Hunt; p49 (t) Katie Hunt; (b) Cath Harries; p50 Cath Harries; p51 Katie Hunt; p52 Ewan Munroe (Flickr); p56-57 HHA124L (Flickr); p59 Felipe KÃ¸s (Flickr); p61 hans s (Flickr); p62 (t) cyesuta (Flickr); (b) John Law; p63 Phil Lowry; p64 & 65 (t) Richard Brooks; p66 Jon Howard; p67 mattbuck4950 (flickr); p68 jonny2love (Flickr); p69 Reading Tom (Flickr); p70 HHA124L (Flickr); p78 jonl1973 (Flickr); p79 (t) Tom Stainer; (b) ianmilne (Flickr); p80-81 Broads Authority/Norfolk Tourism; p83 Katie Hunt; p84 & 85 Martin Pettitt (Flickr); p86 David Merrett (Flickr); p87 ell brown (Flickr); p88 markheybo (Flickr); p89 Warren Wordsworth; p90 (t) Brokentaco (Flickr); p91 ell brown (Flickr); p92 Dave Catchpole (Flickr); p94 & 95 Katie Hunt; p96- 97 andrew_j_w (Flickr); p99 Matthew Black (Flickr); p101 Lee J Haywood (Flickr); p102 shining.darkness (Flickr); p103 Tim Hampson; p104 (t) eyedea (Flickr); (b) Spyke Golding; p105 Cath Harries; p106 (t) Jon's pics (Flickr); (b) Cath Harries; p107 chaosemerald (Flickr); p109 (t) The Rev. Kev. (Flickr); (b) Matthew Black (Flickr); p110-111 Sue HJH (Flickr); p113 Nigel's Europe (Flickr); p114 ell brown (Flickr); p117 Adrian Tierney-Jones; p118 Terry Doran (Flickr); p120 foto footprints (Flickr); p121 Dominic Sayers (Flickr); p122 & 123 ell brown (Flickr); p128 calflier001 (Flickr); p129 calflier001 (Flickr); p130-131 Leftism/Phill (Flickr); p133 psflannery (Flickr); p136 Jonas Smith; p137 (t) eyedropper. co.uk (Flickr); (b) Marcin Chady (Flickr); p139 Adrian Tierney-Jones; p140 (t) Emma Wood / Alamy; p141 leelawrence65 (Flickr); p142 Charlie Dave (Flickr); (b) rbennett661 (Flickr); p143 (t) Charlie Dave (Flickr); p144-145, 148, 149 (t) & 150 Welcome to Yorkshire; p152 (b) Effervescing Elephant; p153 Welcome to Yorkshire; p154 Katie Hunt; p156 Welcome to Yorkshire; p157 Tim Green aka atoach (Flickr); p158 (t) Welcome to Yorkshire; p159 calflier001 (Flickr); p160 (b) ; p162-163 Eric The Fish (2011) (Flickr); p168 Dan Augood (Flickr); p170 Neil Lloyd; p171 (t) ; p172 menu4340 (Flickr); p174 Jozef Mikietyn - Fishing and Angling. / Alamy; p175 (b), 176, 177 & 179 Bob Steel; p180 & 181 Tom Stainer; p182-183 nyaa_birdies_perch (Flickr); p187 Tom Stainer; p191 Conor Lawless (Flickr); p192 kloniwotski (Flickr); p193 Stephen W Conaty (Flickr); p194 milesmilob (Flickr); p195 (t) ahisgett (Flickr); (b) Tomorrow Never Knows (Flickr); p198-199 Shutterstock; p201 CaptainOates (Flickr); p208 www.theedinburghblog. co.uk; p209 (t) lost penguin (Flickr); p211 Shadowgate (Flickr)

CAMRA'S
101

BEER DAYS OUT

Published by the Campaign for Real Ale Ltd.
230 Hatfield Road
St Albans
Hertfordshire AL1 4LW

www.camra.org.uk/books

ISBN 978-1-85249-288-5

A CIP catalogue record for this book is available from the British Library
Printed and bound in China by 1010 Printing International Ltd

Head of Publishing: Simon Hall
Project Editor: Katie Hunt
Editorial Assistance: Emma Haines
Copy Editor: Simon Tuite
Indexer: Jane Coulter
Design/Typography: Linda Storey, Top Floor Design Ltd
Cartography: Mark Walker
Head of Marketing: Tony Jerome

Every effort has been made to ensure the contents of this book are correct at
the time of printing. Nevertheless, the Publisher cannot be held responsible
for any errors or omissions, or for any changes in the details given in this
guide, or for the consequences of any reliance on the information provided
by the same. This does not affect your statutory rights.

Contents

Yorkshire Moors

Cameron's Brewery, Hartlepool

Faversham Hop Festival

Key to book symbols

Breweries and visitor centres   Pubs and pub walks   Festivals   Transport

   Family-friendly Days Out

Haworth,
Yorkshire

Introduction

Walk through almost any town or city in Britain and, if you know what to look for, it will be hard not to uncover some evidence that brewing, or an activity related to it, once took place there – a sign might say Brewery Lane, a building might be called the Malt House or pub could be named Coopers.

Stand in the shadows of one of our great towering cathedrals and you can find pubs where, hundreds of years ago, monks would provide beer as sustenance for weary pilgrims. Visit an old country house and there will be evidence that beer was once brewed for everyone in the household: from the master and his wife to the humblest chambermaid.

Beer runs like a rich golden seam through the culture, history and scientific endeavour of our islands. Beer has contributed to the health of the nation. The people who made it were often at the forefront of technology. The generations of hop pickers who travelled to the hop fields for the annual harvest are part of the rich tapestry of this country's folklore, with a place in our art, music and literature.

But this book is much more than a paean to our beer heritage – it is an opportunity to a visit a new Britain which is once more at the cutting edge of beer innovation, to see and experience some fabulous places from city to country to coast and uncover their beery links, and often to entertain the whole family at the same time. It seeks to show beer as part of a much bigger picture, with the mushrooming of new breweries in recent years part of a growing awareness of and interest in where our food and drink comes from, and the regional differences in it that make travelling through Britain such a gastronomic adventure. And of course for those who want their liquid education to be more than just academic, there are plenty of fabulous places to indulge in the practice of sipping a pint and marvelling at the skill of the farmers, maltsers and brewers who made it happen – not forgetting the people in the pub who make sure it is served properly.

The Albatros, Wells-next-the-Sea

Following beer's fascinating journey

With a history going back thousands of years, beer is this country's, if not the world's most popular drink.

It is liquid bread and a product made with just four natural ingredients, which produce a product of unrivalled variety: just think all those colours, flavour and aromas. And it just starts with water, hops, a cereal – which is normally barley – and the mysterious enigmatic contribution of living yeast. It is with these simple notes that the great brewers with their skill and passion create a symphony of swirling, memorable tastes.

Some regard barley as the soul of beer, for it provides the nutrients that feed the yeast and persuade it to produce alcohol. Fields, where the glorious Maris Otter and other varieties of barley are grown, can be seen at Teddy Maufe's farm and Real Ale shop in North Norfolk (p91), or at High House Farm in Northumberland (p196). This grain provides the staple for many of the country's growing number of Independent brewers.

But before the brewer can use it, the harvested grain has to go to a maltster, who unlocks the sugars in the grain by starting the process of germination and then stopping it before the growing seed has had a chance to use up the sugars locked inside the grain. The traditional back-breaking work of the maltster can be seen at Tuckers Maltings in Newton Abbott in Devon (p72). Modern malthouses might have conveyor belts and computerised operations, but there is something quite evocative about watching men working to turn over the grain in the long, low rooms much as their predecessors did 100 years ago.

Hops are the prima donna ballerinas of the beer world. The bines might grow a towering, winsome five metres

Hops at the Kent Life Museum

tall, but all the brewer needs is minute quantities of the oils and resins from the lupin glands in the small fingernail sized cones, which look like small green flowers on the plant. The hop brings bitterness and aroma to the beer as well as a quality that no other alcoholic drink has – a foaming head. Visit the Kent Life museum near Maidstone (p24) and there is an opportunity to find out much more about these curious plants and how they grow, are harvested, and dried ready for the brewer to use.

With malt and hops ready, the work of the brewer can begin. Many brewers now offer brewery tours, but brewing as the Victorians did it can be experienced at the Hook Norton Brewery in Oxfordshire (p37). Here you can see the mash tun to which the ground malt, known as grist, is added to the heated but not boiling brewing water (known as liquor). Just like the hot water in a

Hook Norton brewery, Oxfordshire

teapot, which draws the goodness out of the tea leaves, the liquor teases the sugar out of the grist.

The sweet liquid now known as wort is transferred to another vessel often called a copper or kettle. The wort is heated up to boiling point and the hops are added releasing their essential oils and resins to the liquid. It is then cooled and transferred into a fermenting vessel, to which hungry yeast cells are added. The yeast voraciously eats the sugars in the wort – expelling carbon dioxide and the by-product which is at the very heart of this book, the alcohol which goes into the drink we call beer. Now, like a well-cooked Sunday roast, the beer needs to rest mature and condition before it is put into casks.

Once beer was stored and served from wooden barrels made by highly skilled coopers. This craft can still be seen at the Theakston brewery in the charming village of Masham in North Yorkshire (p151). Beer is now more likely to be served from steel casks, but either way

it now needs to be taken to a pub: a task once undertaken by horse-drawn drays. These gentle equine giants can often be seen in the historic Wiltshire town of Devizes, where the Wadworth brewery (p60) still keeps some horses in a stables close to its visitor centre.

But where to drink the beer so lovingly produced? In this book there are scores of fine pubs which sell good beer. Some can be visited as part of a country stroll, or on a stunning train ride hauled by a steam engine. Beers can be enjoyed at CAMRA's Great British Beer Festival (p52) or at its extravaganza of darker beer, the National Winter Ales Festival (p169). Beer can be enjoyed in some of London's finest buildings or walking along the canals of Birmingham.

Beer can even be enjoyed while watching bog snorkelling in Wales (p139) or the World Marble Championships in West Sussex (p31), or after a day's fishing in the Ribble Valley (p173). And if just drinking it is not enough, should you feel inspired by your journey to make beer, to become a brewer and take water, malt, hops and yeast and sculpt your own brews – then you can learn to do it like a professional on a course at Brewlab in Sunderland (p187).

From the Orkneys in the north to the foot of Cornwall, the opportunity for a Beer Day Out is as almost as limitless as the variety of beers available to try.

The National Brewery Centre Staffordshire

Beer Days Out calendar

January
- National Winter Ales Festival
  nwaf.org.uk (p169)

February
- Liverpool Beer Festival
  www.liverpoolcamra.org.uk (p172)

March
- Bristol Beer Festival
  www.camrabristol.org.uk (p64)

April
- World Marbles Championship,
  Greyhound, Tinsley Green (p31)
- Maltings Beer Festival, Newton Abbot
  www.tuckersmaltings.com (p72)

May
- Furry Dance, Helston (p78)
- Isle of Man TT
  www.iomtt.com (p179)

June
- Great Welsh Beer & Cider Festival,
  Cardiff
  www.gwbcf.org.uk (p135)
- Scottish Real Ale Festival, Edinburgh
  scottishbeerfestival.org.uk (p207)
- Newcastle Hoppings
  www.newcastle-hoppings.co.uk (p91)

July
- Tramlines Music Festival, Sheffield
  www.tramlines.org.uk (p160)

August
- Great British Beer Festival, London
  www.gbbf.org.uk (p52)
- Kilverts Ale & Literature Festival
  www.kilverts.co.uk (p138)
- Mountain bike bog snorkelling,
  Llanwrtyd Wells (p139)

September
- Bromyard Hop Festival
  www.bromyardhopfestival.co.uk (p127)
- Faversham Hop Festival
  www.thehopfestival.com (p23)
- Minehead Beer Festival
  www.wsr.org.uk (p67)
- National Homebrew Competition,
  Bristol
  www.bristolhomebrewcompetition.org.
  uk (p63)
- Abergavenny Food Festival
  www.abergavennyfoodfestival.com
  (p136)
- Liverpool Pubs Festival
  www.liverpoolcamra.org.uk (p172)
- Amber Valley Beer Festival
  www.derbycamra.org.uk/ambervalley
  (p106)
- St Albans Beer Festival
  www.stalbansbeerfestival.com (p94)

October
- Ascot Beer Festival
  ascotbeerfest.seberkscamra.org.uk
  (p32)
- Nottingham Robin Hood Beer Festival
  and Festival Fringe Fortnight
  www.beerfestival.nottinghamcamra.org
  (p102)
- Norwich Beer Festival
  www.norwichcamra.org.uk (p87)

November
- Guy Fawkes night, Lewes
  www.lewesbonfirecouncil.org.uk (p30)
- World's Biggest Liar competition,
  Bridge Inn, Santon Bridge
  www.santonbridgeinn.com/liar (p177)
- Celtic Beer Festival, St Austell
  www.staustellbrewery.co.uk (p76)

December
- Pigs Ear Beer Festival, London
  www.pigsear.org.uk (p51)

A year of beer festivals

CAMRA's beer festivals are magnificent shop windows for cask ale and they give you the opportunity to sample beers both from the local region and all over the country.

Beer festivals are enormous fun: many offer good food and live entertainment, and – where possible – facilities for families. Some seasonal festivals specialise in spring, summer, autumn and winter ales. Festivals range in size from small local events to large regional ones. CAMRA holds two national festivals, the National Winter Ales Festival in January, and the Great British Beer Festival in August; the latter features around 500 beers.

The festivals listed here are regularly occurring. For up-to-date information, visit the beer festivals CAMRA website www.camra.org.uk/beerfestivals.

January

National Winter Ales (Manchester)
Atherton – Bent & Bongs Beer Bash
Cambridge – Winter
Colchester – Winter
Exeter – Winter
Newark – Winter
Salisbury – Winter

February

Battersea
Chappel – Winter
Chelmsford – Winter
Chesterfield
Derby – Winter
Dorchester
Dover – White Cliffs Winter
Fleetwood
Gosport – Winter
Liverpool
Luton
Pendle
Redditch
Stockton – Ale & Arty
Tewkesbury – Winter

March

Bradford
Bristol
Burton – Spring
Coventry

Darlington – Spring
Hitchin
Hove – Sussex
Leeds
Leicester
London Drinker
Loughborough
Overton (Hampshire)
St Neots – Booze on the Ouse
Walsall
Whitehaven
Wigan
Winchester

April

Barnsley
Bexley
Bury St Edmunds – East Anglian
Chippenham
Doncaster
Farnham
Glenrothes – Kingdom of Fife
Larbert – Falkirk
Maldon
Mansfield
Newcastle-upon-Tyne
Paisley
Thanet

May

Banbury
Cambridge

Colchester
Halifax
Kingston
Lincoln
Macclesfield
Newark
Newport (Gwent)
Northampton – Delapre Abbey
Reading
Stourbridge
Stratford-upon-Avon
Thurrock
Wolverhampton
Yapton

June

Aberdeen
Braintree
Cardiff – Great Welsh
Chappel Cider Festival
Edinburgh – Scottish
Gibberd Garden – Harlow
Harpenden
Lewes – South Downs
Rugby
Salisbury
Southampton
St Ives (Cornwall)
Skipton
Stockport
Tenterden – Kent & East Sussex Railway
Woodchurch – Rare Breeds

July

Ardingly
Bishops Stortford
Bromsgrove
Canterbury – Kent
Chelmsford
Ealing
Derby
Devizes
Hereford – Beer on the
  Wye
Plymouth
Rochford – South East
  Essex Cider Festival
Stafford
Stowmarket
Winchcombe – Cotswold
Windsor
Woodcote – Steam Fair

August

Great British Beer Festival,
  London
Barnstaple
Clacton
Grantham
Harbury
Ipswich
Peterborough
Swansea
Watnall – Moorgreen
Worcester

September

Ascot
Bridgnorth – Severn Valley
Burton
Carmarthen
Chappel
Darlington – Rhythm 'N'
  Brews
Durham
East Malling (Kent)
Faversham – Hop
Hinckley
Jersey
Keighley
Letchworth

Lytham
Melton Mowbray
Minehead
Nantwich
Newton Abbot
North Cotswolds –
  Moreton-in-Marsh
Northwich
Ripley – Derbyshire
St Albans
Scunthorpe
Shrewsbury
Southport
St Ives (Cambs) – Booze
  on the Ouse
Tamworth
Ulverston
York

October

Alloa
Ayrshire Real Ale Festival
  – Troon
Barnsley
Basingstoke
Bath
Bedford
Birkenhead
Birmingham
Cambridge – Octoberfest
Carlisle
Chester
Chesterfield – Market
Eastbourne
Egremont, Cumbria
Falmouth
Gainsborough
Huddersfield –
  Oktoberfest
Kendal
Long Eaton
Louth
Milton Keynes
Norwich
Nottingham
Oxford
Poole
Quorn Octoberfest
Redhill

Richmond (N Yorks.)
St Helens
Sawbridgeworth
Sheffield
Solihull
Stoke-on-Trent – Potteries
Sunderland
Swindon
Thanet – Cider
Twickenham
Wallington
Weymouth
Woolston – Southampton
Worthing

November

Dudley
Heathrow
Rochford
Saltburn
Wakefield
Wantage
Watford
Whitchurch (Hampshire)
Woking

December

Harwich
London – Pig's Ear

Going local for cask beer

We are all going local. There is a growing move towards stocking locally-produced products in our shops, restaurants and pubs. The words "locally sourced" are frequently seen on menus and advertisements.

If offered a choice, most people will say they would rather eat meat or vegetables produced on a local farm. They know the food will be fresh, and its production employs local people and keeps cash in the local economy. Most of us want to see fewer food miles being driven: it is environmental madness that lamb reared on the slopes of the Brecon Beacons in Wales could be sent to a wholesaler in London only to return to be sold in a local butcher's shop.

Well, the same goes for beer. It is a boom time for local brewers. Once there were some parts of the country where breweries were rarer than a hen's tooth. Today, there are more than 900 breweries in the UK, and most of us are likely to live within a few miles of at least one brewery making local beers.

Areas such as Yorkshire have seen an explosion in their number of breweries. Between them East, West, North and South Yorkshire have more than 100, producing quality beers using the finest raw materials – malt and hops – to make their ales. Britain is a great place to be drinking good beer.

Most of the new wave of brewers are very small producers – proud to stand shoulder to shoulder with local butchers, bakers and candlestick makers. One example is Welbeck Abbey Brewery (p107), which is housed in a listed barn on the Welbeck Abbey estate in north Nottinghamshire. Its beers are being made in close proximity to a bakery and a butchery, where many people come and learn the artisanal skills needed to make local products

And be it beer, bread or freshly made sausages, the shop on the estate is proud to sell their wares.

Equally exciting is the Cropton Brewery at the New Inn (p147) in North Yorkshire. When the brewery opened in 1984 it bought much needed jobs to a part of the country which had not had its own brewery for years. Close to the beauties of the North Yorkshire Moors National Park, it has thrived, and keeps outgrowing its capacity, as the demand for its beers has been so high.

Another example of a rural success story is the High House Farm in Matfen in Tyne & Wear (p196), where brewing began in 2003. Farmer-turned-brewer Steve Urwin was desperate to find an alternative form of income for his 200-acre farm, following the devastation caused by an outbreak of foot and mouth disease. His concept of emphasising the links between the farm and the glass, by making a beer from malt made from his own barley harvest has bought some hard-earned success. Many pubs in the area sell High House beers, and the farm itself has become a

Purity ales are made at their eco-friendly Warwickshire brewery

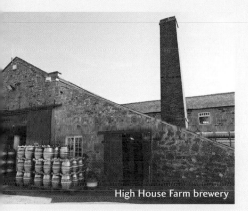
High House Farm brewery

tourist attraction as many travel to visit the brewery and enjoy walking in the dramatic countryside which surrounds it. Some say marriages are made in heaven – well they can now be made in a brewery. High House's latest venture is the acquisition of a wedding licence and they are now getting plenty of booking for weddings and civil ceremonies.

Business is thriving at Purity brewery (p124). The purpose-built brewery is housed in a converted barn in rural Warwickshire. Like most of the new wave of brewers it is proud of its green credentials, and even has its own wildlife sanctuary, which acts as a natural cleaning system for the company's waste water. A system of wetland reed beds and ponds filter and break down the any "nasties" in the water before it is returned into a local stream.

The microbrewery scene is flourishing, with over 250 opening since 2006. Many of the 6,000 beers now being produced by microbreweries are probably only available in a few pubs local to the brewery. This is why being a beer traveller is so rewarding. Yes it is possible to walk into a pub in Dagenham and see the same beers as sold in a pub in Durham or even Dundee, but what is even more exciting is to walk into a pub

and see a CAMRA LocAle sign, which guarantees at least one ale in the pub comes from a local brewery employing local people. And in an era when the large pub companies seem intent on shutting down well-loved locals, many of our small microbreweries are buying pubs, and are breathing life back into local communities.

The Titanic brewery in Stoke on Trent now has six pubs in its fleet. The company has a policy of taking on ailing pubs and turning them into much loved locals selling lots of real ales. The latest is the Roebuck in Leek, Staffordshire. After a much needed refurbishment the once rundown business was reopened in 2011 and it has quickly established itself as the best in town. Up to 10 real ales are regularly on tap.

Another bubbling success is the Acorn Brewery in South Yorkshire. Set up in 2003 it has just bought its first pub. Acorn owners Dave and Judi Hughes have invested £180,000 into the revival of the Old No 7 in Market Hill, which dates back to the 18th century.

Back in 1973 a British economist named Ernst Schumacher wrote a series of essays published as a book called *Small is Beautiful*. The essays were a challenge to an energy crisis – the price of petrol was on the increase – and globalisation was on the march. Does this all sound familiar? He challenged the notion that "bigger is better". In the case of the UK's microbrewing revolution, small is definitely more beautiful than a world dominated by a few international beer brands and chains of plastic pubs, which all seem to look the same. The consumer drive for local beers is empowering hundreds of small eco-friendly businesses using locally sourced ingredients. Small is definitely beautiful.

Beer styles

Once it would have been possible to know the style of beer that people drank by the region they were in.

Very hoppy bitters were found in Kent, London and the Thames valley. London was famed for its darker styles of porter and stout beer. Softer and sweeter bitters were common in the Midlands, whilst fruity flavoursome ales often with a distinctive sulphurous nose hailed from Burton. Malty brews sang their heart out in the valleys of Wales, while Scottish drinkers' palates danced to sweeter brews. The beers of Yorkshire were neither dominated by the sweet biscuity notes of malted barley or the fruity tones of zesty, spicy hops, but were, in a most uncharacteristic Yorkshire fashion, softer and mellower than their fellow beers from the further north or south. In the North East there were tawny ales and pale and dark milds were found in the West Midlands.

City Arms, Cardiff

These regional beers can still be found, often brewed by companies whose roots go back not just into the last century but the one before that. We should treasure these fabulous beers, however today's brewers are inspired not just by the past but by changing consumer tastes and exciting developments that are taking place in countries such as the US, Italy, Denmark and even Japan.

Brewers are no longer bound by rigid classifications. Fruits can be added to beer, as can honey, herbs, heather, spices, and even spirit – brandy and rum feature in a number of speciality beers. One of the best brewers in this country, Sharp's Stuart Howe, says the number of beers styles is limited only by the imagination of the person making the beer.

The skill and craft of these brewers is greater than that of the greatest winemakers. A glass of vintage wine could cost you hundreds of pounds but a glass of beer of an equivalent standard is likely to cost you little more, often less, than a takeaway coffee.

Today, there is no need for brewers to be constrained by an accident of geography to define the beers they make.

In America, experts say there are now nearly 200 different styles of beer. But for the sake of brevity what follow are some broad style definitions. When you go into a pub you will find some, most or even more than the styles listed here. If in doubt ask about the characteristics of an unknown beer from a member of staff behind the bar and don't be shy about requesting a small sample to taste before you make up your mind what to buy.

Bitter

Walk into any pub or bar of note and it should have a bitter on the bar. It is the signature style of British cask beer. It evolved from the hoppy ales developed in the late 18th century.  Typically they will be deep bronze or copper in colour due to the use of slightly darker malts, such as crystal, that gives the beer its fullness of palate. Most brewers produce a range of bitters of different strengths. A few are being produced as low as 2.8% abv. Dubbed the "people's pints", they are being produced to take advantage of a new lower tax for beers of this strength. However, most fall within a band from 3.4% up to 5%.

Golden ale

The first new native beer style to have emerged in Britain since the 19th century, golden ales are particularly popular with the new wave of brewers. They are now so popular that they have their own category in CAMRA's annual Champion Beer of Britain competition. Exmoor Gold and Hop Back Summer Lightning launched the trend in the early 1980s and other brewers quickly followed suit as many drinkers were showing a preference for  lighter coloured beers, which are served lower in temperature than one would expect for a bitter.

Generally, they are brewed with paler malts, which are often used to make lagers. Traditionally, British brewers tended to use English hops such as Fuggles and Goldings for their beers, however, golden ales often use hops from American, New Zealand, Germany, Slovenia or the Czech Republic and lots of them. They tend to be very aromatic beers with lots of spicy, floral notes. The popularity of golden ales has also seen some of the beers in the bitter category make greater use of aromatic hops, though there have always been light coloured easy drinking beers in Britain, such as Boddington's Bitter.

Pale ale and India Pale Ale

Pale ales came into being almost by accident: 17th century brewers were looking to save on the amount of money they spent buying malt,  which tended to be dark in colour and low in fermentable sugar. More efficient, cheaper methods of kilning were developed, which produced malts which were lighter in colour and hadn't had all their sugar content burnt away. These lighter malts produced lighter coloured beers which, with the development of glasswear to drink from, started to prove very popular with drinkers.

 The best known pale ales are India Pale Ales (IPAs), strong hoppy ales which dominated the export trade to India. Bottled Worthington White Shield is a surviving descendant of this style. There has been a renewal of interest in IPAs in recent years, a trend which began in the USA. These new age IPAs are often strong, 7% and up, and are normally very heavily hopped with American hops.

Porter and Stout

Porter was probably the first beer to be produced on an industrial scale, at the start of the 18th century. The use of darker malts tended to create beers full of roasted flavours which were black in colour. However there are few examples of 19th century beers which were also called stouts but they were lighter in colour. In the same way – something which makes it difficult to produce a definitive list of beer styles – it is possible to have a black IPA. The word stout indicated the strength of the drink and not its colour. The strongest version of porter was dubbed stout porter or stout for short. The name porter was the result of the beer's popularity with the porters working the streets, markets and docks of 18th-century London.

The best known example of stout was made by Guinness, and for many years it was the predominant brand for the style in the country and most pubs would serve it. However in recent years many brewers have begun brewing their own version of a stout or porter. Some have been searching through old recipe books as with Hook Norton's Double Stout – a 100-year-old beer bought back to life – others have been creating brand new recipes.

Mild

Mild was once the most popular style of beer in Britain but it was overtaken by bitter in the 1950s. Generally, mild beers are assumed to be mild in terms of hop bitterness or strength, but the original distinction was mild in the sense of fresh, as opposed to beers which had been stored for longer and were likely to be stronger in flavour.

As a general rule, milds are likely to be darker, sweeter than and not as strong as bitter beer. In their heyday these were the beers of the working classes, who needed to rehydrate after a day spent labouring in the fields or in a factory. As this way of life disappeared, the style was in danger of being lost completely as brewers stopped producing a mild. However, campaigning by CAMRA, with promotions like Mild Month in May, has seen a resurgence of interest in the style.

Early milds were much stronger that modern interpretations, which tend to fall in the 3% to 3.5% category, though Rudgate's Dark Ruby Mild at 4.4% is more in keeping with earlier strengths. Mild is usually dark brown in colour, due to the use of well-roasted malts or roasted barley, but there are paler versions such as Banks's Mild, Timothy Taylor's Golden Best and McMullen's AK.

Old ale

Another beer which harks back to the beginning of the industrial revolution,

old ale is generally a beer which has been stored in a large wooden vessel for months or even longer. The storage creates swilling lactic sour flavours from wild yeasts, tannins in the wood and even the yeast with which the beer was first brewed. Old ales were often blended with younger beer to make a beer for sale commercially. Greene King's Strong Suffolk and Fuller's Gale's Prize Old Ale are examples of the style.

Barley wine

A strong, often fruity flavoured ale, which is often more than 8.5% on strength and, at its height, was often produced between 10 and 12% abv. These beers were often kept maturing for long periods of time and were often drunk by the nobility. The best-selling barley wine for years was Whitbread's Gold Label, which was sold in small nip bottles, though today it is only available in cans. Fuller's Vintage Ale, at 8.5% is a bottle-conditioned version of its Golden Pride and is brewed with different varieties of malts and hops every year.

Scottish beers

Scotland had its own beers, styles, which tended to be full of malt flavours and were sweeter and less heavily hopped than English beers. Classically, Scottish brewers made a Light, Heavy and Export, which roughly equates to a mild, bitter and IPA, which were often called 60, 70 and 80 Shilling ales from a 19th-century method of invoicing beers according to their strength. Occasionally a brewer would make a 'Wee Heavy' or 90 Shilling ale, the Scottish equivalent of a barley wine.

Wheat beer

Wheat has been used as an ingredient of beer for as long as barley has. However brewers generally prefer to use barley as it is cheaper and easier use in a brew house. The style is quite common on the Continent, where it is mixed with a proportion of barley malt. Typically a Belgian or Bavarian wheat beer is often unfiltered and might appear cloudy. Often herbs and

spices such as coriander and orange peel are added to it. British variations of wheat beers tend to use only a small proportion of the grain in the mash and brewers will filter the beer so it appears clear.

Lambic

Lambic beers are fermented using wild, non-cultured yeasts and bacteria from the surrounding environment. True Lambic beers are made in a specific area around Brussels in Belgium, though other brewers, especially in America, have left wort open to the elements to see what will happen. The resultant beers tend to be sour and acidic, though they can mellow with time. Sugar can be added to make a faro, or young or old vintages can be blended together to make a gueuze. Traditionally, fruit is added to it to make it more palatable – sour cherries for kriek and raspberries for framboise.

Lager

The British version of lager tends to be stylised as mass produced fizzy beers. However, a lager can be dark in the same way as an ale can

be golden. A true lager is one that has fermented at a lower temperature than ale and then left to condition at low temperature for a period of time. The German word lager means to store. The resultant flavours tend to be crisper than fruiter tasting ales.

A number of British brewers are now producing cask conditioned lagers. Harviestoun's Schiehallion, brewed with lager yeast and Herbsucker hops is probably the best known. Peerless also produces a cask lager called Storr.

South East

Scotney Castle, Kent

1. Buckinghamshire
2. Isle of Wight

Days Out

Introducing the South East

Like the lacing down a just-drunk pint glass of fine ale, beer has left its mark across South East England. Brewing is part of the region's rich history.

In Faversham in Kent there is evidence of brewing as long ago as the 12th century. The town is still home to the country's oldest brewing company Shepherd Neame. In addition, much of the county is dominated by the growing and use of hops, a plant first brought to this country at the beginning of the 15th century by traders from Flanders. Shunned, snubbed and even made illegal by some towns it took a hundred years for the antiseptic and aromatic qualities of hops to be widely accepted. English ale had changed for ever: the hop became a key ingredient of beer.

Over time, of course, the hop industry has changed. It was once a massive force in the area, employing thousands of people, particularly at harvest time, but changing tastes and the end of Britain's pre-eminence as a manufacturing nation saw a massive decline in beer production. The country's workforce was no longer ending each working day with pints of sweet beer, their refreshing liquid bread. Hop gardens closed, but today many have new uses as museums and leisure parks and are a celebration of brewing heritage and the vibrant communities the industry supported. And, it is an inspiration to learn that today's generation of hop growers are not living in the past, but are looking for new varieties to satisfy the demand for flavoursome, distinctive ales.

In the pretty Hampshire town of Ringwood there is a brewery which was once at the forefront of a real ale revolution. Founded in the late 1970s it was a precursor for today's boom in microbreweries. If the handful of owners of breweries such as Ringwood had not campaigned so effectively for tax breaks for smaller producers, most of the new generation of innovative microbrewers would not be in business.

Be it a day at the races at Ascot, bonfire night in Lewes, Sussex, sitting next to members of the Sealed Knot society in Oxfordshire or even watching a tense game of marbles under the flight path of a plane from Gatwick airport, the South East also exemplifies the role pubs and beer play in our evolving communities and culture. We should celebrate and enjoy it.

Oast House, Kent Life museum

1

Shepherd Neame – a story brewing for more than 300 years

Faversham has a fine town square, a creek leading to the sea and the largest number of listed medieval buildings in the country – there are more than 50 of them. It is famous in history for making gunpowder, bricks and beer. The first indications of brewing in Faversham date back to 1147, when the town's (now long-gone) great abbey was founded. Such was the abundance of barley and water many brewhouses set up in the area. Tradition has it that Shepherd Neame dates back to 1698, perhaps having moved to its current spot from another site in the town, making it Britain's oldest brewer. It is unclear when the family-owned company first used the name Shepherd Neame: the first recorded appearance of the name is in an advertisement, which appears in the *Kentish Gazette* in 1865, but while the Shepherds are no longer with us, the Neames are still involved with the company. It is this story and others that are told in the Shepherd Neame visitor centre, which is inside a beautifully restored medieval hall house.

The tour of the brewery takes about 80 minutes and leads people behind the scenes of the working brewer. It is proving to be very popular as more than 25,000 people go on the tour annually. Visitors get to see the age-old traditional mash tuns and taste the water used for brewing that comes from the brewery's own well. There is malted barley to be crunched and aromatic Kentish hops for rubbing and smelling. A magnificent

Shepherd Neame beer and food evening

stained glass window in the brewery shows traditional scenes associated with beer making such as hop picking in Kent. The tour also includes the vaults, once used as a large wine and spirit store. It now features an impressive collection of brewery delivery vehicles, including an old Thorneycroft dray, old pub signs, hop picking equipment and an old cooper's workshop. The tour ends with a tasting of the company's famed hoppy beers. As well as guided tours and tastings there are themed beer and food evenings, murder mysteries, ale samplers' suppers, father's day lunches and even Halloween ghost tours.

Over the first weekend of September the town hosts a Hop Festival, which takes place in the streets outside the brewery. Faversham is also famed for its annual Classic Car Show, held each May. Petrolheads can enjoy a weekend of vintage bus displays and rides, hundreds of classic cars and motorcycles, and even a 1960s steam train.

Visitor information:

Shepherd Neame
17 Court Street, Faversham, Kent,
ME13 7AX
01795 542016
www.shepherdneame.co.uk
Tours of the brewery and tickets for
events must be booked in advance

Getting there and away: Faversham
rail station is 10 minutes' walk from
Shepherd Neame brewery.

A Kentish tradition – the Faversham Hop Festival

Something else Faversham is famous for is its raucous Hop Festival, held on the first weekend of September, which spills out over the town's streets and pubs. The whole town seemingly plays host to this traditional celebration, centred on the medieval town square and surrounding streets. The two-day festival is a vibrant gala in honour of beer and its natural roots, of the hop harvest and of the heyday of hop picking, when thousands of Londoners came down to the Kentish hop gardens every September for a so-called country holiday with pay. Life in London must have been pretty tough if people found picking hops a holiday! Many families returned to the same farms, generation after generation, to be joined by every available local worker to form the largest seasonal agricultural workforce this country has ever seen.

The festival provides a link between one of the natural raw materials that makes beer and the pubs where people drink it. Street corners and pavements become theatres for dance groups and musicians. Vendors sell bines of hops and many people wear garlands of hop cones. Pub gardens become rock gardens and crowds move from pub to pub to hear their favourite bands or look

Colourful parade at the Faversham Hop Festival

for something different. In addition, there are three live music stages in the town showcasing folk groups, rock bands and local musicians. The carnival-like atmosphere offers something for all tastes. And of course there is beer – with Shepherd Neame's products playing a starring role. Its Master Brew Bitter is a sublime example of the British art of brewing lower strength beers which still manage to be full of taste. Not too strong, at 3.7% abv, it is full of rich robust citrus aromas, a deep bitterness and a long, lingering finish from the use of the Kent-grown hops.

It is possible to travel to the festival, and many people do, by steam train from London or other stations in the area. The Spitfire steam train retraces the route of hop pickers from decades earlier. The train, made up of historic carriages from the 1950s and 1960s, features a real ale bar with casks of hoppy Shepherd Neame beer.

3

The Kent Life museum – hopping down in Kent

For families wanting to experience farm life in Kent and see at first hand crops growing, animals grazing and the buildings in which people lived over the last 250 years, the Kent Life heritage farm is the place to come. It also offers an opportunity to learn more about the importance of hop growing. Set within 28 acres, there are plenty of opportunities to see the pigs, chickens, goats, ducks, geese, cattle and, in the springtime, gambolling lambs, all living at the museum, which doubles as a working farm. There is also a collection of historic Kentish farm buildings. These have been saved from destruction, restored and rebuilt on the site. Several of the buildings are used for demonstrations of country crafts. The museum also has two working hop gardens. Here hops are grown, harvested, dried and packed by hand. There is also a working oast house, which has the classic pointed roofs with conical white cowls, recognisable to anyone travelling through the area.

An oast house, for those not in the know, is the place hops were dried and is a design virtually unknown outside Kent and East Sussex; other hop-growing areas have far more prosaic and less attractive buildings for drying hops. Today, most of Kent's remaining oast houses have been converted into chic residences, but the one here is sill being used for its original purpose and is the last in the country to be coal

Hop pickers

fired. Once a year, in September, the fire is lit and used to dry the hops harvested from the museum's two hop gardens. The farm grows Fuggles and Goldings hops; these are the classic bittering and aromatic hops used by generations of British brewers. The Fuggles has a typical English bitter flavour and is frequently blended with Goldings to improve the drinkability of the beer, as it adds roundness and fullness to the palate. The farm also has a display of the hopper huts, the temporary

dwellings once used by generations of itinerant pickers, often traveling down from London for a working holiday. It is hard to imagine what life would have been like in the huts, which seem no bigger than a garden shed, especially as some housed whole families. The great English essayist George Orwell spent two months picking hops in Kent in 1931; if you'd like to read how he got on, much of his experience is recounted in *A Clergyman's Daughter*. He described the hop-picker's hut as being leaky, draughty and worse than a stable. It had no furniture save a heap of straw, and the latrine was 200 yards away. So much for the rural idyll!

If the thought of hops is making you thirsty, then head for the Flower Pot in nearby Maidstone, a freehouse which serves a great range of ales from Kentish micros and others around Britain. Nine handpumps adorn the bar, dispensing ales from the likes of Goacher's, Kent Brewery and Dark Star. The Goacher's Gold Star it sells is an example of the harmonious glory created by a cocktail of floor-malted Marris Otter malt and finest East Kent Golding hops which give a bitter sweet, herbal hoppy finish to this dangerously drinkable ale.

Visitor information:

Kent Life
Lock Lane, Sandling, Maidstone,
Kent, ME14 3AU
01622 763936
www.kentlife.org.uk

Flower Pot
96 Sandling Road, Maidstone,
Kent, ME14 2RJ
01622 757705
www.flowerpotpub.com
12 (11 Sat)–11; 12–10.30 Sun

Getting there and away: Kent Life is close to Junction 6 on the M20.

Oast houses, Hop Farm Family Park

4

Hop Farm Family Park – quite a dray out

Once this place was a thriving hop farm. How times have changed, as it is now a vibrant leisure park, and though some might find some of its facilities brash, it really does offer a fun family day out.

The Hop Farm Family Park is one giant playground for children, with jungles, dinosaurs, a pirate cove, a maze and all manner of other attractions. However, it still pays more than a passing nod to its one-time important role in the brewing of beer. In the heart of Kent, between Maidstone and Tonbridge, the Hop Farm is situated in a largely rural area. It was bought by the Whitbread brewery in 1920 as a farm for its hops. With its collection of 32 cowl-topped oast houses, which are home to an exhibition of the history of hops, it has long been a Kent landmark and is now one of the region's most popular tourist attractions.

The farm was also formerly home to the Whitbread dray horses, and horses still form an important feature at the attraction. Shires are the gentle giants of the animal world. They evoke images of a world long gone, when these were the workhorses of farms and industry and as commonplace as the Transit van.

Just seeing shires in a field or delivering beer is one thing, but touching them and learning more about these placid animals is something else. The Hop Farm offers shire horse experience days when people can learn how to groom a horse and plait its mane. There is a chance to harness the horse and hitch it to a wagon before having a go at driving it, and later unharnessing and giving it a feed. It is tiring work both for the horse and the willing participants.

Thankfully, about 10 minutes' drive away there are two great real ale pubs at which to quench your thirst. The Halfway House in Brenchley is a picture-book pretty pub. Built in 1790, this former coaching inn has a large garden and is renowned for its barbecues, beer festivals and tug of war competitions. Inside, it is a maze of small, interconnecting rooms on different levels, all exhibiting a degree of antiquity and cosiness that is the hallmark of this pub, which has up to eight different ales crowded onto the bar. Often on the bar is Goacher's Fine Light Ale, brewed in nearby Maidstone. A pale amber light bitter, almost straw in colour, it has a tantalising floral hop character which comes, of course, from the locally grown hops.

Just down the road is the Hopbine, in the quiet hamlet of Petteridge. Small and largely unspoilt, it has an attractive traditional Kentish white boarded and tiled exterior and has been listed in CAMRA's *Good Beer Guide* for 25 years. The two-bar pub is a great place to try a K&B Bitter, brewed by Hall & Woodhouse. Once upon a time this beer hailed from the Sussex town of Horsham; it now comes from Blandford Forum, in Dorset. A lightly hopped beer, it has a refreshing taste and is satisfying without bowling people over with unnecessary bitterness or strength.

5

Hop growing – Westerham and Scotney Castle

Hop growing is no small beer in the county of Kent; in fact, it's hard to get away from it, as you may have gathered by now. And, at the National Trust's Scotney Castle, they hope it is going to be good for business. The estate gives you two houses for the price of one: at the top of a hill is a Victorian-built Elizabethan-style house, at the bottom are the entrancing ruins of a 14th-century castle and moat. In addition, it is also a working farm; the Little Scotney farm has several large hop gardens. The fields are distinguished by their distinctive ranks of twine-strung wooden poles, more than 6 metres high, up which the hop bines annually climb, always in a clockwise direction. Large the plants might be, but it is only the small flowers, or cones, which the brewer is looking for. These give beer much of its citrus flavours and bitterness and, as they possess antiseptic qualities, they help stop it going off. But hops are not the only things growing in the estate's gardens; it is celebrated for its spectacular displays of rhododendrons, azaleas and kalmias in May and June. Many of the plants grow on the side of an old sandstone quarry to give the effect of an Alpine garden. The estate is open all year, offering a variety of walks through beautiful parkland, woodland and farmland. There is also a shop in which beers made using the estate's harvest of hops are sold, although they have to travel to another National Trust property for the brewing to take place.

Once the hops are harvested and dried they make the 23-mile journey

Visitor information:

Hop Farm Family Park
Paddock Wood, Tonbridge,
Kent, TN12 6PY
01622 872068
www.thehopfarm.co.uk
Shire horse experience days must be
pre-booked

Halfway House
Horsmonden Road, Brenchley, Kent,
TN12 7AX
01892 722526
www.halfwayhouse-brenchley.co.uk
🍺 12–11.30 (11 Sun)

Hopbine
Petteridge Lane, Petteridge,
Kent, TN12 7NE
01892 722561
🍺 12–2.30, 6–11; 12–3,
7–10.30 Sun

Getting there and away: The Hop Farm is on the A228 near Paddock Wood, and signed from the M20 and M25.

Scotney Castle

to the Westerham Brewery, which is at Grange Farm in Crockham Hill, near Edenbridge. The brewery was set up in 2004 by Robert Wicks, who gave up a well-paid life in the financial sector to follow his dream to become a brewer. He converted an old dairy at the farm into a microbrewery. Keen to use Kent-grown ingredients in his beers, he began talking to Scotney Castle's hop farmer Ian Strang about using his hops in a brew. He then created Scotney Pale Ale and Scotney Best Bitter, both of which are sold at the castle. However, real ale fans might prefer to seek out the bottle-conditioned Viceroy India Pale Ale, which is made not just with National Trust hops but with malted barley that comes from National Trust farms too. The organically grown Target and Prospect hops provide lots of tangy citrus flavours to the fulsome beer.

Each autumn Little Scotney Green Hop Harvest Ale is brewed as a homage to the hop. This beer uses undried green hops from Scotney. A mild-tasting, mid-gold best bitter, it has a wonderful sappy flavour and is worth seeking out.

Visitor information:

Scotney Castle
Lamberhurst, Tunbridge Wells, Kent, TN3 8JN
www.nationaltrust.org.uk

Westerham Brewery
Grange Farm, Pootings Road, Crockham Hill, Kent, TN8 6SA
01732 864427
www.westerhambrewery.co.uk
🕐 Shop: 10–8 (9 Fri & Sat);
11–8 Sun
Tours by arrangement – minimum 30 people

Getting there and away: Scotney Castle is signed from the A21 at Lamberhurst.

Little Scotney farm, which grows the hops used in Westerham's beers

6

The Bluebell Railway – let off steam and drink first class beer

Real ale, jazz and a steam train ride though the Sussex countryside – what could be better? The **Bluebell Railway** is now the only all-steam standard gauge railway in the country. So whenever you travel on it you are guaranteed a steamy experience – there are certainly no diesels to be found on this line. And on several evenings throughout the year, the volunteers who run the line offer jazz and real ale events, with music playing at Horsted Keynes station.

The 18-mile return journey from Sheffield Park station via Horsted Keynes to Kingscote takes approximately one and a half hours, giving rattling good views of the countryside as it travels through the heart of the Sussex High Weald. The route crosses bridges over the River Ouse, through a tunnel at Sharpthorne Village, on to 1950s vintage Kingscote Station before returning to its starting point. Extensions are currently underway to push the line a further two miles to East Grinstead. But have no fear, if you cannot make one of the jazz evenings then you will find that real ale is on sale at buffet bars at both Sheffield Park and Horsted Keynes stations throughout the year.

Sheffield Park is the headquarters of the line and it also includes a museum and a sight of the many engines which are undergoing restoration. The small bar at the station is called the Bessemer Arms. It is named in honour of a local woman who campaigned for the line to remain open after British Railways announced its closure at the end of the 1950s. The bar usually stocks a couple of real ales, often from local breweries, with the number increasing when special events are running on the line. The beer that hit the spot on my visit was Hammerpot's Martlet. The brewery is located on the South Downs, two miles east of Arundel and close to the hamlet of Hammerpot. It is has been brewing since 2005 and is one of the new wave of local brewers. Its Martlet is a light-coloured ale that looks like burnished gold. Light and easy to drink, it is 3.6% abv, and has a distinctive and refreshing citrus hop character.

Real ale-loving parents can be reassured that the line offers a full range of activities for children, including magic shows and games of Find the Teddy Bears. Other special events include Mother's day cream teas, vintage transport weekends, wizard weekends, Victorian picnics and Bluebell family fun weekends.

Bluebell Railway carriage

Visitor information:

Bluebell Railway
Sheffield Park Station, Uckfield,
East Sussex, TN22 3QL
01825 720800
www.bluebell-railway.co.uk

Getting there and away: The Bluebell Railway is accessible by bus from East Grinstead and Haywards Heath stations.

Flaming Lewes – and a trip to Harveys Brewery

Lewes might not have a cathedral, but it does have a cathedral of beer in its magnificent traditional tower brewery. It also holds one of the largest displays of bonfires on Guy Fawkes night, when the townspeople march in torchlight processions, carrying effigies for burning on one of the many bonfires which blaze. The town boasts seven bonfire societies and is dubbed the firework capital of the world. Six of the societies hold their celebrations on bonfire night on 5 November or, when the 5th is on a Sunday, on the previous day. The other society holds its celebration in mid-October. The flaming processions celebrate – if that is the right word – the uncovering of the Gunpowder Plot in 1605, when English Catholics tried to blow up the Houses of Parliament, and also commemorates the burning at the stake of 17 protestant martyrs from the town of Lewes itself in the 1550s. The processions begin through the busy streets at about 5pm and the last one ends at about midnight. Each bonfire society has its own costumes, ranging from North American Indians to Mongol warriors. The effigies have included Guy Fawkes, a 17th-century Pope and, one year, Osama bin Laden. One society has even made effigies of people who it believes are against the procession or are nationally reviled.

It is highly unlikely that an effigy would ever be made of anyone from Harveys Brewery. The townspeople are mighty proud that they have a local brewery, especially one with a history going back to 1790.

The town's pubs can be crowded as more than 60,000 visitors cram into the town's steep and narrow streets on bonfire night. A perfect place to enjoy the celebrations is the John Harvey Tavern, which is opposite the brewery and the river Ouse, into which, at some point in the evening, a flaming barrel of tar is rolled; this symbolises the throwing of magistrates into the river after a reading of the riot act. Who says the English do not know how to party? This is wilder than Rio's Mardi Gras. The pub is also hallowed as the place the founder of Harveys first brewed a beer.

Another pub to seek out – the town does have many good ones – is the Lewes Arms, which is home to the World Pea Throwing Championships and dwyle (or dwile) flonking competitions. And if you've never flonked a dwyle, suffice it to say that it involves dodging out of the path of a soggy beer-soaked piece of rag.

Tours of the brewery won't be happening while the bonfire societies are marching; in fact, they are as rare as a hen's tooth. As it stands there is a two-year wait to get on one of the trips (for which currently no charge is made), which take place on two evenings each week. But the wait is worth it, as the brewery is one of the most picture-perfect in the country and was designed by William Bradford who was also responsible for the Hook Norton Brewery in Oxfordshire (see p37). It is one of the great seminal moments in the life of any beer fan to be able to see the vessels and touch the raw materials that go into to a pint of Harveys Sussex Best Bitter. It's a sublime, complex beer, which simultaneously refreshes and stimulates with its beautiful, aromatic, hoppy aroma balanced by a biscuity, crisp malt character.

Visitor information:

Harveys Brewery
  Bridge Wharf Brewery, 6 Cliffe High Street, Lewes, East Sussex, BN7 2AH
  01273 480209
  www.harveys.org.uk
  🏪 Shop. 9.30–5.30; closed Sun
  Tours by arrangement

John Harvey Tavern
  Bear Yard, Cliffe High Street, Lewes, East Sussex, BN7 2AN
  01273 479880
  www.johnharveytavern.co.uk
  🏪 11–11; 12–10.30 Sun

Lewes Arms
  1 Mount Place, Lewes, East Sussex, BN7 1YH
  01273 473152
  www.thelewesarms.co.uk
  🏪 11–11 (midnight Fri & Sat); 12–11 Sun

Getting there and away: Lewes rail station is 10 minutes' walk from Harveys brewery.

8 🪧

Greyhound pub losing (or winning) your marbles

Pubgoers definitely knows how to keep our old traditions alive. Every Good Friday the best marble players in the world head to the **Greyhound** pub on Tinsley Green in Crawley, West Sussex. Hundreds of spectators gather to watch teams of marble players cabbage, fudge and nose drop as they fight it out to be declared the best in the world. According to local legend, it is an event that has been taking place since the 16th century when, in 1588, during the reign of Elizabeth I, two men from Surrey and Sussex engaged in an epic marble melee for the hand of a local maid. Today, under the flight path to Gatwick Airport, competitors – male and female – from around the world fight it out to become a mighty marble maestro. This is no playground fun: the **British & World Marble Championships** is a serious business and one which takes the 3,000 year old game into a highly competitive arena. The tradition of playing marbles was revived at the pub in 1932, after an absence of some 50 years, and the championship has been played here most years since. When the current pub was built in 1938, the owners at the time, the now long-since-closed Mellersh & Neale Brewery from nearby Reigate, put in a purpose-built circle on the ground so that the tradition could continue.

To play the game 49 marbles are placed in a ring about 2 metres in diameter. Each team has six players, with four marbles per person. The team that knocks 25 marbles out of the ring

British & World Marble Championships

wins. It sounds easy. However, the skilful marbles player must have an accurate aim and a rock-steady hand. To propel a marble it must be placed in the crook of a bent forefinger; the thumb is put behind the forefinger. The player then holds their hand on or close to the ground, takes aim, and flicks their thumb sharply forward to shoot the marble at its target. The player may squat or kneel on one or both knees to obtain the best aiming position. Any forward movement of the hand while shooting the marble is strictly against the rules. And, of course, to help the players steady their nerves, celebrate success or drown their sorrows, the pub hosts a beer festival, which runs until the beer runs out. Appropriately for such a time-honoured event, most of the beers at the festival are served in the best and most traditional way – straight from the barrel.

British & World Marble Championships
www.greyhoundmarbles.com
Held on Good Friday.

Getting there and away: Gatwick Airport rail station is 3.5 miles from the Greyhound.

Visitor information:

Greyhound
Tinsley Green Road, Tinsley Green, West Sussex, RH10 3NS
01293 884220
11–11; 12–10.30 Sun

9

A day at the races – Ascot Racecourse Beer Festival

It is a racing cert that real ales fans will have a good time at **Ascot Racecourse Beer Festival**, which is held over a Friday and Saturday in October at the Berkshire track. For the two days at least 200 thoroughbred real ales, ciders and perries are available, and if anyone does tire of the beers there is some cracking Group One racing taking place too. The beer festival coincides with the Ascot Festival of British Racing, which includes the Queen

Elizabeth II Stakes. This was the festival when, in 1996, Frankie Dettori won all seven races and famously dismounted with an extravagant flying leap. The race festival is regarded as the climax of the British flat racing season, designed to increase the sport's public profile and to rival the Arc weekend in France and the US Breeders' Cup by attracting the best horses. The 300-year-old Ascot track is used to glamorous events, as in June it also hosts the three-day Royal Ascot Festival renowned for the extravagant outfits and elaborate hats many women wear on Ladies' Day.

The dress code at the beer festival is rather more relaxed. Organised by CAMRA's Berkshire South East branch, the festival has been running since 2007, and was originally conceived by Ascot's head of sales and marketing, John Blake, as a way of getting real ale drinkers to go horseracing for the first time and also to get racegoers, better known for glugging champagne and sparkling wine, to give cask a try. John, a CAMRA member, was recognised for his efforts by being named the Campaign's first Real Ale Campaigner of the Year in 2008. Since its inception, the festival has gone from strength to

strength, progressing from selling 6,500 pints in its first year, to more than 23,000 at the last festival. And the festivalgoers get a chance to pick a beery winner before turning to the horses, as there is a vote for the ale of the festival. CAMRA members are entitled to half-price entry to both days of the festival, which includes access to the racing and the live music.

Gates open at the racecourse in the High Street at 11am before the racing, which takes place from 2pm until about 5pm. Ascot is easily reached by train as it is on the line from London Waterloo to Reading; there is also plenty of car parking at the track.

Visitor information:

Ascot Racecourse Beer Festival
ascotbeerfest.seberkscamra.org.uk
Held Fri–Sat at the beginning of October. See website for details of dates and venue. Tickets available from www.ascot.co.uk

Getting there and away: Ascot rail station is seven minutes' walk from the Racecourse.

Horses and dray at Ascot Beer Festival

10

Oxford inspires – six of the best

The Radcliffe Camera, Oxford

Oxford's small and intimate city centre is a delight to explore on foot. It is precisely as described by the 19th-century poet and writer Matthew Arnold: 'that sweet city with her dreaming spires'. With every step one can follow in the footfall of literary giants, stand in the shadow of some great fictional characters, or sit and sup a beer in the same pubs where students who went on to become world leaders once downed a pint. Old and ancient, the centre is dominated by the 'gown' as most of the buildings are owned by Europe's second oldest university; only the Sorbonne in Paris is more senior. The city's medieval conflicts, when town and gown waged fierce fights and even killed each other, are long gone. The two coexist in harmony and can be seen drinking together in the city's pubs.

On Broad Street, the site each September of the St Giles Fair, is the Eagle & Child. A popular pub with tourists, it is the small, intimate front bars which are of interest. Here once sat *Lord of the Rings* creator J. R. R. Tolkien and *Narnia* writer C. S. Lewis. Both Oxford dons, they were also part of a literary group called The Inklings. It is easy to imagine them in these homely, dark brown rooms drinking ale and talking about their literary creations.

On the other side of the road is the Lamb & Flag, owned by St John's College. It was saved from conversion into student accommodation by a vigorous campaign run by CAMRA's Oxford branch. It has been an ale house since 1695, and Thomas Hardy is reputed to have written *Jude the Obscure* here. Who knows if it is true, but the pub does have close links with the West Country as house beer, Lamb & Flag Gold, is brewed by Palmers of Bridport, Dorset (see p69). In its home county the beer is sold as Palmers Dorset Gold; it is more complex and thirst-quenching than many golden beers, and has some banana and soft fruit flavours.

The walk to Broad Street takes people past the Ashmolean, a museum with one of the oldest collections in the world, and which is particularly renowned for its 300-year-old display of ancient Egyptian artefacts that can now be viewed in a brand new gallery. Fans of TV's *Inspector Morse* and *Lewis* will no doubt recognise many of the buildings on this street, which are frequently used as locations for the programmes.

The White Horse is on Broad Street, a road famous for its colleges, Blackwell's bookshops and the Christopher Wren-designed Sheldonian Theatre built in 1664. The pub claims to be Oxford's smallest. Britain's wartime Prime Minister, Winston Churchill, used to drink here. If he came back today he could try Shotover Prospect, a pale-copper-coloured local brew, which is not too strong but has plenty of taste.

The **Kings Arms** at the end of Broad Street is a large friendly pub, with a warren of rooms and much loved by locals, students and tourists. The rooms really have to be explored before investigating the pub's wide range of ales. It frequently stocks a couple of beers brewed in the county, including some from Oxfordshire Ales.

The friendly Kings Arms

Nearby is the hard-to-find **Turf Tavern**, but it is well-worth the search. It was built on the last remaining part of the city walls and sells a fabulous collection of British beers. It was once used by President Clinton and the former Prime Minister of Australia, Bob Hawke, who drank a yard of ale (a glass containing about three pints of beer) here. The flagstoned drinking areas outside are much larger than the small front bar of this ancient pub and they are frequently crowded, with people warming themselves by the braziers on colder evenings. Its delightful house bitter comes from another Oxfordshire brewer, White Horse.

The small and friendly two-bar **Bear** is located on a narrow lane between Christ Church and Oriel Colleges off the High Street. It claims to be oldest pub in Oxford and gets its name from

having been built on the site of a former bearfighting pit. It is also one of the city's most famous pubs as the walls are decorated with a collection of the cut ends from more than 5,000 ties, which were all allegedly given in exchange for a pint of beer. Sadly, the tradition has died out and anyone wanting a pint of Fuller's mouth warming ESB will have to use real money.

Visitor information:

Eagle & Child
49 St Giles, Oxford, OX1 3LU
01865 302925
www.nicholsonspubs.co.uk/
theeagleandchilddoxford
🕐 11–11 (midnight Fri & Sat);
12–10.30 Sun
Lamb & Flag
12 St Giles, Oxford, OX1 3JS
01865 515787
🕐 12–11
White Horse
52 Broad Street, Oxford, OX1 3BB
01865 204801
www.whitehorseoxford.co.uk
🕐 11–midnight
Kings Arms
40 Holywell Street, Oxford, OX1 3SP
01865 242369
www.kingsarmsoxford.co.uk
🕐 10.30–midnight
Turf Tavern
4–5 Bath Place, Oxford, OX1 3SU
01865 243235
www.theturftavern.co.uk
🕐 11–11; 12–10.30 Sun
Bear
6 Alfred Street, Oxford, OX1 4EH
01865 728164
🕐 11–11 (midnight Sat); 11.30–
10.30 Sun

Getting there and away: Oxford rail station is 15 minutes' walk from the Eagle & Child.

11

England's Civil War – two historic pubs

When sitting in the tranquil garden of the Castle Inn it is hard to imagine the carnage which once took place 210 metres below, at the foot of Edgehill.

On a bleak autumn day in October 1642 the first bloody action of the English Civil War took place here. More than 25,000 cavaliers and roundheads locked together in a gory, mauling brawl. With musket, pike and staff, and to the sound of drums the King's men and the Parliamentary army clashed. That day as the battle raged on foot and horse, neighbours and families fought to the death, with more than 3,000 people dying in an indecisive battle.

Today, it is not uncommon to find heavily armed roundheads and cavaliers sitting side by side in the pub's garden supping pints of Hook Norton ale. The Sealed Knot, a Civil War re-enactment group, use the pub for meetings and all is brotherly and sisterly love. The King's men and Parliamentary troops might argue over the merits of different beers, but that it is as bad as it gets. Inside the pub there are two bars, one containing replicas of armour and weapons used during the battle.

For walkers there are many nearby public footpaths and bridle paths, and there is a maze of trails in the woods close to the inn, where you can follow in the footsteps of the ghosts of the battle who are reputed to haunt the area.

Many pubs in the area claim links with the war. Soldiers of either side were billeted there or Oliver Cromwell spent the night in them. However, only eight miles away by road is Banbury and Ye Olde Reindeer in Parson Street, which played a significant part in the war.

The attractive Hook Norton pub's pride and joy is a somewhat dour, brown room in the back known as the Globe Room. It is a superb example of a 16th-

The delightful garden of the Castle Inn, Edgehill

century oak-panelled room, but it is by more luck than judgement that it can be enjoyed today. During the Civil War, the room was used by Oliver Cromwell as the headquarters of his army. It also served as a courtroom where he sat in judgment over the Royalist trials

Ye Olde Reindeer, Banbury

that took place as he laid siege to the town's castle. It is even said Cromwell planned the battle of Edgehill here. In 1912, the superb room was gutted and dismantled and was all set to be sold to sold to the United States. It took more than 50 years, but historians in the town eventually came to realise what a treasure Banbury had lost. They began what few expected would be a successful search to find the Globe Room.

After futile searches in America, the panels were rediscovered almost by chance in 1963 in storage in London. It seems they had never crossed the Atlantic. The ceiling was destroyed during a bombing raid during World War II, but the rest was in good condition.

Today, the panels are now back in their original place and the ceiling has been restored. Neither the roundheads nor the cavaliers would have drunk Hook Norton beer in either of these two pubs, their time was long before Hooky's beers were first produced, but if they had I bet they would have enjoyed Hooky Gold. It is a golden, crisp beer, with lots of citrus and fruity flavours.

Despite being a thoroughly modern beer, it's absolutely at home in its 17th-century surroundings.

Visitor information:

Castle Inn
Edgehill, Oxfordshire, OX15 6DJ
01295 670255
www.castleinnedgehill.com
🕐 11.30–11
Ye Olde Reindeer
47 Parson Street, Banbury,
Oxfordshire, OX16 5NA
01295 264031
www.yeoldereindeer.co.uk
🕐 11–11; 12–3 Sun

Getting there and away: Banbury rail station is 15 minutes walk from Ye Olde Reindeer.

12 🛢

Hook Norton – where progress is measured in pints

The village of Hook Norton in North Oxfordshire is used to the melodic clip-clop of the brewery's horsedrawn dray delivering beer to local pubs. It is a potent sound rooted in another era, when the world was less bustling and people had time to enjoy the finer things in life. There is something magical about this pretty village which makes it the perfect base for any visitor exploring the Cotswolds, the city of Oxford, or for hopping over the border to Stratford-upon-Avon in Warwickshire. However, for any beer lover the highlight has to be the **Hook Norton Brewery**, which is still run by the fifth generation of the family who

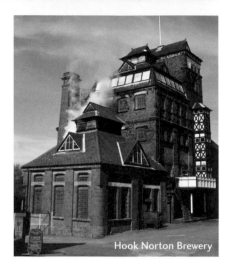
Hook Norton Brewery

from Monday to Saturday, and is in the converted 1849 maltings once owned by John Harris, the maltster who went on to found the brewery. A tour of the brewery can be arranged but must be booked beforehand; it lasts two hours and consists of a trip around the brewery and village museum, followed by a beer sampling.

For the traveller, two of the village's pubs – the Pear Tree and the Sun – offer accommodation. The Pear Tree, at the bottom of Brewery Lane, is the nearest pub to the brewery. It has a single, beamed bar with welcoming log fire. A quintessential English pub, the brewery's staff can often be found here sampling the beers. Most customers choose either a Hooky Bitter or the Old Hooky. The Bitter is a classic example of the British brewer's art and skill, full of taste yet not too strong. It is a golden bitter, hoppy to the nose, malty on the palate and very moreish. The Old Hooky is full of bold fruit and hoppy flavours and the tang of crystal malt.

The Sun stands in the centre of the village. A beautiful English inn, it is built from Cotswold stone with original flagstone floors, oak beams and an inglenook fireplace.

founded it. Brewing began on this site more than 160 years ago, and the 'new' brewery, completed in 1899, is a near-perfect example of a Victorian tower brewery. William Bradford, the doyen of the era's brewery architects, designed it. Harveys Bridge Wharf Brewery in Lewes (see p30) is another surviving and active example of his work. Both breweries share the architect's signature decorative elements based on a Queen Anne revival style, including ironwork, an ornate roofline and fenestration. The Hooky brewery still has in working order the steam engine installed in 1895. Although not much used these days, it is often fired up on the brewery's open days.

The making of Hook Norton's beers is a tactile, aural and visual experience, where tradition, craft, science and technology are bought together in creative harmony. Only the finest Maris Otter malted barley is used in the mash tun, and when the wort is drained off the grist needs to be manually dug out by a sweating brewery worker. The seemingly magical transformation of sweet wort into alcohol takes place in the brewery's hardworking open fermenters. The Visitor Centre is open

Visitor information:

Hook Norton Brewery
Brewery Lane, Hook Norton,
Oxfordshire, OX15 5NY
01608 730384
www.hooky.co.uk
Brewery tours at 11 and 2 Mon–Fri,
and 10.30 and 1.30 Sat.
Tours cost £9.50, and must be
booked in advance.
Pear Tree
Scotland End, Hook Norton,
Oxfordshire, OX15 5NU
01608 737482
11.30–11.30 (1.30am Fri & Sat)

Sun Inn

Sun
High Street, Hook Norton,
Oxfordshire, OX15 5NH
01608 737570
www.the-suninn.co.uk
🕐 11.30–3.30 (midnight Fri & Sat);
11.30–11 Sun

Getting there and away: Banbury rail station is 6 miles from Hook Norton. Stagecoach bus 488 links the towns.

13 🚂

All aboard the Watercress Line – a steamy adventure

Rattling along the Watercress Line while supping a pint of bitter must be one the best ways of enjoying the beautiful rolling Hampshire countryside. Things get steamy twice a month on the Real Ale Train as it sets off from its Alton base on a round trip journey to Alresford. One of the carriages pulled by the steam locomotive is a restored bar carriage, and on board are up to two cask beers, often from Hampshire breweries.

I am on the Mid-Hants Railway, known by everyone as the Watercress Line. Saved by a bunch of rail enthusiasts in 1973, the train clicks and clacks the 10

miles between two market towns. It rises up towards the highest station above sea level in Southern England, Medstead & Four Marks (home of the Triple fff Brewery), before heading back towards sea level. The line gets its name from the fact it was one used to take watercress from Alresford up to London for sale in the markets.

But all good train journeys should end in a pub. The Railway Arms in Alton is a gem. Before entering, take a look at its exterior. The pub's sign is a railway engine thundering through the front wall. The sculpture is a 2-metre-long model of a Drummond M7 locomotive, which was created by local artist Richard Farrington. He was inspired by a painting by the Belgian impressionist Rene Magritte called 'Time Transfixed'. The pub is the tap for the Triple fff Brewery and a second, bronze sculpture, of two brewers labouring under the weight of a heavy barrel, is an insight into the musical inspirations of the brewery's founder, Graham Trott. The sculpture is called 'Stairway to Heaven', after the 1971 Led Zeppelin song, and is also the name of a Triple fff beer.

The Railway Arms

Another fff beer is Pressed Rat and Warthog, named after a song from a few years earlier by Cream. Another of

The Watercress Line combines steam and ale

its beers with a clear musical heritage is Moondance – the name of a Van Morrison song. Inside the friendly pub is a large collection of rail memorabilia, a wide range of beers from microbrewers, and of course Triple fff's range of beers. It also offers a chance to try Alton's Pride, a former CAMRA Champion Beer of Britain. Its floral hop notes soar as high as any Eric Clapton guitar solo, but underpinning it is the steady driving force of Jack Bruce's malty bass and the clean crisp finish of Ginger Baker's driving drums.

The range of beers on the train varies, but Bowmans and Itchen Valley brews are frequent travellers. They are good companions, especially as the train encounters other themed trains on the line. Often passengers on other trains will be dressed in period costumes and it is great to be able to raise a glass to them and yell "cheers" as they pass by. And when the train pulls back into Alton station, there is still time for a beer at the Railway before catching a mainline train back home. In the words of the song: 'Well it's a wonderful night for a Moondance.'

Visitor information:

Watercress Line
www.watercressline.co.uk
Triple fff Brewery
3 Magpie Works, Station Approach,
Four Marks, Hampshire, GU34 5HN
01420 561422
www.triplefff.com
Group tours by arrangement
Railway Arms
26 Anstey Road, Alton,
Hampshire, GU34 2RB
01420 82218
12–11; 11–midnight Fri & Sat

14

Ringwood Brewery – and a visit to a country charmer

For fans of Britain's modern real ale revolution the **Ringwood Brewery** should hold a special place. It was founded in 1978 by a man who brewed a thumping good pint and who is widely regarded as the inspiration for a generation of today's new wave of brewers. Peter Austin is now in his 90s, but he was instrumental in forming independent brewers association SIBA in 1980, and became its first chairman. Peter's brewing career began in 1942, during World War II, at the Friary Brewery in Guildford. He moved to the Hull Brewery, where he was head brewer, before retiring in 1975. But brewing was in his blood and his work was far from over. He was intrigued by a small brewery opened by a former Watney brewer, Bill Urquhart, who started the Litchborough Brewery in Northamptonshire in 1974, in a barn next to his house. At the time there were only a handful of small brewers in the country. Peter, along with other early brewing pioneers of the micro revolution, including Simon Whitmore (Butcombe) and Nigel Fitzhugh (Blackawton) came to Urquhart to find out how to do it.

In 1978 Peter opened the Ringwood Brewery in Hampshire, creating some iconic beers including Old Thumper, voted Champion Beer of Britain by CAMRA in 1988, and Fortyniner. He showed that it was possible to build a new brewery with limited capital, and this played a key role in facilitating the growth in the number of small brewers. He installed 24 breweries in the UK, the US, Bavaria, Belgium and Ireland. Today his legacy is a thriving scene for small, local brewers, which now number more than 900 in the UK. Since 2007 his beloved Ringwood Brewery has been owned by Marston's, but it still retains an independent and iconic air and is a tribute to Peter's success. The tour of the brewery takes in the tastes of malted barley and allows a sniff of the fragrant hops, while the genius of the yeast at work can be seen in the fermentation room. A taste of the beers takes place in the Pin Room, but where else can the beers be enjoyed?

It is hard to find a better place better than the Royal Oak in Fritham. It is just over 20 miles driving distance from Ringwood but it is worth it, even for a non-drinking driver. A thatched jewel at the end of a track in the New Forest, it is a treasure trove of low beams and log fires, with its beers served through a hatch. The area is well-used by walkers, cyclists and even ponies. The food is perfect for lunchtime; good pies and cheese ploughmans were invented to be eaten in a pub like this country charmer. But what to drink? Well, Old Thumper of course – a powerful beer (let someone else do the driving!), it is a rock and roll of malt tastes, and is so good you often have to have two.

Visitor information:

Ringwood Brewery
Christchurch Road, Ringwood,
Hampshire, BH24 3AP
01425 471177
www.ringwoodbrewery.co.uk
Shop: 9.30–5; closed Sun
Brewery tours at 12, 2 and 4 on Sat and 2.30 on Sun May–Sep. Tours must be pre-booked.

Royal Oak
Fritham, Hampshire, SO43 7HJ
023 8081 2606
11.30–2.30 (3 summer), 6–11;
11–11 Sat; 12–10.30 Sun

London

Greenwich Park

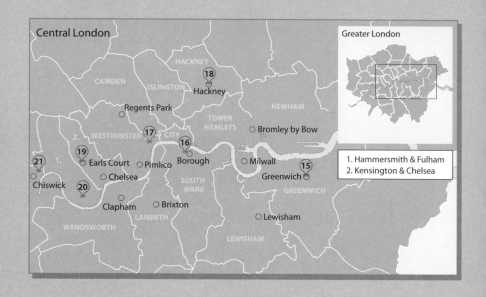

Central London

Greater London

HACKNEY
18
Hackney

CAMDEN
ISLINGTON

Regents Park

NEWHAM

TOWER
HAMLETS
WESTMINSTER CITY 17
Bromley by Bow

19 16
21 Earls Court Pimlico Borough Milwall 15
1. Chelsea Greenwich
Chiswick SOUTH GREENWICH
-WARK
20
Clapham Brixton

LAMBETH
WANDSWORTH Lewisham

LEWISHAM

1. Hammersmith & Fulham
2. Kensington & Chelsea

Days Out

Introducing London

London is one of the world's most vibrant cities. It is also one of the most important when it comes to telling the story of beer.

More than two hundred years ago London pioneered brewing on a massive scale, seeking to satisfy not only the thirsts of the many people who lived and worked in the capital, but also the thirsts of the empire. Beer was sent to the four corners of the world, following in the wake of the army, civil servants and traders who left these shores.

But by the start of this millennium the empire was a thing of the past and most of the breweries had closed. As a beer revolution started to sweep the rest of the country, it seemed London's brewing tradition was very much history.

Then things started to happen – new brewers appeared to join real ale stalwart Fuller's, which was still flying the flag for cask ales from its Chiswick site. New bars at the leading edge of beer culture began to appear.

In London's Borough Market the best of the old and new can be experienced. The Market Porter is gloriously old-fashioned and it is easy to imagine it being used by local workers seeking refreshment from a night spent carrying goods for the area's fruit and vegetable traders and wholesalers. Almost cheek by jowl is the Rake. In the few years it has been open it has acquired a reputation for selling great beers from around the world while showcasing many of London's newest brews.

At the Old Brewery in the grounds of the Old Royal Naval College in Greenwich, London brewer Meantime has opened a stunning bar and restaurant, which puts beer at the very heart of all that happens. It's modern, smart and it is a testament to the importance of beer as part of our culture. Here the brewery isn't hidden away for no one to see, but dominates the dining area in all its shining glory.

London is also home to CAMRA's flagship Great British Beer Festival. Each year thousands of people descend on London to come and drink the country's best beers. It is an experience that is not to be missed.

Great British Beer Festival

15

Greenwich – time for a pint

The thoroughly modern Old Brewery

People really should make time to visit Greenwich. And one of the best ways to get there is to take one of the regular and relatively cheap modern-day clippers which travel the river, with frequent stops, taking passengers from the London Eye down to the O2.

A journey on one of these commuter and pleasure boats gives people a view of the city shared with the generations of sailors for whom the Thames was once a river of gold, bringing riches from the world into England.

The ingredients of beer were once bought up the river to the city's many brewers. Hops came from Kent, the garden of England, and barley was bought in by nimble seaworthy barges from Essex and Suffolk.

Would those sailors have thought, as their cargo boats sailed by on the incoming tide, that the place they were passing would one day be recognised with World Heritage status?

Greenwich has so much maritime history: the Royal Observatory, the *Cutty Sark*, Greenwich Park and the Nautical Museum. You can easily spend a day just exploring the sites, but we're here for the beer. Close to the Thames Clipper's stop is the Gypsy Moth pub, named after the ketch used by Sir Francis Chichester, the first man to sail around the world alone, with only one port visit, in 1967. The boat has long since gone, but the name lives on at the pub. A popular meeting place it is close to entrance to the Thames Tunnel that leads walkers to and from the Isle of Dogs. However the area, with its great riverside walks, has even more pubby delights.

Next to the nearby Discover Greenwich visitor centre is the Royal Hospital's Old Brewhouse, which has been brought back into use after 140 years by the Meantime Brewing Company.

Once a brewhouse for retired seaman living in the Royal Naval Hospital, who had a two-quart daily ration of beer; it is now home to Meantime's fabulous Old Brewery, a restaurant, bar and café, with a microbrewery which brews historical and modern beers. This place takes beer to new heights. Try the Kellerbier, a fresh and vivacious upstart of a beer, brewed on the premises. Zesty, tangy, with a hint of orange and with a refreshing satisfying malty finish it is a near perfect pick me up.

Also in the grounds of the Old Royal Naval College is the annual Greenwich Comedy Festival. Held in September, this fantastic festival has presented big name acts such as Russell Howard, Bill Bailey,

Jo Brand and Reginald D. Hunter. Beer and a laugh – what could be better?

A short walk down river is the Trafalgar, a pub which has sweeping views of the endlessly moving river. It is famed for its whitebait dinners when, 100 years ago, rival barges full of politicians would travel down Westminster to party in the pub. Unsurprisingly, whitebait is still served in the pub's restaurant. Who knows, writer Charles Dickens may even have come to drink here, as the bar's staff tell me he did. It is a great place.

Nearby, continuing down the Thames Path towards the Thames Barrier, is the Cutty Sark pub. It is hard to avoid its large name emblazoned on the building's imposing Georgian façade. Built in the early 19th century, many cargo boats carrying goods from the Empire must have passed this building by. Inside, a large sweeping staircase takes customers up from the intimate downstairs wood-beamed bar to panelled rooms with panoramic views of London's financial centre. A freehouse, the pub sells Fuller's London Pride. Brewed 20 miles upstream, it is full of malt biscuit flavours, some toffee notes and a glorious floral hoppy aroma. Like the beer we should be fiercely proud of pubs like this.

Visitor information:

Gipsy Moth
60 Greenwich Church Street, Greenwich, SE10 9BL
020 8858 0786
www.thegipsymothgreenwich.co.uk
🍺 12–11 (midnight Fri & Sat); 12–10.30 Sun

Old Brewery
Pepys Building, Old Royal Naval College, Greenwich, SE10 9LW
020 3327 1280
www.oldbrewerygreenwich.com
🍺 11–11; 11–10.30 Sun

Greenwich Comedy Festival
www.greenwichcomedyfestival.co.uk
Held for a week in early September (check website for dates). Entry to the festival is free, with tickets to the comedy shows individually priced

Trafalgar
Park Row, Greenwich, SE10 9NW
020 8858 2909
www.trafalgartavern.co.uk
🍺 12–11 (midnight Fri & Sat); 12–10.30 Sun

Cutty Sark
4–7 Ballast Quay, Greenwich, SE10 9PD
020 8858 3146
www.cuttysarktavern.co.uk
🍺 11–11; 12–10.30 Sun

Getting there and away: Greenwich is accessible from central London by Tube, Docklands Light Railway, National Rail and Thames Clipper.

16 🍺

Borough Market – a bon viveur's paradise

Borough Market is close to the south side of London Bridge and the oldest cathedral building in the capital, the 600-year-old Southwark cathedral.

The market, with a history that stretches back more than 1,000 years, is a foodie's delight, with its clamour of vibrant market stalls. From organic Cumbrian lamb to spicy sausages from Spain or rustic handmade breads and freshly-picked samphire, it can all be found here. A favourite brunch is freshly cooked Lincolnshire sausage served on a slice of locally baked sourdough

Borough Market and the Market Porter

bread, or a couple of Whitstable Bay oysters (when in season). Beer lovers should head for the Utobeer stall, where they will find many unusual and rare beers from all over the world. And if the stalls are not enough to enthral, then the many film crews which always seems to be working in the market should provide interest. The market is also a golden triangle for beer fans, with three of London's finest pubs almost within touching distance of each other – the Market Porter, Brew Wharf and the Rake. Each is different in style and character and each is an exemplar of the diversity and quality of beer.

The **Market Porter** is one of London's great real ale pubs. It featured in the film version of *Harry Potter and the Prisoner of Azkaban* as the Third Hand Book Emporium. Opening as early as 6 in the morning, the pub always seems to be busy, and customers often throng onto the pavement. It is the perfect place to enjoy a glass of Harveys sublime Sussex Best Bitter, a complex beer full of citrus hop character and biscuit malt.

Underneath the nearby railway arches is **Brew Wharf**. It is a large, modern brewpub, together with a large restaurant and an excellent paved area outside for sitting. The brewing kit can be seen though a large window. Here stand large stainless steel tanks, inside which the yeast is doing its mysterious work of converting the sugar from the malt into the alcohol we call beer. The brewer is always keen to explore the outer reaches of the beer universe in his desire to find new tastes, so be prepared for something different.

When the diminutive **Rake** opened in 2006 it was at the forefront of a beer revolution in London. The covered decking area outside is bigger than the bar. The same people as own Utobeer run it, so its large and extensive beer list is second to none. On sale are speciality beers from around the world. It is a true beer experience, where beer is chosen with care, savoured and discussed. Rare cask-conditioned beers, Lambics, Trappist and champagne beers – they can all be found here.

Visitor information:

Borough Market

www.boroughmarket.org.uk
Borough Market is open year round
on Thursday and Friday afternoons
and all day Saturday

Market Porter

9 Stoney Street, Borough, SE1 9AA
020 7407 2495
www.markettaverns.co.uk/The-
Market-Porter
6am–8.30am, 11–11; 12–11 Sat;
12–10.30 Sun

The Market Porter

Brew Wharf

Brew Wharf Yard, 14–16 Stoney
Street, Borough, SE1 9AD
020 7378 6601
www.brewwharf.com
12–11; 12–4 Sun

Rake

14 Winchester Walk,
Borough, SE1 9AG
020 7407 0557
www.utobeer.co.uk
12 (10 Sat)–11; 12–8 Sun

Getting there and away: Borough
Market is immediately adjacent to
London Bridge tube and national rail
stations.

17 🍺

Three of the best – central London's finest pubs

London's one-day travelcard is a
marvellous and easy way to move around
the city, especially if you enjoy sitting on
the upper floor of a double-decker bus.
However, the walking distances around
London are often shorter than you
might think, and sometimes it is good
just to stroll and explore the streets.

The area of Belgravia was one of the
great building projects of the 1820s,
which has at its heart the glorious
elegance of Belgrave Square, which was
built by the visionary developer Thomas
Cubitt. The once boggy area was drained
and reclaimed using the spoil from the
newly dug St Katharine's Dock near the
Tower of London.

The rich lived in the large houses
facing out from the square; behind were
the quarters for the horses and servants.

At the end of a now quiet cobbled
mews, behind Belgrave Square, is one of
the country's greatest pubs. Beer shines
brightly at the Star Tavern. It is one of

The exceptional Star Tavern

only a handful of pubs that have been listed in every edition of CAMRA's *Good Beer Guide*. For anyone wanting a venue with an old-world atmosphere the Star is peerless, a pub that looks like a pub. Music and TV would be out of place in the downstairs bar; the emphasis is on Fuller's beers and good food. Upstairs there is an excellent dining room.

The Harp in Covent Garden, close to Charing Cross railway station, is a bit of a rarity. It is a truly local pub, even though it is in the tourist heart of the capital. The owner is Bridget (Binnie) Walsh, a celebrated real ale pioneer. Her vibrant pub is a near-perfect example of how the London cask beer scene is reaching out to new drinkers, and this place always has a varied range of beers on offer. In 2011 it was named CAMRA's National Pub of the Year, the first time in CAMRA's history a London pub had won the accolade. The pub is often so crowded with drinkers they have to spill out on to the pavement. Mirrors, theatrical memorabilia and portraits adorn the walls of the narrow bar. There is no intrusive music, TV or fruit machines, and a cosy upstairs room provides a refuge from the clamour in the main bar.

A short walk away is a pub with a different temperament. Big, bold and just a bit brash, the Porterhouse is a barn of a pub where you probably don't go for a quiet pint, you go to enjoy the company of loud friends, to eat, to drink and to experience the craic. In the heart of Covent Garden, it is a rambling cavern of a bar, full of dark alcoves and intrigues, over several different levels. It is a place to meet friends, lose and find them again. The décor looks as if created by Heath Robinson after a glass or two of the suds, as large copper pipes sweep across the wall and an eccentric clock marks time over the main bar. It describes itself as an Irish bar; well, it sells 11 draft brews, all from the Porterhouse microbrewery in Dublin – three stouts, three ales, three lagers and an idiosyncratic Weissbier. The beers are non-pasteurised and anything but bland and, for anyone with a group of friends who are unsure what to try, just order the sample tray of nine beers.

Visitor information:

Star Tavern
  6 Belgrave Mews West, Belgravia,
  SW1X 8HT
  020 7235 3019
  www.star-tavern-belgravia.co.uk
  🕑 11 (12 Sat)–11; 12–10.30 Sun
Harp
  47 Chandos Place, Covent Garden,
  WC2N 4HS
  020 7836 0291

www.harpcoventgarden.com
10.30–11.30 (11 Mon);
12–10.30 Sun
Porterhouse
21–22 Maiden Lane, Covent Garden,
WC2E 7NA
020 7379 7919
www.porterhousebrewco.com
11–11 (11.30 Thu–Sat);
12–10.30 Sun

Getting there and away: The Star is
15 minutes' walk from London Victoria
tube and national rail stations.

18

Pig's Ear – worshiping beer in the East End

Pig's Ear Beer & Cider Festival

Lower Clapton's unusual Round Chapel, off lower Clapton Road, was built in 1869-71. Once, its congregation thrived and the space would have been filled with worshippers. But the neighbourhood changed, the people then living there moved away, and the building fell derelict. Thankfully, in the 1990s, the money was found to renovate the magnificent building and restore it. Today, it is an arts centre and considered to be one of the finest non-conformist buildings in London, and is Grade II* listed. It is also currently home once a year to a different congregation, one of London's friendliest beer festivals – the Pig's Ear Beer & Cider Festival. Held in the first week of December, it offers more than 200 beers, some of which are specially brewed for the festival. It is also an opportunity for the new wave of London's brewers to show off their considerable creative skills. The festival

is organised by CAMRA's East London and City branch and it is renowned for its bottled beer bar.

Nearby is the Lee Navigation and views over Walthamstow marshes, a site of special scientific interest. Here, in 1909, the aircraft pioneer Alliott Verdon Roe (the man behind the Avro Air Company later famous for such planes as the Avro Lancaster and Vulcan bombers) made the first flight in a British-built machine across the marsh in his tri-plane. A blue plaque in a railway arch he used as a workshop, on the other side of the river, marks his achievement. The river-hugging path is a must for any keen walker or cyclist, and it is possible to follow it right into the heart of London.

One nearby nigh-essential stopping-off place is the Anchor & Hope. People who use this wonderful, small single-roomed pub say it has two bars – inside and on the riverbank. This no-gimmick, traditional hostelry is one of the smallest in the Fuller's estate and it soon fills up. Outside there is always plenty to see. Traffic on the river is busy, and both pleasure boats and brightly painted barges pass by. Rowers and scullers use this stretch of water too. It is a perfect place for sipping on a pint of Fuller's London Pride.

If you need to stretch your legs after all that beer, a short walk away is Springfield Park, which was formed in 1905 from the gardens of three large houses. It is a marvellous green lung, within a heavily urbanised inner city area, and runs down from Upper Clapton to the river's edge.

Springfield Park, Clapton

19 🍺

Great British Beer Festival – drink Britain's best beer in the biggest pub in the world

The world's biggest festival for beer drinkers, the Great British Beer Festival (GBBF) wows the crowds every August with its impressive selection of British brews. Organised by CAMRA and staffed by over 1,000 volunteers, it calls itself the biggest pub in the world, when a large and echoing exhibition hall is transformed into the ultimate giant temple to the pleasures of malt and hops. The first GBBF was in 1977, at Alexandra Palace in north London, and it has been held every year since, other than in 1984. Over the years the festival's venue has been in Leeds, Birmingham and Brighton, but London has been its permanent home since 1991, when it was held in the Docklands Arena, and then at various times at both Olympia and Earls Court.

Today, the festival sells more than 600 beers from the UK and around the world, though its prime focus is real ale, of which there will be more than 450 from UK brewers. The festival's Bières Sans Frontières has become a showcase for quality beers from many countries, including Belgium, the Czech Republic, Germany and the USA. There is also a strong showing from the makers of traditional British cider and perry, with than more than 100 available, all served by gravity straight from the barrel.

The festival is usually held during the first full week in August and runs from Tuesday to Saturday, with more than

The Great British Beer Festival at Earls Court

60,000 enthusiastic drinkers attending. And mindful that so many beers are available, many visitors choose to drink from a third-pint glass rather than a half or full pint, in order to sample a greater number of different delights – rather like going for the gourmet menu of mini courses at a top restaurant! There are also food stalls, book stalls, and several places to try some traditional pub games. In the evenings bands play, there is a family room for children under the age of 18, and Thursday is the day when traditionally everyone wears a funny hat. Another festival highlight are the tutored tastings, where some of the world's greatest beer experts swirl, sniff and sip some of the world's greatest brews. The festival is also home to the Champion Beer of Britain awards, which come as the climax of a year of local tasting panels and regional heats. Finally, at the GBBF, one beer is crowned the Champion Beer of Britain. And you can get to try it!

Visitor information:

Great British Beer Festival
gbbf.camra.org.uk
Check website for venue and dates.
Discounted entry for CAMRA members

20 PUB

The Beer Academy – become a beer gourmet

Beer, beautiful beer. Want to learn more about it? How beer is made; what makes it different; how to taste it professionally; how to enjoy it with food; how to present it, and much, much more? Wine courses and experts are seemingly two a penny. Nothing wrong with that, but 10 years ago a bunch of guys got together who wanted beer to have its share of the limelight. Beer might have more colours, aromas, flavours and styles than wine, but the common perception was that wine was the drink of sophistication, culture and history. And, when it came to food, wine should be the drink of choice.

The Beer Academy exists to help people – from the beer virgin right up to a sommelier – understand, appreciate and enjoy a glass of the suds. Courses can last an afternoon, a day, or even longer, but one of its 90-minute taster sessions offers a great opportunity to learn more about beer – in all the forms

Beer Academy tasting event

Visitor information:

Beer Academy
www.beeracademy.co.uk
Other Beer Academy course are
frequently held outside London.
Check website for details
White Horse
1–3 Parsons Green, SW6 4UL
020 7736 2115
www.whitehorsesw6.com
🍺 9.30–11.30 (midnight Thu–Sat)

Getting there and away: The White
Horse is a minute's walk from Parsons
Green tube station.

in which it is produced. It doesn't just look at cask beer, but takes a sipping canter through the beer scene. So be prepared to sup a keg beer or an internationally-known lager – all in the cause of education, of course!

Normally led by a brewer, the course is a beginner's guide to the history and culture of beer. It takes people through beer's different styles and flavours and the contribution that each of the ingredients makes to the final drink. The course looks at the difference between ale and lager and what makes cask beer so special. It also gives participants an understanding of beer and food matching. Because of beer's rich tapestry of styles and flavours, a well-chosen ale will often make a better partner to a specific dish than wine.

The courses, which normally take place monthly, are held in the White Horse in Parsons Green, south-west London. The pub is dedicated to quality beers from the four corners of the world. It regularly runs beer festivals, such as its well-known Old Ale festival. Its renown is such that brewers will often meet up here for a pint when they are in London. The grand pub, in a fine Victorian building, is worth a visit in its own right, but for anyone who wants to understand more about what they see on the bar, or wanting to give a beer-lover the perfect present, a Beer Academy course would be ideal.

21 🛢

Fuller's – London's oldest brewery

Fuller Smith & Turner is a glorious exponent of the brewing of cask beer, and has the unique distinction of being the only brewer to have won CAMRA's Champion Beer of Britain on four occasions with three different beers. Situated by one of London's busiest road junctions, brewing has taken place on the site of the Griffin brewery in Chiswick, southwest London, close to the banks of the River Thames, for more than 350 years. Tours of the Fuller's Brewery must be booked in advance, and they offer the opportunity of seeing the capital's oldest and biggest wisteria into the bargain.

The brewery's first CAMRA Champion Beer of Britain winner, Extra Special Bitter (ESB), was launched in 1971, though it was initially brewed in 1969 as a seasonal beer known as Winter Beer, replacing another seasonal beer named Old Burton Ale. A strong, highly complex beer, it is brewed from pale ale and crystal malts and a heady cocktail of Target, Challenger, Northdown and Goldings hops. It is said many of America's craft brewers were inspired to make beer because of Fuller's ESB. As an experiment, Fuller's current brewer John Keeling has been storing ESB and others of the company's beers in wooden whisky casks, which lend luxurious, smoky, peaty flavours to the beers. Annually, since 1997, the company has produced a limited edition bottle-conditioned beer – Vintage Ale – always brewed with different malt and hops. These bottles are recommended for keeping for many years and can be bought from the brewery shop.

The fabulous, if heady, ESB can be supped in the Mawson Arms, also known as the Fox & Hounds, which is cheek by jowl with the brewery and is the brewery tap. The dual names are said to come from an era when a pub needed a different licence to sell beer and spirits.

The closeness to the flowing Thames offers a short walk to two great riverside pubs, the Old Ship and the Dove, both on the nearby Upper Mall.

A historic pub, the Old Ship was first recorded in 1722. Always popular, its terrace and balcony quickly fill with people watching the river and chatting.

The Dove is a 17th-century riverside gem close to Hammersmith Bridge,

which was almost destroyed by fire in 2009. The Scottish poet James Thomson is believed to have written 'Rule Britannia' while lodging here.

Visitor information:

Fuller's Brewery
Chiswick Lane South, Chiswick, W2 2QB
www.fullers.co.uk
Brewery tours: 11 – 3 Mon–Fri. Tours must be booked in advance

Mawson Arms/Fox & Hounds
110 Chiswick Lane South, Chiswick, W4 2QA
020 8994 2936
1 – 8; closed Sat & Sun

Old Ship
25 Upper Mall, Hammersmith, W6 9TD
020 8748 2593
www.oldshipw6.com
9am – 11; 9am – 10.30 Sun

Dove
19 Upper Mall, Hammersmith, W6 9TA
020 8748 9474
11 – 11; 12 – 10.30 Sun

Getting there and away: The Mawson Arms is 25 minutes' walk from Turnham Green tube station. The Old Ship and the Dove are about 15 minutes' walk from Hammersmith tube and bus stations.

Fuller's Brewery sits on the banks of the Thames

South West

West Bay, Bridport

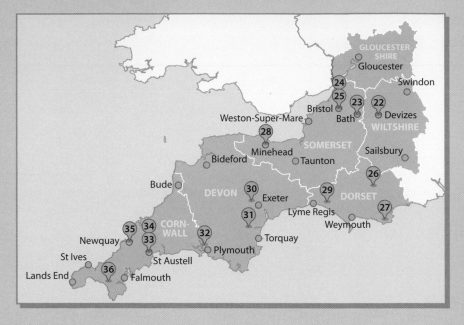

Days Out

Introducing the South West

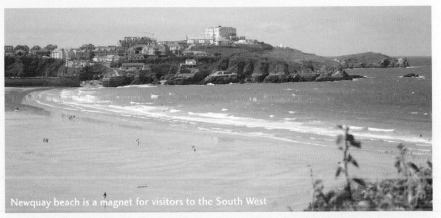

Newquay beach is a magnet for visitors to the South West

Forget the notion that the South West of England is all about cider. Beer is made in this region too, and plenty of it: some in old breweries with origins which go back more than a hundred years, some in establishments which are only months old.

But all the brewers involved share a passion and belief that beer is part of our cultural heritage and pretty good to drink too. For these people beer is a drink of style and some sophistication. There probably isn't a town in the region that does not bear some trace of the region's brewing heritage, and there are some exceptional brewery visitor centres where the story of beer is told. Still thriving are St Austell, Hall & Woodhouse, Palmers and Wadworth. Thankfully, they are far from ancient history, and their commitment and longevity firmly shows the importance of beer and brewing to a community. The region is also home to scores of microbreweries and long-established brewpubs who are bringing an excitement to the mash tun and winning over a new generation of beer drinkers.

The South West also hosts a national competition for home-brewers, who are the new kids on the block and part of a movement developing beers with new tastes and aromas. Some of these people are professional brewers, but most are quite ordinary folk – IT engineers, teachers and even accountants, who are all excited by the potential that the palette of malt, hops, water, yeast and their imagination can bring to beermaking. Old or new, all these people are pushing back the barriers of brewing. Be they big, small or one man and a dog, the mash tuns, coppers and fermenting vessels of the South West are producing some great beers.

And then there are the pubs and the beer festivals. Whether they are deeply rural with views over the Tamar valley, town-centre pubs in Devizes, or a station platform in Minehead, there are pubs and festivals with great quality and vitality. For the beer traveller the pubs and festivals are the ultimate destinations. These are places to sit, drink and contemplate the excellence of the beers in the South West.

22

Devizes – Wadworth brewery and a shooting match

The Wiltshire town of Devizes is home to one of the country's great real ale champions, Wadworth. The company's 19th-century red-brick brewery dominates a junction on the northern edge of the town's centre. Old it might be, and yes, beer is still delivered locally using a horse-drawn dray, but it is a brewery with its feet firmly planted in the 21st century. A newly opened visitor centre, which forms part of the brewery's bustling shop, is full of interactive displays which tell the story of brewing in this ancient town, help you name the parts on a dray horse, and explain the work of the brewer's cooper.

Tours of the brewery normally happen twice a day and here you can see old brewing vessels (including a copper from 1885) cheek by jowl with the modern equipment in use today to brew Wadworth's lipsmacking ales. The old equipment is still used once

a year to brew a seasonal harvest ale. Each September the brewer makes the journey to a Herefordshire hop farm for a supply of freshly picked Goldings. Undried and still full of the smells of the countryside, they are added to the boil of malt and hops and bring a spicy, fruity piquancy to the finished beer.

Devizes is a fine market town. It oozes with tradition and its streets and alleyways are a delight to explore, as are the walks along the Kennet and Avon Canal watching the barges negotiate the many locks.

Not far from the brewery, on the other side of the marketplace, is the town's oldest pub. From outside the Lamb Inn looks like any other welcoming pub. But inside the inn has an explosive secret: guns, bullets and an indoor target range. The Devizes and District Miniature Rifle League is one of Wiltshire's best-kept secrets – and it's been going for more than 100 years. The league was founded by Staff Sergeant Gregg of the Royal Army Medical Corps in 1906. He wanted to improve the aim of troopers in the Wiltshire Regiment, which barracked in the town. The range at the Lamb is an 8-metre metal tube with a hole at one end to fire the 22-calibre rifle down. The tube runs through the

Wadworth brewery boasts great traditional ale and a modern visitor centre

ladies and gents toilets before hitting a paper target, behind which there is a sturdy steel plate to stop the bullets. The soldiers have long gone, but the tradition of marksmanship lives on, and from October to March rifle club members will be testing their skills at a number of pubs and clubs in the area which also have ranges and still carry on the tradition.

A good beer to have in your sights is Wadworth 6X. Since the formation of CAMRA some 40 years ago, 6X has been regarded as a standard-bearer for real ale, and it became well known far beyond its Wiltshire heartland. It can often be found locally served out of an oak cask. The beer has the malt aroma often associated with a Waddies brew. The beer has dark raisin and blackcurrant-like notes, and finishes with a mellow bitterness from a duet of Fuggles and Goldings hops, before giving way to a lingering but satisfying malt finish. It certainly hits the target.

23

Bath – beer gastronomy

Beer is a wonderful companion to food, yet often it is wine that we revere and celebrate. But beer, as an aperitif, an accompaniment to fine food, or at the end of a meal instead of a brandy is, like Caesar's wife, beyond reproach. Beer has a greater range of colours, aromas and flavours than wine can ever have. Indeed, there are many that argue that wine should step out of the limelight and let beer take centre stage.

The style and elegance that beer can bring to the dinner table is matched only by the elegance of the most celebrated of English spas – Bath. This city, with its sweeping Georgian terraces and Roman heritage, is a place well-worth exploring on foot. The pillared houses on Bath Street and the Pulteney Bridge are as magnificent as anything found in the Italian city of Florence, and will be familiar to many as the setting for

SOUTH WEST

Visitor information:

Wadworth
Northgate Brewery, Devizes, Wiltshire, SN10 1JW
www.wadworth.co.uk
Shop and visitor centre: 10–5.30 Mon–Fri (4.30 winter); 10–4 Sat
Tours by arrangement
Lamb Inn
20 St John Street, Devizes, Wiltshire, SN10 1BT
01380 725426
11–midnight (1am Fri & Sat)
Devizes and District Miniature Rifle League
22rifles.djpc.net

Getting there and away: Trowbridge rail station is 10 miles from Devizes. Stagecoach bus 49 links the two towns.

Iconic Georgian terraces in Bath

Roman baths offer another form of refreshment

Jane Austen novels and their small- and big-screen adaptions, depicting a time when it was the height of fashion to come to Bath and 'take the waters'. Many still come to the city to take the waters at the Pump Room and make a tour of the Roman baths. Others prefer their water to have hints of malt and hops.

The Hop Pole is opposite the Royal Victoria Park, one of the city's great green lungs. The pub is worth seeking out for its beers alone; they come from Bath Ales. The beer list includes Gem, a pint with a soft caramel taste which gives way to a burst of fruit in the finish. On the other hand the Barnstormer is as exciting a fast fairground ride, rising and twisting through its peaks of dark chocolate malts and sticky toffee, which are offset by some hints of vanilla. Once a month these and other beers are taken to sublime heights with the pub's supper club. Each month the people who run the pub create an evening at which food and drink are the stars. The evening is normally dedicated to a famous chef or gastronome. Past champions include Elizabeth David, one of the first people

to introduce the people of Britain to the delights of Mediterranean food, and fish guru Rick Stein. This is the theatre of pub food at its very best.

Beer and cheese are perfect partners. In fact beer is a much better partner to cheese than wine. The combination of sausages and mash with ale is well-known. However you may not have though of pairing seared salmon with a glass of Bath's SPA. The effect is extraordinary, with the citrus flavour of the hoppy beer complementing the delicate flavours of the fish.

The food in the pub's bar is an equally exhilarating experience. Many of the dishes are sold tapas-style, for sharing, like good beer and conversation. In beer and food matching there are no right answers, only opinions, and discovering what you think is your personal favourite is a great experience.

Visitor information:

Hop Pole
7 Albion Buildings, Upper Bristol Road, Bath, BA1 3AR
01225 446327
www.bathales.com/pubs/hop-pole.html
🕐 12–11 (midnight Fri & Sat)

Getting there and away: Oldfield Park rail station is 15 minutes' walk from the Hop Pole.

24

The Bristol home-brewing competition

My heart sank when I read the e-mail: 'Tim, just to remind you that you agreed to join us at our next meeting'. I had been invited to attend a meeting of the Oxford Brewers Group. Members of the group describe themselves as enthusiastic home-brewers. I remembered my own feeble efforts at trying to turn the ingredients of beer bought as a home-brewing kit from a high-street store into something drinkable. Disastrous would be too good a word. The group was holding its third taste and swap session, which is now an annual event, where members meet to share, drink and enthuse about beer. So on a Saturday afternoon I found myself in a Scout Hall in East Oxford. Normally, members of the group set themselves a brewing challenge – in this case, a common grist in which were included some Maris Otter Pale Ale malt, some Crystal and wheat malts.

Within moments I was won over – as each brewer lead a brief tasting of their beer. This was no homage to the shop-bought home-brew kit; it was brewing at its most exciting and creative, showing just some of the wide palate of colours, flavours, aromas and tastes that can be produced from similar recipes. Some used Styrian hops, some used Cascade, others chose Sovereign or Northern Brewer. I then went on to try a stout which was as smooth as velvet and the equal – if not better – of many commercial brews. Its excellence was equalled by an American pale ale. The grist was a cocktail of malts: pale, Maris Otter, Munich, Vienna, wheat and roasted barley. The hops were

Amarillo Gold, Centennial and Cascade, providing marvellous lemon citrus and floral notes. Then there was a brown beer, to which Brettanomyces yeast had been added, producing marvellous, soaring Lambic-style flavours.

In the US home-brewers are at the vanguard of a brewing revolution, with many vital conversations taking place between professional and home-brewers. They hold a massive annual national home-brewing festival, with hundreds of brewers showing off their creations. Well, there is now a British equivalent of this competition, which is normally held in Bristol each September. Organised by home-brewer Ali Kocho-Williams, the National Homebrew Competition attracts more than 120 brewers, who bring with them some fabulous creative and experimental brews. Even

commercial brewers can take part providing their beers are made at home using non-commercial equipment. This is where members of the Oxford Brewers Group, and others like them across the country, can have their recipes tested against the very best in the land. The beers presented on the festival's public day are about passion, commitment and taste. Bland is not a word often used to describe the beers served here. If you like beers and the magical journey of exploration brewers are on, then Bristol is a must-visit event.

Visitor information:

National Homebrew Competition
The competition is held on
Saturday in mid September. See
the website for details. www.
bristolhomebrewcompetition.org.uk

25

Ship-shape and beer Bristol fashion

Bristol may be one of the country's best cities for pubs, but it is also home each March to one of the country's best beer festivals. To get in to the Bristol Beer Festival you really have to be two things: a member of CAMRA and well-organised. There is a limit on the number of people the venue can hold, consequently all the tickets are sold in advance and the first tranche of tickets can only be bought by Campaign members. Oh, and you might have to be prepared to queue too, such is the demand for tickets. But as you will be in the company of other beer fans, the conversation is good.

The festival takes place in the Brunel-designed, Grade I-listed, Passenger Shed, Temple Meads. It is a great space for supping beers. It was here that steam railway engines use to fill their empty tanks with water; today, during festival weekend, drinkers can fill their boots from a choice of more than 130 ales. The festival has grown from strength to strength each year, especially its LocAle category; more than 20 brewers now compete for the accolade of being the best brew in the area.

As with all CAMRA festivals, to ensure it runs ship shape and Bristol fashion, it needs volunteers. More than 150 members of the fraternity and sorority of CAMRA give up their free time to make it happen, even if many only work for a few hours during festival week. Work begins on the Tuesday. Someone has to ensure the beer is delivered. It then has to be racked and stillaged, signs need to be put up and glassware needs to be sorted. And once the festival opens it is CAMRA members behind the bars serving beer and cider, selling tokens for the drinks, and acting as stewards. And on Sunday, when the punters have gone, barrels need to be emptied and the venue tidied up. As one of the organisers says, many come back year after year, as volunteering at the festival is great fun. You get to work with people who share your enthusiasm for ale and support CAMRA's aims. There are also plenty of opportunities to introduce

The Bristol Beer Festival is always a sell out

fellow festival-goers to your favourite ale, and share your love of all things cask. On top of all that, you can sup your favourite and new tipples – sensibly, of course. Anyone wanting to go the festival as a volunteer or who wants to buy tickets should go to the Bristol branch's website for more information.

A festival volunteer

Visitor information:

Bristol Beer Festival
Held Thu Sat in mid March. Check the website for details of dates and ticket sales. www.camrabristol.org.uk/festival.html

Getting there and away: Bristol Temple Meads rail station is 5 minutes' walk from Brunel Passenger Shed.

26

Ancient and modern – Hall & Woodhouse brewery

In the handsome town of Blandford Forum stands the Hall & Woodhouse brewery. There is always something evocative about an old brewhouse, especially one as well preserved as that which forms part of the Hall & Woodhouse brewery tour. Once, at a time before most people have even woken up, the brewers would have begun their first mash of the day. It is a scene that was repeated many times over the 100 years the room was used. The malted barley would have been crushed in a mill installed in 1899. The grist would then be mixed in the mash tun with the heated water, or liquor as brewers call it, from the brewery's own well 50 metres underground. There then would have been that marvellous elemental moment as the warmth of the water started to release the goodness and sugars in the malt – and the air was filled with the soft aroma of Ovaltine and the swirl of steam.

Mash tuns at Hall & Woodhouse brewery

Visitors walk up and down stairs where, since the time Queen Victoria reigned, generations of brewery workers would also have walked. The brewery's old coppers are still in place, having put in a collective 150 years of making beer, but they too became tired and worn out. Once every town of any pride would have had its own family brewery, and the malty aromas from the mash tun would have been commonplace. Most are now long gone. But Hall & Woodhouse is so much more than a brewery with a past, it clearly has a future too, as its well-loved brewhouse has been gracefully retired and replaced by a brand new £5 million brewhouse, which stands nearby. The work of today's brewers can be seen through a large viewing window. The owners of the brewery hope their new investment will have a 100-year lifespan too.

In the brewery's visitor centre the range of the company's Badger beers is available. This includes Tanglefoot, a beer reputedly named by the company's redoubtable head brewer John Woodhouse in the 1980s. After sampling a test brew of the beer he struggled to his feet and fell over – the name was born. Flagon malt is used in the beer, it is bittered with Admiral and aromatic Goldings hops, and these add to the cocktail of fruity notes created by the brewery's distinctive yeast, introduced in 1934. Light, almost golden in colour, it has hints of pears and lemon on the palate, which competes with a malty biscuit taste. The beer proved an instant hit and was voted the Best Beer in the World at the Brewing Industry's International Awards in 1987.

27
The Square & Compass – a view to die for

What can be better than sitting with a pint of Palmers Copper Ale looking out over St Aldhelm's Head and the stunningly pretty village of Worth Matravers, which is hiding in the valley. For anyone wanting a day relaxing enjoying coastal walks or even just staring out to sea, this is the place to be. On a fine day the views are as harmonious as the malt and hops double act in the Copper Ale which just sings in the glass. Little has changed at the Square & Compass since the Newman family took over the pub in 1907 – well, there is now a roof on the toilets and electricity. It is a living gem, which offers the timeless qualities of a classic rural English pub in a stunning location: a decent pint, simple food and wonderful company. Inside, staff serve the beer straight from barrels through a hatch, as there is no bar. Two small rooms lead off

Visitor information:

Hall & Woodhouse
Blandford St Mary,
Blandford Forum, Dorset,
DT11 9LS
www.hall-woodhouse.co.uk
Shop: 9–6 Mon–Fri (5 Sat)
Brewery tours by arrangement

Getting there and away: Poole rail station is 15 miles from Blandford Forum. Wilts & Dorset Bus X8 links the two towns.

View from the Square & Compass

and both, aged by time, feel and look like well-worn comfortable brown shoes. On a clear day most of the pub's customers sit outside using the weatherbeaten and bleached wooden benches or tables and chairs cut from local stone.

Drinkers at the Square & Compass are a mixture of high Tory and hippy, with top-of-the-range Porsches and battered VW camper vans vying for the limited parking space. Sensible people park in the village's car park a few moments' walk away. However cycle riders often make it here along the narrow lanes, and walkers travelling the South West Coast Path stray off it and walk up a steep incline to the pub. The food is beautifully uncomplicated – cheese and onion pie or a pasty – with perhaps a bag of crisps as a starter.

The pub's name derives from the typical tools of the many stonecutters and masons who lived in the area. The solid Norman-built St Nicholas church, in Worth Matravers and one of Dorset's oldest, is an example of their work. The local Purbeck stone was also used in Westminster Abbey and Salisbury Cathedral. Each year in August the pub hosts a stone-carving fortnight, with some choosing to camp in a nearby field. In October the pub holds a beer and pumpkin festival which also maintains a slightly tenuous stonecutting link, often challenging people to carve out scary monsters from their vegetables.

Next to the bar is a small museum of fossils and archaeological artefacts collected by the redoubtable Chapman family for more than 60 years.

The Square is a hard pub to leave, but the compensation is the stunning view of Corfe Castle from the A351 Wareham to Swanage road. Close to the castle is the Greyhound Inn, which is one of the most photographed pubs in the country. Hardly surprising, as the craggy ruins of the castle provide a dramatic milieu to the 16th-century pub.

SOUTH WEST

28
Steam and ale – Minehead beer festival

Steam trains at Minehead station

When my friend Adrian Tierney Jones said: 'You should go to the Minehead Beer Festival, it is flipping brilliant' I listened. I hadn't been to this seaside town in Somerset since I was a small child. Like so many children over the years, I remember asking my Dad: 'Where does the sea go when the tide goes out?'. I'd never seen such a large beach before. Well that hasn't changed;

the sea still disappears into the far horizon at low tide.

The town's railway station was there when I was a child, but it wasn't used as a venue for a beer festival. Now, for one weekend in September the station, which is the northern terminus of the West Somerset Railway (WSR), is the venue for a festival of ale and steam.

Why is there a such a close link between trains and beer? At Minehead, coal-fired steam engines help stoke the excitement of drinkers. Indeed, many of the festivalgoers choose to take one of the puffing and chuffing steam or diesel trains to the line's southern end at Bishops Lydeard, 20 miles away (there is a special discount for CAMRA members). The steaming train takes the strain, passing along the Exmoor Coast and up into the Quantock Hills. The buffet cars each have a different Somerset real ale and some bottled Cotleigh Old Steamer and GWR175, both brewed especially for the WSR.

More than 100 beers are served at the festival, but the best part is that it is likely that at least one beer from every Somerset brewery will feature. It doesn't seem that long ago that a festival of Somerset brewers might have been a festival of one or two. How times change! Good beer is essential to the quality of life. There are now around 20 brewers in the county, and they have a passion for brewing. Brewing excites them and they are looking for beers with big flavours. If we want taste in our beer, then we need brewers like these in Somerset. Suited accountants do not run these small concerns, nor do marketing-led focus groups; it is the big brewers who follow this kind of business plan, which is why so many international brands are bland and similar. So expect to discover beers full of taste and character: dark beers, light beers, fruit beers, spiced beers, American-style IPAs and wood-aged beers are all likely to be found.

When I was a child I never found where the sea went, but with the high tide it's back again, as I will be next year!

Visitor information:

Minehead Beer Festival
Held Sat–Sun in mid Sept. Free entry. See website for dates. www.wsr.org.uk
West Somerset Railway
www.west-somerset-railway.co.uk

Getting there and away: Taunton rail station is 5 miles from Bishops Lydeard, the southern terminus of the West Somerset Railway.

The expanse of sand at Minehead beach

Palmers brewery in Bridport

29

Palmers – a thatched brewery on the dramatic Jurassic coast

The town of Bridport is in the heart of the Jurassic coast in southwest Dorset. One of England's first World Heritage sites, it is also home to Palmers brewery. Founded in 1794 in a former mill, it is the only brewery in the country with a thatched roof and a 6-metre diameter working water wheel, which today is purely decorative and no longer supplies power to the brewery.

Two Palmer brothers, John Cleeves and Robert Henry, bought the brewery in the 1890s. Over a century on, the company is still run by two Palmer brothers, John and Cleeves. Break open a piece of the local sandstone rock and you are likely find an ancient fossil; break open the brothers and the word 'Dorset' will probably run though both of them. They are fiercely proud of their brewery and the role it and the company's 50 plus pubs play in the local community.

Tours of the elegant brewery can be arranged and visitors will see the fine wooden mash tuns and one of the best views of a working brewery from its viewing gallery. The tour takes in every stage of the brewing process and includes a tasting of the English pale and crystal Maris Otter malts, which gives the Palmers beers their distinctive taste. Sweet to taste and with a hint of biscuit maltiness, it is the sugars contained within the malt which the yeast converts to alcohol. You also get to sniff the aromatic whole leaf English Goldings and Slovenian Styrian hops, with their different degrees of citrus and spicy flavours.

The tour ends with a tasting of the company's beers, but as good as drinking in a brewery always is, sometimes trying it in a pub is even better. Palmers has many fine pubs and several with dramatic coastal locations. About a mile away is the town's port of West Bay. Situated at the western end of the stony Chesil Beach, the coastline here is a breathtaking sweeping landscape, dominated by towering fossil-filled sandstone cliffs. There is something almost old fashioned about this seaside location. Its small harbour was once dominated by fishing vessels and boats exporting ropes made in Bridport. The beers served in the West Bay Hotel are anything but ropey. While sitting and watching the comings and goings on the quay or enjoying the pub's fishy menu, there are few better things to drink than

West Bay, Bridport

30 🚂
The Tarka Line – follow in the wake of the world's most famous otter

a glass of Palmers Tally Ho! A rich beer, it is ruby in colour. Try to remember the taste of the malt in the brewery and the aromas of the hops, and see if you can pick up the deep maltiness and even some banana flavours in the beer, balanced by the lingering, spicy finish from the hops.

The Tarka Line follows the rolling river valleys of the Taw and Yeo. Little seems to have changed since the days when the author Henry Williamson's creation, Tarka the Otter, hunted for frogs and swam the waters. The classic tale of life and death in the countryside, published in 1927, gives the line its name.

Tarka would have taken much longer to make the journey, but the train takes 60 minutes to travel from the south of Devon to the north, linking Exeter with the ancient market town of Barnstaple. People travelling from Exeter often put bikes on the train and explore the countryside around Barnstaple or cycle on part of the Tarka Trail. Others choose to break the 39-mile journey with a stop off at Crediton, a thriving market town with a variety of interesting shops, or get off at Eggesford and walk from the station into the magnificent Forestry Commission woodlands. Others get off at Newton St Cyres and sup a pint brewed by Devon's oldest brewer.

A good place to start a journey, or even end it, is the Great Western, close to Exeter's St David's station. It sells the largest selection of real ales in the city, with offerings from Dartmoor, O'Hanlon's and RCH. In the railway-themed pub's Loco bar there is an excellent selection of LocAles.

Newton St Cyres is home to the Beer Engine. Directly opposite the station it is the county's oldest microbrewery, and opened in 1983. The original brewer, Ian Sharp, can still be seen hard at work in

The scenic Tarka Line

the brewery, through a window from the pub. His beers all have a railway theme. One of the most popular is Rail Ale; with a golden colour, it has a fruity aroma and a soft malty finish. Yeast and beer from the brewery is used to bake the pub's own bread.

People getting off at Crediton will not be disappointed by the Crediton Inn, which is a 10-minute walk away. For 30 years the pub has had the same landlady, the effervescent Diane Heggadon. And she delights in selling local ales. She runs a good beer festival each November, and should you be feeling competitive there is a skittles alley. The pub's sign depicts St Boniface, who went on to become the patron saint of Germany and is believed to have been born in the town.

Anyone visiting Barnstaple should take a moment to see Butchers Row. Built in 1855, it originally comprised 33 near-identical butchers' shops with an overhanging roof to keep them cool. Nearby is the excellent Panniers pub. Owned by J.D. Wetherspoon, it organises a beer festival for local CAMRA branches in March.

Just over half a mile from Barnstaple Station is the Reform Inn. A popular local, it is the brewery tap for Barum brewery, and hosts regular beer festivals. The Barum IPA should have enough hops in it to satisfy most hopheads and fans of American-style IPAs.

Visitor information:

Tarka Line
For a map of the route and a booklet to collect stamps from the pubs visit www.railaletrail.com/tarkamap.htm

Great Western
St David's Station Approach, Exeter, Devon, EX4 8NU
01392 274039
www.greatwesternhotel.co.uk
11–11; 12–10.30 Sun

Beer Engine
Newton St Cyres, Exeter, Devon, EX5 5AX
01392 851282
www.thebeerengine.co.uk
11–11; 12–10.30 Sun

Crediton Inn
28a Mill Street, Crediton, Devon, EX17 1EZ
01363 772882
www.crediton-inn.co.uk
10–11; 12–3, 7–10.30 Sun

Panniers
33–34 Boutport Street, Barnstaple, Devon, EX31 1RX
01271 329720
9am–midnight (1am Fri & Sat)

Reform Inn
Reform Street, Pilton, Barnstaple, Devon, EX31 1PD
01271 323164
11.30–11 (midnight Fri & Sat); 12–11 Sun

31

Tuckers Maltings – releasing the soul of beer

All beer is made with a malted grain, usually barley. But there are few opportunities in Britain to see the essential process which begins to unlock the sweet sugars from the hard grain. Newton Abbot's oldest company, Tuckers Maltings, began life as a seed merchant in the 1830s before beginning to malt barley in the 1870s. The town was a centre for clay mining and there would no doubt have been hundreds of workers in the area thirsting for a beer and many brewers keen to secure a supply of quality malt. The company built the existing malthouse in 1900. Today its malt supplies many of the country's microbrewers as well as the resident Teignworthy Brewery.

Traditionally, all malt was probably made as it still is at Tuckers. The first step the visitor sees is the wetting of the grain, a process known as steeping. This starts germination within the grain. To make beer the brewer needs the goodness – the natural sugars generated by the germination process – in the grain; yeast lives on this and, as part of its lifecycle, produces alcohol as a by-product.

Once the steeping is completed, the grain is laid out on the 120-metre-long floor of the malt house in a bed 20 centimetres deep. It is a strange, quiet, low-ceilinged room, but then the process of malting is itself mysterious. The room soon heats up from the germinating grains, but the maltster does not want it too hot, as this will kill the grains. The temperature is controlled by simply opening and closing the many small, distinctive windows which run the length of the room. The heat is also dissipated by raking the beds of grain twice a day. It can be back-breaking work.

When the grains have formed little rootlets, the germination has to be stopped. If the growth continues for too long then too much of the sugar sweet goodness that the brewer needs will be gone. The germinating grain, sometimes known as green malt, is moved by hand to the floor below, where it is kilned for two days at temperatures in excess of 150°C to ensure the growing stops. The grain is now ready to go to the brewer.

After the tour, the results of what happens in the brewery can be tried at a tasting of one of the Teignworthy beers. A good time to visit is when Tuckers hosts its annual three-day Maltings Beer Festival in April. Organised by local members of the Society of Independent Brewers (SIBA), it features more than 300 different brews, many of which use Tuckers malt.

The maltings also has a large shop which stocks a selection of more than 250 bottled beers, many of which are bottle conditioned.

Visitor information:

Tuckers Maltings
Teign Road, Newton Abbot, Devon, TQ12 4AA
www.tuckersmaltings.com
10–5 Mon–Sat.
Tour times: 10.45, 1, 2 and 3.15

Maltings Beer Festival
Held Thu–Sat in mid April.
See website for dates.
www.tuckersmaltings.com

Getting there and away: Newton Abbot rail station is five minutes' walk from Tuckers Maltings.

32 🚂

The Tamar Valley Line – and an area of outstanding natural beauty

What a train ride! From Plymouth to Gunnislake, the Tamar Valley Line snakes and turns for 15 scenic miles along the border between Devon and Cornwall. It is easy to see why so much of the area is designated as an Area of Outstanding Natural Beauty.

The Rising Sun is about a 10-minute walk along Stony Lane from Gunnislake station. A cosy pub with some nice views, it offers a chance to try Amber ale from the Otter brewery. Brewed in a deeply rural location in the Blackwood Hills near Honiton, it looks as pretty in a glass as the hills do outside. It's a complex well-rounded beer full of fruity hoppy flavours that might give you the energy you need to walk through the tree-lined valley to Calstock station, which is about two miles away.

A five-minute walk down a steep hill from Calstock station is the Tamar Inn. Once it was supposed to be a meeting place for smugglers, an accolade it seemingly shares with most waterside pubs in Devon and Cornwall. It has some great views of the Tamar and is a good start and end point for some walks along the riverside. The St Austell HSD on the bar is hard to resist. It is a full-bodied brew, as complex as the brickwork in the inspiring Calstock viaduct which traverses the river.

Back on the Tamar Valley line, the Ferry House Inn and the nearby Royal Albert Bridge Inn in Saltash Passage, where once a ferry crossed the river, are about a 10-minute leg stretch from St Budeaux station. Located close to the Brunel Bridge, they offer some stunning views over the Tamar.

To round off the day go to the Providence Inn near Plymouth rail station. It might be small but it has a big heart. The one-bar pub is a great supporter of local ales and always sells one from the South Hams brewery. Try the Wild Blonde if it is on. It is a light-coloured golden beer, which is brewed during the spring and summer months.

Viaduct on the Tamar Valley Line

The use of Styrian and Goldings hops make the nose as aromatic as a bowl of soft fruits.

Visitor information:

Tamar Valley Line
For a map of the route and a booklet to collect stamps from the pubs visit
www.railaletrail.com/tamarmap.htm

Rising Sun
Gunnislake, Cornwall, PL18 9BX
01822 832201
www.rising–sun–inn.co.uk
🍺 12–3, 5 (7 Sun)–11

Tamar Inn
The Quay, Calstock, Cornwall,
PL18 9QA
01822 832487
www.tamarinn.co.uk
🍺 12–2.30, 6–11.30; 12–midnight
Fri & Sat; 12–10.30 Sun

Ferry House Inn
888 Wolseley Road, Plymouth,
Devon, PL5 1LA
01752 361063
🍺 12–midnight

Royal Albert Bridge Inn
930 Wolseley Rd, Plymouth,
Devon, PL5 1LB
01752 361108
🍺 10–11; 12–10.30 Sun

Providence Inn
20 Providence Street, Plymouth,
Devon, PL4 8JQ
01752 228178
🍺 11–11

33 🛢 👪

St Austell Brewery – and a glass of white gold

When Walter Hicks decided to mortgage his farm in 1851 for £1,500 and set up a maltings in a shed, some of his relatives probably thought him mad. But entrepreneurial Victorians were full of big ideas and grand visions – it was a time of great energy and innovation. So the step from farmer to maltster to owning pubs, and then to building a brewery, would have seemed quite logical to Hicks. His philosophy, and one that is still embodied in the company, is that each generation is investing in something for the next generation to enjoy. The story of Walter Hicks, and how the company he founded went on to become the **St Austell Brewery** and one of Cornwall's oldest surviving companies, is told in the brewery's visitor centre. A tour through the brewery reveals that some Victorian vessels are still in place, but that over the years the family has continued to invest in new equipment. At the end of a tour, beer can be enjoyed in the appropriately named Hicks bar.

Hicks' beer must have been drunk by generations of workers mining Cornwall's white gold. Huge reserves of china clay, which was used by the porcelain and paper industries, were found in the granite rock north of St Austell. Much of the china clay would have been taken to the pretty port of Charlestown, which is just over a mile down the road from the brewery. Built by Charles Rashleigh in 1791, the town's largest pub is named after him. Most visitors head down to the harbour, which will seem faintly familiar to fans of period dramas such as *Mansfield Park* and *Hornblower*, as this much-preserved Georgian settlement is often used as a location for filming.

Sitting in the sometimes very busy Harbourside Inn, it is easy to see why the quay is so popular as there is usually at least one elegant square-rigger tall ship moored outside. The modern pub is a great supporter of Cornish ales and sells beers not just from St Austell, but also Sharp's and Skinner's. St Austell's Tribute is usually on the bar. It was first brewed as a seasonal beer in 1999 to mark the total eclipse of the sun at 11am on 11 August. It was then called Daylight Robbery and, for reasons no one precisely understood at the time, became the brewery's best-selling beer. The two-month sale period became three and then four, and so it went on. The beer was renamed Tribute in 2001, when it became a permanent feature in the company's portfolio.

Its success is undoubtedly down to the beer's look and taste. A thoroughly modern beer, it is a glass of white gold with a complex floral and citrus aroma

St Austell visitor centre

and more than a hint of elderflower, which comes from a cocktail of Willamette Fuggles and Styrian Goldings hops. It also used the comparatively new Cornish Gold malt made from barley grown in the county, which was especially malted for St Austell by Tuckers in Newton Abbot (see p72).

Hicks bar at St Austell Brewery

Of all the companies the maltster supplied when it was first founded, only St Austell survives. CAMRA members receive a discount on St Austell's brewery tours, which includes two free halves of beer.

Visitor information:

St Austell Brewery
   63 Trevarthian Road, St Austell,
   Cornwall, PL25 4BY
   www.staustellbrewery.co.uk
   🍺 Shop: 9–5 Mon–Fri; 10–4 Sat
   Tours by arrangement
Harbourside Inn
   Charlestown Road, Charlestown,
   Cornwall, PL25 3NJ
   01726 76955
   🍺 11–11 (midnight Fri & Sat);
   12–11 Sun

Getting there and away: St Austell rail station is 10 minutes' walk from St Austell brewery.

34 🍺
St Austell – a Celtic beer festival

There is a labyrinth of cellars and corridors underneath the St Austell Brewery. Once, the vaults were used to store hundreds of barrels of wine and spirits, but now for most of the year they are empty or just used as a place to put things no one can decide what to do with. But, for one day in November, the Victorian vault becomes the location for one of the South West's, if not the country's, best beer festivals. For 12 hours the brewery rocks to a celebration of beer and music at the St Austell Celtic Beer Festival. More than 150 beers are available to try, but the

Celtic beer festival

real treat is the opportunity to sample some of experimental beers produced by St Austell's head brewer Roger Ryman and his team.

Ryman arrived at the brewery in 1999. A very modern brewer, he brought with him from Scotland, where he was assistant head brewer at Maclays, the ability and skills to make a new beer every two months and then just move on. He also had an appreciation of what brewers in other countries were doing. He was undoubtedly influenced by the books of beer writer Michael Jackson, who was one of the first to describe to a wider audience brewing trends from America, where many brewers were using citrusy, tangy hops from Washington and Oregon. Suddenly English hops seemed so sober and staid. So at the festival people can expect the different and the unexpected as the brewing team draws inspiration from around the world. The only boundaries are the knowledge, imagination and cultural enlightenment of the brewers. The air is full of malt, hops and spice. Warm soft flavours seem to hang from the subterranean crypt's ceilings.

The festival is a university for new beers – a fame academy for different ingredients. One of the festival's earliest graduates was Clouded Yellow, which was created by Ryman for the first Celtic Festival in 1999 and named for a migrant butterfly. It seems almost unimaginable that a seemingly somnolent regional brewer should produce a German-style wheat beer full of spicy apples and banana flavours. However, it has gone on to be a regular brew.

Each year there will always be something different on the bar: it could be an IPA brewed with New Zealand and Australian hops or a Strawberry Blonde: a Cornish lager matured with strawberries. Drinkers might try a Grand Imperial Chocolate Stout which is full of burnt mocha coffee flavours intertwining and caressing with concentrated cocoa notes.

One year a barrel of Tribute Extra was aged for two months in a wooden cask previously used for maturing bourbon whiskey, to which a Belgian trappist yeast was added. This produced soaring notes of orange and whisky flavours. There have been Belgian Triples, American IPAs, and super-chilled pints of Proper (Cool) Job. This is a raucous celebration of the ability of brewers, which is as loud and exciting as the music playing on the stage.

Revellers at the Celtic beer festival

35 🚂

Atlantic rail ale trail – Newquay to Par

The Atlantic Coast Line links the northern town of Newquay with Par in the south. It is an iron road connecting the rolling waves of the Atlantic with the charms of a small port on the English Channel. Rail travellers can start in Newquay, Par or at any of the intervening stations on the 20-mile line. If you buy a rover ticket you can get on and off wherever you want. With seven stops on the line, there are more than a dozen pubs which are easily accessed from the stations. There also numerous walks and cycle paths offering something for people who want to add a little exertion to a rail ale excursion.

To make the journey is an opportunity to try some of the many beers now produced in Cornwall. Locals will tell you Newquay has Cornwall's best beaches but is the county's ugliest town. It is famed for its white-topped fast-moving breakers, which are beloved by surfers worldwide. St Austell's Proper Job is sold in the Great Western, close to the station. Like the rolling breakers, it looks at its best when it has a crisp white head. The beer is a British-style American IPA. It has the strength, at 5.5% abv, one would expect from a beer dubbed an IPA. However, American Willamette, Chinook and Cascade hops provide the bitterness and aroma. It is full of fruit flavours with the citrus notes from the Cascade harmonising like a Cornish male voice choir with the fruity pineapple and melon notes from the Chinook hop.

The Quintrell Inn is two minutes away from Quintrell Downs station. Here rail alers can try Skinner's Betty Stogs,

Newquay beach

The CAMRA Kernow Branch and the Cornwall and Devon Rail Partnership, have produced an online rail ale guide to the route, including details of some of the pubs you can visit on the way.

which is brewed in Truro. Named after a Cornish folk legend, the beer is the colour of copper, a metal that was once extensively mined in this area. The beer has refreshing hints of citrus from the hop and some soft apple flavours. The bitter finish develops slowly but takes its time to fade.

The train passes through the Luxulyan valley, which has great walks and some now quite beautiful, former industrial sites where once copper, tin and China clay were mined. The cogs and wheels of large pieces of machinery can clearly be seen, and the industrial waste seems as beautiful as the brooding Barbara Hepworth outdoor sculptures at her former studio in St Ives.

The Royal Inn in Par is a free house which sells a wide range of ale including Sharp's Doom Bar. Now owned by Molson Coors, it is still very much a Cornish beer, and is brewed in Rock. It is the prince of the company's brews; the mantle of king has to go to the Burton-on-Trent-brewed White Shield. Doom Bar is a flowery flavoured beer with a hint of blackberry and a satisfying bitter dryness in the finish.

36 🍺
Helston – dancing with the devil

The town of Helston, right down in Cornwall between Falmouth and Penzance, almost at the point where the land gives way to the Atlantic Ocean, has two claims to fame. Firstly, it is home to one of the country's oldest breweries and secondly, on 8 May, the streets are filled with swaying, vibrant dancers celebrating Furry Dance day.

Both the brewery and the day of dance are survivors from a different era. The Blue Anchor is one of only a handful of pubs to have been included in every edition of the *Good Beer Guide*. Dating from the 15th century, it started life as a dormitory and hospital for monks, who provided religion to save the souls of travellers and beer for their nutrition. When CAMRA was founded it was one of only four pubs to still brew on the premises. How times have changed; today there are scores. The hand of time has touched little in the pub. It is a surviving thatched, granite relic from another age. The floors are covered with granite flagstones. A series of small rooms lead off a main corridor, which heads out to a skittle alley, the small Spingo brewery and a covered beer garden.

One of the beers brewed here, Braggot, comes from an ancient brewing heritage, which would not seem out of place in a modern American brewer's portfolio of radical brews. Braggot was first brewed in 2001, in celebration of the first charter granted to the town in 1201. Trying to define a braggot beer is not easy: it is an ancient beer which sees an ale infused with flavours of honey, apple and spice. Monks certainly drank mead, so perhaps they did drink a beer like this. Some historians believe the braggot's roots, like the origins of the dancing on Furry day, are pre-Christian and pagan in origin. Certainly, there are 3,000-year-old archaeological remains which provide evidence that grain and

honey drinks were produced in Bronze Age Ireland, Wales and Denmark, so why not Cornwall?

But as the beers flow so do the conversations about the dancing taking place in the streets outside. The first begins at 7 in the morning as the church clock strikes the hour. They go on throughout the day, with the final dance seeing most of the townsfolk and visitors joining in one gyrating, pulsating mass. The dances come from old and forgotten traditions. Some say the dances are to celebrate the devil being driven out of the town, others claim it marks the day when a roaring dragon dropped a rock on the town, still others that it is a celebration of the end of winter. Who knows, but the stories are as good as the Spingo beers.

Furry Dance day, Helston

Visitor information:

Blue Anchor
50 Coinagehall Street, Helston, Cornwall, TR13 8EL
01326 562821
www.spingoales.com
🕐 10.30–midnight (11 Sun)

Getting there and away: Camborne rail station is 10 miles from Helston. First bus 39 and Travel Cornwall bus 445 link the two towns.

Eastern

Sunrise near Oulton broad, Norfolk

Days Out

Introducing Eastern England

St Albans Abbey

From glorious winter walks on the windswept north Norfolk coast to exploring Roman history in St Albans, home of CAMRA's HQ, there is always a lot to do and see in Eastern England.

In some places there are fields of barley as far as the eye can see. The staple ingredient of most beers, barley malt provides the soul and body to the greatest long drink in the world. And many of the region's brewers are proud that the malt they use in their beers is made with grain grown close to their brewery. Grain's journey from the ground to the glass can be appreciated at Branthill Farm. The barley growing on the farm's fertile land is used in many of the beers sold in their Real Ale Shop.

However, there are also places seemingly miles from civilisation, places of heath, marsh and solitude, where a good walk is rewarded with the discovery of a warm, welcoming pub and its reward of a pint of freshly poured ale. The wetland Broads are unlike any other part of England and they offer the opportunity to experience the vibrancy of our wildlife as the wetlands teem with birds and butterflies.

The chalky, flint-filled soil which covers much of the region gives Eastern England much of its architectural charm and character: many of the region's churches and houses are extravagantly decorated with flint.

Once great oak trees grew where there are now miles of hedgeless fields. The wood was used to build and decorate many fine buildings, but it was also used to make ships and boats, and the coast never seems that far away. At Southwold, home to the glorious Adnams brewery, it is an awesome experience to climb the steps of the lighthouse or feel the rush of foam and salt blowing in from the sometimes endlessly roaring North Sea.

For many years Norwich was regarded as a beer desert. However, today it is part of the great beer renaissance which has swept the land. The county of Norfolk now has more than 30 small brewers and many of their beers can be found in Norwich's numerous fine and independently run pubs.

The ancient city of Bury St Edmunds is home to the region's biggest brewer in Greene King with its stunning Art Deco style brew house and also, reputedly, the country's smallest pub, the Nutshell.

37 🛢

Southwold – and Adnams Brewery

A pier, a lighthouse and beach huts all help make the intimate town of Southwold a perfect seaside town. This historic and picturesque resort is certainly one of the most popular in East Anglia, with many visitors coming to see the handsome church, with its 30-metre tower, dedicated to the last king of East Anglia, St Edmund. Others can be found walking on Gun Hill admiring the six seaward facing cannons, placed as a reminder of a 17th century sea battle – the Battle of Sole Bay – fought off the coast. Still others visit the nearby lighthouse, with 113 steps to the top, which has given safe passage to sailors since 1890. However, a stone's throw from the lighthouse is the site where, in 1345, the ale-wives of the town made beer. Today it is home to the town's most famous export, Adnams Brewery. In 1872, two brothers, George (who was later eaten by a crocodile in Africa) and Ernest Adnams bought the brewery, with a little bit of help from their father's money. Today, the Adnams family still own the brewery (not to mention a few other businesses in the

town), which has the reputation for making some quintessential English ales and for being the 'greenest' brewery in Europe. Regular brewery tours, taking 1½ hours, are held, which have to be booked in advance.

Unsurprisingly, given the age of the town and its closeness to the sea, it has some atmospheric pubs, which you can retreat to after an afternoon exploring the town's delights, such as the pier, home to a collection of unique slot machines, or the Sailors' Reading Room and museum. The Lord Nelson, named after the region's favourite son who was born not too far away, is popular with locals and visitors, and is a perfect place to enjoy a pint of dry and refreshing Adnams Bitter. It is a marvellous beer and almost the quintessential English pint. Robust, with hints of earthy sulphur vapours, it is a harmony of orange notes from the hops, dark fruits and the sweetness from the malt.

Another pub worth seeking out is situated under the lighthouse. The Sole Bay Inn is the nearest pub to the brewery and is just two minutes away from the shimmering sea.

The Harbour Inn, a riverside pub, is about a mile south of the town centre. A mark on the wall shows the level reached by floodwaters in 1953, and the place can be almost impossibly busy on sunny days.

Southwold pier

Nearby a foot ferry and footbridge provide access to Walberswick. Here is the famed **Anchor**, run by Sophie and Mark Dorber. A family-friendly hostelry, it's a welcome retreat for all who enjoy good conversation, food and drink.

38 🚂
The Poppy Line – a rail tour through north Norfolk

Anyone who travels the 10½ mile round trip from Sheringham to Holt will soon realise how the **Poppy Line**, more properly the North Norfolk Railway, got its name. In the warmer months, there are always plenty of flowers to be seen: in the spring and early summer there are primroses, bluebells and bright yellow gorse, which then give way to mauve heathers and the blood red of the poppies.

The train travels through Weybourne, a restored country station in a pretty, coastal village. A mile down the hill from the station is the **Ship**. The pub prides itself on sourcing locally-produced Norfolk ales and food; Grain and Humpty Dumpty beers are often on the bar. The pub is close to the Muckleburgh Military Vehicle Museum, which is worth a visit. From Weybourne it is possible to take the three- to four-mile coastal footpath back to Sheringham.

The next station is the Kelling Heath Park with its moorland nature trail walk. Because of the station's gradient only diesel trains, not steam, stop here on the way to Holt. Passengers wanting to travel to Sheringham will have to wave the train down to make it stop.

The Georgian town of Holt is at the western end of the line. In summer months the Holt Flyer, a former London Routemaster bus, will take people the one-mile journey into town. In December the town is renowned for it display of Christmas lights. On the High Street is the Grade II-listed **King's Head**, which with ease mixes the old with the contemporary, the community and the

Visitor information:

Adnams Brewery
East Green, Southwold,
Suffolk, IP18 6JW
01502 727225
brewerytours.adnams.co.uk

Lord Nelson
42 East Street, Southwold,
Suffolk, IP18 6CJ
01502 722079
www.thelordnelsonsouthwold.co.uk
🍺 10.30–11; 12–10.30 Sun

Sole Bay Inn
7 East Green, Southwold,
Suffolk, IP18 6JN
01502 723736
www.solebayinn.co.uk
🍺 11–11; 12–10.30 Sun

Harbour Inn
Blackshore Quay, Southwold,
Suffolk, IP18 6TA
01502 722381
🍺 11–11; 12–10.30pm Sun

Anchor
Main Street, Walberswick, Southwold,
Suffolk, IP18 6UA
www.anchoratwalberswick.com
01502 722112
🍺 11–11

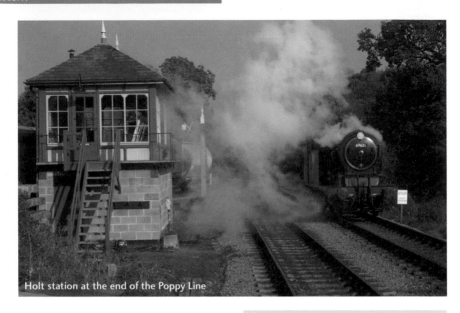
Holt station at the end of the Poppy Line

visitors. A fine supporter of Norfolk beers, its range includes Woodforde's and Yetman's. For most, Yetman's will be an unknown brewer and therefore worth trying. Set up in a medieval barn in 2005, the beers are named after colours, other than its stout, which is just called Stout. The Orange's amber hue, almost the colour of a well polished table comes from the use of crystal malt. The full malt flavour is balanced by the classic English combination of Fuggles and Goldings hops, which provide a fruit bitterness.

Many take the train back to Sheringham, though some prefer, having bought their bike with them, to cycle the five-mile downhill road journey. Dogs are welcome on the train.

Once back in Sheringham, the **Crown** offers a perfect end to the journey. Located next to the lifeboat museum, it has fantastic views over the beach to the surging North Sea. A range of five real ales is usually available to choose from. Each Easter the line holds a steam gala, when engines from other lines add to the fleet of locomotives.

Visitor information:

Poppy Line
www.nnrailway.co.uk
Ship
The Street, Weybourne,
Norfolk, NR25 7SZ
01263 588721
www.shipinnweybourne.co.uk
🕐 11–3, 6–11; 11–midnight Fri & Sat;
11–11 Sun
King's Head
19 High Street, Holt, Norfolk,
NR25 6BN
www.kingsheadholt.org.uk
01263 712543
🕐 10.30–11; 11–10.30 Sun
Crown
East Cliff, Sheringham, Norfolk,
NR26 8BQ
01263 823213
www.crown-sheringham.co.uk
🕐 10 (12 Sun)–11

Getting there and away: Sheringham railway station is 2 minutes' walk from Sheringham Poppy Line.

39

Norwich – the UK's city of ale

Norwich is quite a city for beer and has some fine pubs. A recent survey by a team of CAMRA volunteers heroically visited 136 pubs in the city on one summer's evening and found 215 different ales on sale. CAMRA's Norwich & Norfolk branch now claim Norwich is the top city in the UK for real ale, per head of population, toppling recent claims made by Sheffield and Derby. The survey was masterminded by CAMRA member Ian Stamp, who was sitting in Command HQ, a.k.a. the Murderers, one of the city's famed real ale pubs, which sources beers from brewers large and small across East Anglia. The meandering pub, which is full of nooks and crannies, is also popular with footie fans as it has several screens for watching games.

Many cities have one beer festival, but, supporting the claims that it is the top and thriving place for real ale, Norwich has two. For more than 30 years the CAMRA's Norwich & Norfolk branch has been organising the Norwich Beer Festival, so theirs wins the claim for seniority. Currently held for six days in October in the St Andrew's and Blackfriars' Halls, it features more than 200 different real ales. In addition, for the first time in 2011, the city authorities organised their own festival, the City of Ale, starting in May and running for 10 days, celebrating local brewing talent by featuring beer brewed within 30 miles of the city. Several pub trails and other events were organised with the express intention of getting people back into pubs. The idea for this festival fits in with the Norwich *Evening News*'s Love Your Local campaign. The campaign highlights the role pubs play in the community and warns punters to 'either use them or lose them'.

Also worth seeking out is the Fat Cat, an outstanding example of a real ale pub, which features beer not just from its own brewery but 25-plus guest ales from across the country. The pub houses a large collection of brewing memorabilia, so there is always something to capture the eye and start a beery conversation.

The King's Head is an understated gem. Its charm is its urbane simplicity together with a large range of excellently kept, locally-brewed beers. Shunning keg beers, the house bitter comes from the city's Winter's Brewery. Like many modern beers, the dry, rewarding finish is preceded by nose tingling zesty citrus notes of lemon and grapefruit flavours.

EASTERN

Murderers, Norfolk

Visitor information:

Murderers/Gardeners Arms
2–8 Timberhill, Norwich,
Norfolk, NR1 3LB
01603 621447
www.themurderers.co.uk
🕐 10–11.30 (1.30am Fri & Sat);
12–10.30 Sun

Norwich Beer Festival
www.norwichcamra.org
Held Mon–Sat in late October.
See website for dates. Free entry
for CAMRA members
City of Ale
cityofale.org.uk
Fat Cat
49 West End Street, Norwich,
Norfolk, NR2 4NA
01603 624364
www.fatcatpub.co.uk
🕐 12–11 (midnight Thu–Sat)
King's Head
42 Magdalen Street, Norwich,
Norfolk, NR3 1JE
01603 620468
www.kingsheadnorwich.co.uk
🕐 12–midnight (11 Sun)

Getting there and away: Norwich rail station is 15 minutes' walk from St Andrew's & Blackfriars' Halls.

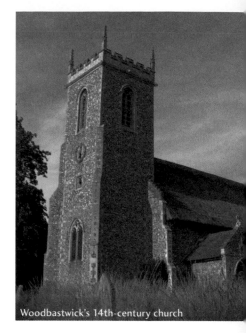

Woodbastwick's 14th-century church

40

Woodbastwick – Cockshoot Broad and Woodforde's brewery

When it comes to a gentle walk, there can be few better places than the pretty village of Woodbastwick. It is for good reasons that the village has twice won a best-kept village award. It has a restored 14th-century medieval flint church with a thatched roof, some pretty cottages, a fine pub and the award-winning Woodforde's brewery's visitor centre. Woodbastwick is also the home to one of the earliest herds of British White cattle. The breed claims a link back to the country's ancient indigenous wild white cattle. The herd has bred in the parish since 1840.

However, a visit to Norfolk would be incomplete without seeing one of its famed Broads. A half-hour's stroll from the village takes the visitor to Cockshoot Broad. The Norfolk Wildlife Trust has transformed it into a tranquil nature reserve, famed for its waterlily beds and the damselflies it attracts. A boarded walkway snakes around the Broad and there is a bird hide from where it is possible to catch closer glimpses of the abundant wildlife.

A good walk is even better if at the end of it there is a prospect of a thirst-quenching pint of Woodforde's Wherry and some food created with locally-produced ingredients. Back in Woodbastwick is the thatched Fur & Feather pub, which is the tap for the adjacent Woodforde's brewery. Wherry was the first commercial beer brewed by home brewers Ray Ashworth and Dr David Crease when they set up the brewery in 1981. The business partners were part of a new wave of brewers in the United Kingdom, inspired by stories of American home brewers who were beginning to push at the boundaries of brewing – a classic example of traditional British skills being rediscovered in the New World and re-exported back to the old country. Then, Norfolk was often described as a beer desert as there were no brewers left in it – and little choice of cask beers in local pubs. Ashworth and Crease wanted to rebel against what they saw as the relentless blandness of larger brewers' products. Well, bland Wherry is not, as the beer is a clean, zesty, refreshing bitter, which is golden to the eye and has a tingling, hoppy, floral aroma with hints of lemon. The beer, named after a type of sailing boat used to transport people and goods on the Norfolk Broads, has carried Woodforde's to success as it is a former CAMRA Champion Beer of Britain. The brewery's visitor centre is open most days and tours of the brewery can be booked in advance.

Visitor information:

Cockshoot Broad
Open year round, dawn to dusk.
Free entry
www.norfolkwildlifetrust.org.uk

Fur & Feather
Slad Lane, Woodbastwick,
Norfolk, NR13 6HQ
01603 720003
www.thefurandfeatherinn.co.uk
10–10.30 (11 Fri & Sat)
Woodforde's
Broadland Brewery, Woodbastwick,
Norfolk, NR13 6SW
www.woodfordes.co.uk
Visitor centre: 10.30 (11.30 Sat & Sun)–4.30
Tours of the brewery by arrangement (Tue & Thu evenings). Brewery open days are also held

41

Laxfield – medieval village

The people who live in the rural village of Laxfield are lucky: they still have two thriving pubs and a history that traces back to Saxon times. It must have been a place of some importance as it merits a mention in the Domesday Book. Once, the settlement had more than eight pubs, but changing lifestyles and rising house prices saw most of them call last orders, and today only two remain.

Most visitors make a beeline for the thatched King's Head, which is also known as the Low House. The 16th-century pub has seemingly been untouched by time. It is a warren of dark wooden rooms and high settles polished by generations of bottoms sitting upon them. It is also one of the very few pubs left in Britain that has no bar counter. People go into the taproom towards the back, where beers are drawn straight from the barrel. It is one of those elemental places where

Guildhall in the attractive village of Laxfield

years of conversation, swapped stories and laughter are held forever within the walls. With a large garden, it also hosts beer festivals in May and September.

However, the village's other pub should not be forgotten, as the Royal Oak also champions real ale. The main part of the pub comes from the 16th century but parts of the building have been developed over the years.

But there is much more to the village than just its pubs. Many visitors park their cars before wandering around to see its historic buildings. The church has a magnificent freestone and flint tower. Opposite is the attractive 15th-century Guildhall, which is also home to the Laxfiend & District museum. The collection includes some early 20th-century shop interiors and a kitchen from the 1900s, together with window displays, artefacts, costumes and information on domestic life of the same period. Also on display are some memorabilia from the Mid-Suffolk Light Railway, which once terminated in the parish. A popular outing in summer is a horse-drawn carriage ride from nearby Tannington Hall, an Elizabethan manor house and hotel. Laxfield also has one of the biggest communal playing fields in Suffolk, at almost eight acres, which includes a large children's play area and a bowls green.

Visitor information:

King's Head/Low House
Gorams Mill Lane, Laxfield,
Suffolk, IP13 8DW
01986 798395
www.laxfieldkingshead.co.uk
🌑 12–3, 6–midnight; 11–midnight
Fri & Sat summer; 12–4, 7–11 Sun

42 🛢

Wells-next-the-Sea – the Real Ale shop and a North Sea clipper

A remote North Norfolk barley farmer, on the Holkham Estate, is the owner of one of the best real ale shops in the country. Like many struggling farmers, Teddy Maufe was looking for a way to diversify, and it had to be one that related to the work he was doing on his farm. The idea of a shop selling tawdry trinkets for the tourists appalled him; he wanted something that reflected what he was growing on his farm – barley – and the use it was put to. He was aghast that most people didn't realise that the barley he was growing made beer. He wanted to help people understand the farm-to-glass connection by opening a shop selling bottle-conditioned beers brewed in Norfolk, often made with his farm's barley. His inspiration was a trip to Napa Valley, California, where he toured a vineyard and saw the pride with which winemakers showcased their products. Today the Real Ale Shop sells more than 60 different beers, most from the region but a few from farther afield. And the majority are not available in supermarkets, so it is a wonderful place to finds some hard-to get brews. Maufe has now installed a small floor maltings in the farm. It is only a tiny operation, malting a mere 25kg at a time, but it is designed to show visitors to the shop how malting is done. However, he plans

Albatros floating restaurant and bar, Wells-next-the-Sea

to put the pale malt, made from Maris Otter barley grown on his 1,000-acre farm, to good use, as it will, he says, produce a range of extraordinary beers. The remote farm offers somewhere to stay too – either in the farmhouse bed & breakfast or in the self-catering cottage.

In nearby Wells-next-the-Sea there is a curiosity of a pub where some of the beers brewed with Maufe's malt can be tried. Built in 1899, the Albatros pub first plied its trade as a cargo boat carrying goods to Holland. In World War II it rescued Jews and political dissidents from Nazi-occupied Denmark and took them to neutral Sweden, carrying back guns and explosives for the Danish Resistance crammed in amongst her cargo. Now it has joined the small but select national fraternity of water-borne beer outlets, and the craft's former cargo hold is a restaurant and bar, serving a variety of traditional Dutch pancakes and some fine real ales. On a day when the wind is bracing there can be few better beers than Woodforde's Nelson's Revenge. A bold, rich beer it almost has some sherry like character, more than enough to keep the wind at bay.

Visitor information:

The Real Ale Shop
Branthill Farm, Wells-next-the-Sea, Norfolk, NR23 1SB
01328 710810
therealaleshop.co.uk
🌐 10–6 (4 winter); 12–4 Sun; closed Mon

Albatros
The Quay, Wells–next–the Sea, Norfolk, NR23 1AT
07979 087228
www.albatros.eu.com
🌐 12–11

43 🛢

Bury St Edmunds – and Greene King brewery

The town's motto is: 'Shrine of a King, cradle of the law'. Today, perhaps, a third

Beautiful and relaxing Abbey gardens, Bury St Edmunds

element should be added: 'Home of a world-famous brewer'. History seems to ooze from every pore of this picturesque market town. Its famous abbey gardens, built on the site of a great Benedictine abbey, are at the very heart of Bury (as the locals call it). Free to enter, the gardens are renowned for their stunning floral displays.

The gardens are framed by the abbey wall that runs from the ancient Abbot's Bridge via the imposing Abbey Gate to St Edmundsbury Cathedral. Inside are some magnificent formal gardens, the largest of which consists of a great circle filled with flowerbeds set in well-kept lawns. There are also the more secluded areas, such as the old English rose garden, a permanent memorial to the American servicemen, many of them based at airfields in the area, who fought in World War II; or the water garden and the blind garden, where scent is everything. Inside are craggy remains of the former abbey's buildings and cloisters.

Also in the town's centre is the Greene King Brewery, located near a site where beer was brewed as far back as 1086. The Great Abbey's *cerevisiarii*, or ale brewers, are mentioned in the Domesday Book. Greene King is a highly traditional English brewer, which only makes ales. It has been brewing on this site since 1700, using the fresh water drawn from chalk wells deep underneath the town. The visitor centre offers a shop and museum. Tours of the brewery include sight of the 'new' Art Deco brewhouse, built in 1938. Few would think a space in a brewery could look so beautiful or sumptuous. Weather permitting, people are taken to the very top of the brewery, where they can stand outside and enjoy the best views in the town, before sampling a few of the beers in the Brewery Tap.

Greene King is probably one of the country's biggest traditional real ale

brewers; it vies for the number one position with Marston's. So it is fitting that the town that has the biggest brewery should also be home to England's smallest pub. The Nutshell has been serving beer from its 5 metre by 2.5 metre bar since 1867. The walls are crammed with historical items, photos and memorabilia, but you might not get to look around: it often gets so crowded that drinkers have to spill out into the street to drink their pints of Green King Abbot Ale.

Greene King Brewery

Visitor information:

Greene King Brewery
Westgate Street, Bury St Edmunds, Suffolk, IP33 1QT
01284 714 297
www.greeneking.co.uk
 Brewery tours: 11 (not Tue) & 2 (not Mon), Mon–Fri; 11, 12.30 & 2 Sat; 11.30 Sun

Nutshell
17 The Traverse, Bury St Edmunds, Suffolk, IP33 1BJ
01284 764867
www.thenutshellpub.co.uk
 11–11; 12–10.30 Sun

Getting there and away: Bury St Edmunds rail station is 20 minutes' walk from the Greene King brewery.

Historic Boot Inn and 15th-century clock tower, St Albans

44

St Albans – home of CAMRA

There is much to explore in the city of St Albans. It's an ancient city, with tiny, twisting, undulating streets; parts of it are positively picturesque. It was once one of the country's most important Roman towns and there is still much evidence of its importance and status. The remains of the Roman city of Verulamium, as they called it, are now part of a fine museum which includes recreated Roman rooms and some of the best Roman mosaics and wall plasters outside the Mediterranean.

The skyline of the city is dominated by an impressive cathedral, which can be seen from miles around. Constructed partly from brick taken from the remins of the Roman city, it was built on the site where the martyr Alban was beheaded in the 4th century.

St Albans is also home to CAMRA. The Campaign has established close links with the people and pubs of the city since its inception more than 40 years ago. Consequently, many of its pubs have an excellent reputation for serving good beer. It would take a much larger guide than this one to do justice to all of the great pubs in the city.

Close to the Verulamium museum, the Six Bells is a 16th-century pub and the only freehouse within the walls of

Roman Verulamium. It's a regular entry in the *Good Beer Guide* and Oakham JHB, Tring Ridgeway and Taylor Landlord are the regular beers, as well as rotating

guests. The menu is also well-regarded. Nearby are some fine old timber-framed houses. It is also within walking distance of the Verulamium Park, which is home to yet more Roman city walls, as well as a mosaic floor and hypocaust, both of which are open to the public.

In the Market Place, the Boot Inn dates back to the 1400s and has lots of open beams set into its low ceilings. Another *Good Beer Guide* regular, there

Ye Olde Fighting Cocks

are five regular beers and three guest ales. Nearby is the 15th-century clock tower, which faces the endearing High Street. The tower's bell, which still strikes the hours, is older than the tower itself. It is near here that two fierce battles took place during the Wars of the Roses. The clock tower is open to visitors on summer weekends, and you can climb the 93 steps to the top of the tower for a fine view over St Albans.

Sopwell Lane runs parallel to the river; it has some fascinating small houses and the ivy-covered ruins of Sopwell Nunnery. It is also home to the White Lion, a 16th-century, two-bar pub which holds a fine beer festival every August. Nearby are a number of other fine back-street pubs – see your *Good Beer Guide* for details.

Ye Olde Fighting Cocks vies with the Ye Olde Trip to Jerusalem in Nottingham (see p103) as being the oldest pub in England. The pub, which is listed in the *Guinness Book of Records*, is an 11th-

century structure set on an 8th-century site. It was originally located close to St Albans cathedral and was moved to the present site after the dissolution of the Abbey in 1539.

CAMRA's South Hertfordshire branch runs the fine St Albans Beer Festival in the city, which takes place at the end of September for four days, and brings ale-lovers flocking to the city.

Visitor information:

Six Bells
16–18 St Michaels Street, St Albans, Hertfordshire, AL3 4SH
01727 856945
www.the-six-bells.com
12–11 (11.30 Fri & Sat);
12–10.30 Sun

Boot Inn
4 Market Place, St Albans, Hertfordshire, AL3 5DG
01727 857533
12 midnight (1am Fri & Sat);
12–11.30 Sun

White Lion
91 Sopwell Lane, St Albans, Hertfordshire, AL1 1RN
01727 850540
www.thewhitelionph.co.uk
12–11

Ye Olde Old Fighting Cocks
16 Abbey Mill Lane, St Albans, Hertfordshire, AL3 4HE
01727 869152
www.yeoldefightingcocks.co.uk
11–11.30 (midnight Fri & Sat);
12–11.30 Sun

St Albans Beer Festival
www.stalbansbeerfestival.com
Held Wed–Sat in late September (check website for dates). Free entry for CAMRA members

Getting there and away: St Albans City rail station is 15 minutes' walk from the Boot.

East
Midlands

Monsal Head, Peak District

1. Rutland

Days Out

Introducing the East Midlands

From the below sea level flatlands of Lincolnshire and its seemingly endless horizon to the inspiring 600m-high hills of the Peak District, there is much to attract the eye a lot for the beer-lover to enjoy in the East Midlands.

For foodies it offers a lot – with a proud tradition of regional creations using locally-sourced ingredients – sausages, cheeses and tarts are all made in the area and many towns still have their own bakeries. It is also home to many fine breweries. Some, like Batemans where brewing began in 1874, are among the oldest in the country and still run by the fourth generation of its founding fathers. Others, like Thornbridge, are newcomers to the brewing scene, and have helped beer throw out its old-fashioned image and made it smart and chic. Its visitor centre in Bakewell is shiny, bright and modern. Old or new, these breweries share an enduring passion for creating beers from the simplest of raw materials: malt, hops, water and yeast.

And for anyone wanting to enjoy a cask conditioned beer it is to a pub or beer festival you will have to go. The region has some great pubs, where beer is served with pride and understanding. Nottingham is home to Ye Olde Trip to Jerusalem, a contender for the title of oldest pub in the country – certainly a place where beer has been served for hundreds of years. The city also has examples of how a pub can breathe new life into a building which faced demolition. The Canalhouse is a fantastic example of an old building

which has found a new life as a thriving, vibrant pub. In Lincoln it is possible to walk through medieval streets, which have changed little since they were first built, before enjoying a pint. Derby, dubbed Britain's real ale capital, claims to sell more real ales than anywhere else in the country.

Old and new, ancient and modern, there are plenty of places for beer hunting for the real ale lover.

Thornbridge Hall

45 🍺 👥

Batemans Brewery – Lincolnshire's theatre of beers

BATEMANS BREWERY

Batemans Brewery and visitor centre

This brewery should be on every beer lovers wish list of places to go to. A Union flag flies proudly above the Salem Bridge Brewery, in deeply rural Wainfleet, Lincolnshire. Home to **Batemans Brewery**, the flag, which is mounted on a former windmill on the bank of the river Steeping, is a potent symbol of the Bateman's family's pride in still running a brewery established by their forebears more than 137 years ago. In 1874 farmers George and Suzanna Bateman, the great grandparents of today's managing director Stuart Bateman and marketing director Jaclyn Bateman, decided to sell their farm and rent a small brewery in Wainfleet. The industrial revolution was underway and across Britain a new breed of entrepreneurial Victorians wanted to use the latest technology to brew sufficient beer to slake the thirsts of the country's growing number of rural labourers and industrial workers. George and Suzanna moved to the brewery's current site in 1880.

In 1985, a family rift almost saw the end of the brewery. The brother and sister of George Bateman, chairman at the time, wanted to sell their shares, a move which could have led to the end of family involvement in the brewery. But a determined and spirited two-year fight by the chairman saw him raise the money to buy the shares and ensure the company's independence. In 1986, at a moment when the future of the brewery seemed most in doubt, it won CAMRA's Champion Beer of Britain award, an accolade which encouraged George to work even harder to save his beloved brewery and to continue to brew his acclaimed ales. Subsequently it has won the award four more times.

In 2000 a visitor centre was opened and in 2002 a new brewhouse, named the Theatre of Beers, was built, reinforcing the family commitment to remain an independent family brewery for many years to come. With a shop, large garden and bar, it is a great place to relax in the beer garden, play traditional pub games and enjoy a glass or two of their 'good honest ales'. For theatre in a glass there are few beers better than Batemans Triple XB. A classic British-style ale, American Liberty hops have been added to the traditional cast of Goldings and Challenger. The American hops add a subtle banana spiciness and floral notes to the beer, which stand up to the nutty performance of the locally grown malt. The first was so good, I had to have an encore.

East Midlands

Visitor information:

Batemans Brewery
Salem Bridge Brewery, Mill Lane,
Wainfleet, Lincolnshire, PE24 4JE
01754 882009
www.bateman.co.uk
 Visitor centre: 11.30–4 Wed–Sun
and bank holidays; 11.30–2.30 Oct
Dec & Feb–Mar. Children must be
accompanied by an adult. Free entry
 Brewery tours: 12.30 and 2.30
Wed–Sun (2.30 only Oct–Dec &
Feb–Mar; closed Jan). Evening and
weekend tours available

Getting there and away: Wainfleet
rail station is 5 minutes' walk from
Batemans Brewery.

46
Lincoln – a city pub walk

Lincoln is an old and beautiful medieval city, dominated by a dark, brooding, castle and one of the country's largest cathedrals. It is also ideal for a walking tour. The oldest part of this historic city stands 60 metres up on a limestone prominence above the River Witham. In Celtic times, it provided a position of great strategic advantage for warring tribes, who named it Lindon – the hill-fort by the pool. The castle was founded by William the Conqueror in 1068. With walls of between 2 and 3 metres thick and more than 6 metres high, it was built to intimidate anyone threatening the city and to protect the people who lived within its guarded six acres. The castle also has a copy of the original the Magna Carta on display.

Lincoln cathedral

Close to the castle's West Gate is the Victoria, a pub rightly proud to have been in CAMRA's *Good Beer Guide* for more than 27 years. Built at some time in the 1840s, it's a cracking pub, with a nice garden, which also offers accommodation.

Nearby, and also in the shadow of the castle in the historic cathedral quarter, is the Strugglers, a supporter of CAMRA's LocAle scheme. The pub's name allegedly comes from it being the place where condemned prisoners came for a last pint before facing the hangman. The large garden which faces the castle wall even has a big screen TV for sports events.

Lincoln cathedral was built in 1092; however, most of it dates from the 13th century when it was rebuilt in the Gothic style. It is the third largest cathedral in England, after York Minster and St Paul's in London. Towering above the city, it is a prominent landmark for miles around. Down a narrow, steep, street from the cathedral is a small Samuel Smith's pub, the Widow Cullen's Well, that you could easily pass by if you hadn't been told about it. It is said to be named after a woman in the 17th century who allowed neighbours to draw water from her well. Small and intimate, it always keeps one cask ale from one of the country's most enigmatic brewers.

EAST MIDLANDS

101 BEER DAYS OUT | **101**

The **Jolly Brewer** in Broadgate is the local CAMRA Pub of the Year 2011 and a supporter of beers brewed in the county. It is decorated in a curious Art Deco style. A fiercely independent pub, it is a great supporter of local musicians, with two music nights every week.

Ten real ales are sold in the timber-framed **Green Dragon**. Dating back to the 16th century, on a Monday evening the prize for winning the pub's quiz is a gallon of beer. On a similarly generous scale, the pub is renowned locally for its ample Sunday carvery lunches.

Close to Lincoln station is the **Ritz** pub. Once a cinema, in 2004 it opened as a pub. A modern classic, it is decorated in a smart and highly attractive Art Deco style which is augmented by photos of the many stars whose films flickered in what is now an imposing bar. A J. D. Wetherspoon pub, it is one of the many fine buildings around the country which has been saved from demolition by the company and given a new lease of life. One of the benefits of being a CAMRA member is that Wetherspoon's gives all members £20 worth of vouchers a year for use in its pubs. With regular beer festivals and a large range of real ales, there is plenty to choose from.

Visitor information:

Victoria
6 Union Rd, Lincoln, LN1 3BJ
01522 541000
11–midnight (1am Fri & Sat);
12–midnight Sun

Strugglers
83 Westgate, Lincoln, LN1 3BG
01522 535023
12–11 (midnight Tue & Wed;
1am Thu); 11–1am Fri & Sat

Widow Cullen's Well
29 Steep Hill, Lincoln, LN2 1LU
01522 523020
1–11

Jolly Brewer
27 Broadgate, Lincoln, LN2 5AQ
01522 528583
www.thejollybrewer.co.uk
12–midnight (1am Fri & Sat);
12–11 Sun

Green Dragon
Magpie Square, Broadgate, Lincoln, LN2 5BH
01522 567155
www.greendragonpub.co.uk
11–11 (midnight Fri & Sat);
12–10.30 Sun

Ritz
143–147 High Street, Lincoln, LN5 7PJ
01522 512103
9am–midnight (1am Fri & Sat)

Getting there and away: Lincoln railway station is 5 minutes' walk from the Ritz.

47

Nottingham – castle and beer festival

Nottingham Castle

If Robin Hood really did have a merry band of men, it is probably because they had been drinking at **Nottingham Robin Hood Beer Festival**. Held for three days over a long weekend in October in the fantastic grounds of Nottingham

Nottingham Castle caves

Castle, more than 850 different cask ales feature at the festival. Organised by the local CAMRA branch, the occasion claims to hold the world record for offering the largest selection of real ales at any festival. And, unsurprisingly for a city whose local branch pioneered CAMRA's LocAle initiative, which encourages pubs to stock locally brewed beer, more than 200 of the beers for sale are from breweries located within 20 miles of the festival. The City Council have embraced the event, and are now supporting a Festival Fringe Fortnight (FFF), which involves more of the local community. For participating pubs the rules are simple and are based on the LocAle scheme: they must sell at least one cask beer that has been brewed within 20 miles of the city centre. In 2011, nine pubs took part in the FFF, with events that included matchings of locally produced beer and food.

However, no one visiting the city outside festival time will be disappointed. The castle, founded in 920AD to keep the Danes from sailing further down the Trent, is built on a tall bluff of sandstone, with a sheer cliff that provides a natural defence. Underneath are many caves and tunnels cut into the soft stone, which can still be explored by anyone willing to descend the 300 steps through hundreds of years of history. The caves proved to be a boon for the city's brewers. Sandstone caves maintain a constant temperature of around 14°C and made excellent cellars for the storage of ale. Also carved into the rock

at the foot of the castle, is Ye Olde Trip to Jerusalem pub, reputed to be one of the oldest pubs in the country, founded in 1089. Legend has it that knights on their way to fight in the Crusades would often stop for refreshment here. Tours of the pub's extensive labyrinth of cellars and caves can be arranged, by booking seven days in advance.

The city has many other fine pubs to enjoy – another carved into the rock is the Hand & Heart. A free house, the dining area extends back into a sandstone cave. It usually features six real ales on the bar and offers a discount to CAMRA members.

The Canalhouse is an unusual pub in a former canal museum. It must be unique among pubs as the canal extends inside the building and provides moorings for some narrow boats. The pub is owned by the Castle Rock Brewery, which was founded in 1977 by former CAMRA chairman Chris Holmes. Castle Rock's Harvest Pale is a former CAMRA Champion Beer of Britain. First brewed for a CAMRA festival in 2003, it quickly became a regular brew. A golden beer its colour is as yellow as a field of ripening barley. It has an aroma which explodes in the mouth with zesty lemon flavours, which comes from the cocktail of American hops. The malt has slight hint of toffee apple sweetness. The finish is long and totally refreshing.

Visitor information:

Nottingham Robin Hood Beer Festival
Held Thu–Sat in mid–October (check website for dates). Tickets are available at the gate and in advance through the website.
www.beerfestival.nottinghamcamra.org

Festival Fringe Fortnight
Takes place in pubs around the city either side of the festival weekend.

🍺 12–11 (midnight Thu; 1am Fri & Sat); 12–10.30 Sun

Getting there and away: Nottingham rail station is 5 minutes' walk from Ye Olde Trip to Jerusalem.

48 🍺

Derby – Britain's real ale capital

Ye Olde Trip to Jerusalem
Brewhouse Yard, Nottingham, NG1 6AD
0115 947 3171
www.triptojerusalem.com
🍺 11–11 (midnight Fri & Sat)

Hand & Heart
65 Derby Road, Nottingham, NG1 5BA
0115 958 2456
www.thehandandheart.co.uk
🍺 12–12 (11 Mon; 2am Fri & Sat); 12–10.30 Sun

Canalhouse
48–52 Canal Street, Nottingham, NG1 7EH
0115 822 5317
www.canalhousebar.co.uk

Canalhouse

There is much more to Derby than its industrial heritage. Its roots are Roman; the invaders knew a thing or two about the strategic importance of its location on the River Derwent. However, it was the railways, Rolls Royce and the silk industry which came to give the city its industrial heart. Currently the Derby Museum of Industry and History, which is housed in a former 16th century silk mill, is mothballed. However, when it reopens it will have plenty of exhibits to keep plane and train spotters happy. The city also boasts an 18th-century cathedral, graced with large windows which flood the large interior with light. Look out for the peregrine falcons nesting on the 64-metre-high tower.

Locals will tell you that every day is a beer festival, making it the country's capital city for real ale. A recent count by the local CAMRA branch found 161 different ales on sale in the 68 pubs visited. It is said there is a pub on every street corner. Indeed, the city offers an unmatched choice of old and new pubs, street-corner boozers, modern bars, pubs matching beer and food, and six pubs that brew their own beer.

The city's centre presents the strolling beer lover with a near-perfect pub walk. Close to Derby station – it is 200 metres away – the **Brunswick** was built as a watering hole for railway workers in 1842. It later fell into disrepair and was shut for many years. Thankfully, while still retaining the air of a down-to-earth street-corner boozer, it is thriving and vibrant again. It now has its own brewery, and food matching evenings are offered in a room upstairs.

Brewery Tap, Derby

Housed in an old Victorian building, the **Brewery Tap** is a stylish modern interpretation of what a modern pub, with lots of exposed brickwork and wooden flooring, should look like. On fine days, the roof terrace offers great views across the river.

The **Olde Dolphin** is the city's oldest pub. The front patio is modern but inside it creaks and oozes with warmth and character. Each July it hosts a famed beer festival.

The nearby **Old Silk Mill** is the CAMRA Derby branch's Pub of the Year for 2011. In the last two years it has been transformed from a closed, run-down building into a thriving city centre, traditional pub.

The **Flowerpot** is home to the Black Iris Brewery and, at weekends, more than 25 ales will often be on sale. The pub is also well known as a music venue.

The **Falstaff Tavern** is a former coaching inn, which also brews its own beer, and the pub's rooms are crammed with brewery memorabilia, as well as the odd ghost or two. The house beer Falstaff Fistful of Hops is as exactly as it says on the label, it is very hoppy. The final addition of dry hops into the cask, add a floral, and orange piquancy to this tongue curling brew.

Visitor information:

Brunswick
  1 Railway Terrace, Derby, DE1 2RU
  01332 290677
  www.brunswickinn.co.uk
  11–11; 12–10.30 Sun
Brewery Tap – Derby's Royal Standard
  1 Derwent Street, Derby, DE1 2ED
  01332 366 283
  www.derbybrewing.co.uk
  1–11 (midnight Thu; 1am Fri & Sat)
Olde Dolphin
  5a Queen Street, Derby, DE1 3DL
  01332 267711
  10.30–midnight; 12–11 Sun

Olde Dolphin

Old Silk Mill
  19 Full Street, Derby, DE1 3AF
  01332 255308
  www.theoldsilkmill.com
  11–midnight; 12–11 Sun
Flowerpot
  23–25 King Street, Derby, DE1 3DZ
  01332 204955
  11–11 (midnight Fri & Sat); 12–11 Sun

Falstaff Tavern
74 Silverhill Road, Derby, DE23 6UJ
01332 342902
www.falstaffbrewery.co.uk
🕐 12–11 (midnight Fri & Sat)

Getting there and away: Derby railway station is five minutes' walk from the Brunswick Inn.

Falstaff Tavern brewpub

Midland Railway Centre

49 🚂

Amber Valley – a beer festival and a rail tour

It's full steam ahead for one of the newest and friendliest beer festivals in the country, Amber Valley Rail Ale Festival. The first festival took place in 2009 and since then it has grown steadily in size and popularity. Located at Butterley station in Ripley, the festival provides an opportunity to try some great local beers in preserved railway carriages and experience a steam train ride though one of the most beautiful parts of Derbyshire. Ale and steam train enthusiasts can take the short train ride to Swanwick Junction on Saturday and Sunday afternoons, where they will see the main site for the

growing museum, which contains a large collection of steam and diesel locomotives. And, like many of the best festivals, music is a key feature, and drinkers can expect to experience the delights of local Morris sides, folk musicians and tribute bands. The railway museum, which is open for most of the year, regularly runs steam and diesel passenger trains, with one of the highlights being the causeway crossing over the middle of the Butterley reservoir. During the summer months both the Narrow Gauge Golden Valley Light Railway and the Butterley Park Miniature Railway operate most weekends. Indeed, a trip to the Midland Rail Centre here, irrespective of the time of year, offers the opportunity to try out two nearby impressive real ale pubs.

The Talbot Taphouse in Ripley is a renovated Victorian flat-iron site. It is home for beers from the exciting Amber Ales. The brewer loves to experiment with new brews – so expect beers made with North American yeasts, or German malts, and flavourings like chocolate, ginger and vanilla.

In Marlpool is the Queen's Head, another marvellously restored pub, which has become something of a beer temple, where the promise is to make every day a beer festival. More than 14 real ales are likely to be on tap at any time, including beers from Castle Rock, Thornbridge and Oakham Ales, along with 20 real ciders.

Butterley station, Ripley

50 🛢

Welbeck Abbey – real ale, cheese and bread

What is more mysterious – the stories which abound about Welbeck Abbey or the enigmatic, elemental life cycle of a yeast cell? One of the most curious tales of the Welbeck Estate, home to the Portland family, is about the 5th Duke, who was as mad as a box of frogs. A mid-19th-century coal baron, he was something of a recluse, somewhat akin to American billionaire Howard Hughes. Under the grounds of the extensive estate he used his miners to dig an extensive and elaborate network of tunnels, so that he could travel unseen in his horse-drawn carriage. The tunnels still exist and are in perfect working order, though all most visitors see are the glass skylights at ground level, which pave the estate's roads. The family-owned Welbeck Estates acts to conserve, protect, and develop an evolving and sustainable estate. It is also home to the School of Artisan Food, which includes a bakery, a patisserie and a cheese-making set up. Bakers, cheesemakers, and their students tease yeast into life to make the most glorious creations. The breads are so tasty and crunchy they can be eaten on their own, without the need for butter. A range of organic, hand-made cheeses are made, including an unpasteurised Stichelton cheese, using organic milk from a herd of Holstein-Friesian cows at Collingthwaite Farm on the estate.

Recently the estates added Welbeck Abbey Brewery to its family of yeast-derived products. Housed in a converted former carriage workshop, it has been developed by one of the country's best

Wellbeck Abbey First Brew

Tours of the brewery, by arrangement, on Tuesday, Wednesday and Thursday evenings, 7.30–9, £5 a head

Getting there and away: Welbeck is off the A60 between Mansfield and Worksop.

51 🛢

The Peak District – Thornbridge Brewery and Bakewell

brewers, Dave Wickett, the founder of the Kelham Island Brewery and owner of the legendary Fat Cat pub in Sheffield. Here can be seen the brewer's art and craft. The current brewster, Claire Monk, takes such simple natural raw materials – malted barley, hops and water – and, with the magic of yeast, turns them into the symphony of tastes and colours that we call beer. Modern in outlook, she often looks to the US and New Zealand for inspiration, and delights in using flavoursome hops from these countries to add extra taste to the beers. Currently the brewery produces four different beers, which are available on draught in local pubs or are hand-bottled and sold in the Welbeck Farm Shop. The shop also sells freshly made breads, cheeses and meat. The site is also home to the Harley Gallery, a craft shop, a garden centre and a café.

The wooded, rolling hills which surround the village of Bakewell on the Derbyshire Wye River are near perfect for anyone wanting to spend a day walking or cycling. Until recently the pretty town, with many of its buildings in the local warm, brownish stone, was famed for its eponymous pudding and the fact that Jane Austen stayed at the Rutland Arms Hotel. Now it has a third claim to fame as, since 2009, it has been home to the renowned Thornbridge Brewery.

The state-of-the-art Riverside Brewery is located about 10 minutes' walk away from the town's centre. The source of many legendary beers, including Jaipur IPA, Saint Petersburg Imperial Russian Stout and Wild Swan, the staff here pride themselves on their innovation and passion. The brewers delight in showing that their beers are not old-fashioned but are as stylish and chic as the brewery is.

Nearby is Thornbridge Hall, where the company started brewing in 2005. It took old recipes and added a modern twist, with a wide range of malts, hops and herbs foraged from the hall's garden.

Bakewell, Derbyshire

The formula has worked well as it has won more than 250 awards nationally and internationally since it began. Brewing still takes place at the hall, where a traditional infusion mash is used, but the emphasis is on experimentation. In the old days brewers served beer aged in oaken casks. Now brewers are rolling back the barrels for flavouring beers. At the hall, several beers are gently ageing in flavoursome wooden barrels once used to store spirits, in the same way that many whisky distillers do. As the beers grow older so intensity, acidity and spirit notes will be added to their taste. Thornbridge Hall is set in 102 acres of parkland within the Peak District National Park. It is a private house but has occasional special events, and is perhaps best known for being open to the public on a Saturday in July when it hosts an annual charity garden party.

Thornbridge beers can be drunk at the visitor centre, but many prefer to take the short drive or half an hour's good walk to the village of Longstone and the cosy Packhorse Inn. Now owned by Thornbridge, it welcomes muddy boots, kids and dogs. Try the Thornbridge Wild Swan, its pale colour belies the complexity of the citrus fruity beer. It's the perfect refresher after a good walk.

Nearby is Monsal Head, with some of the greatest views of Monsal Dale, the famed Headstone railway viaduct, and up the Wye Valley where the river hits a stratum of hard rock forcing it to make a sharp turn southwards through the softer limestone.

Visitor information:

Thornbridge Brewery
  Riverside Business Park, Buxton Road, Bakewell, Derbyshire, DE45 1GS
  01629 641000
  www.thornbridgebrewery.co.uk
  Shop: 9–4 Mon–Fri. Brewery tours available by arrangement, Wednesdays at 1pm and 3pm. Admission £7.50 (£3 for under-18s)

Thornbridge Brewery tour

Thornbridge Hall
  Ashford in the Water, Derbyshire, DE45 1NZ
  01629 641006
  www.thornbridgehall.co.uk
Packhorse Inn
  Main Street, Little Longstone, Derbyshire, DE45 1NN
  01629 640471
  www.packhorselongstone.co.uk
  12–3, 4.45–11.30;
  12–11.30 Sat & Sun

Getting there and away: Thornbridge Brewery is off the A6, near Bakewell.

EAST MIDLANDS

Shugborough Estate

West Midlands

Days Out

Introducing the West Midlands

The West Midlands has made a huge contribution to the art and science of beermaking. The town of Burton upon Trent is world famous for the production of pale ales. The water from the Trent which percolates up to the surface through layers of gypsum gives a natural effervescence and clarity to the beer and brings out the best flavours from the region's malt and hops.

In the 19th century the region's railways and canals helped transport pale beers from Burton worldwide and started to challenge the might and power of the London brewers, famed for making porters and stout. At Marston's you can see the wooden 'unions', a development which saw brewers from around the world visit Burton to marvel at the technology and see how beer was made. The region is also home to two of the famous four brewpubs, the All Nations and Three Tuns, which kept the tradition of public house brewing alive in the 1970s. Critics said they were an anachronism and would soon close; however, they went on to inspire a generation of licensees to create hundreds of locally brewed beers. The region is also the birthplace of the Industrial Revolution – and at Ironbridge it is possible to see the first bridge made of cast iron, testament to a developing technology which was utilised by many of the new wave of commercial brewers to build larger and more efficient breweries. At Purity brewery in Warwickshire you can visit not just a modern brewery developing new beers tailored to today's tastes, but one which is also showing how beer can be produced in a sustainable and environmentally friendly way

Hops too are vitally important to the region; each year thousands of people from industrial Birmingham used to travel to the area around Bromyard to help with harvest. Without the back-breaking labours of these people, the thick dark old ale of England might never have been transformed into bright beer. Perhaps some of the seasonal hopworkers who were part of this social phenomenon, which lasted several centuries, drank in the pubs which feature in the tour of some of Birmingham's best city pubs.

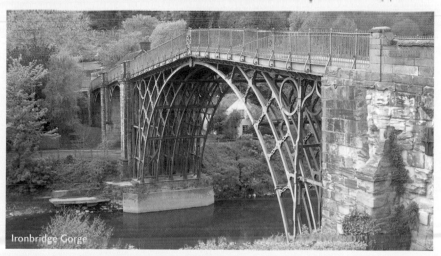
Ironbridge Gorge

Shugborough Hall, with its revived brewery

52 🛢 👨‍👧

Shugborough Estate – a titanic story

In its heyday, the Shugborough Estate must have been quite a place. Its zenith was probably the 19th century. There must have been a real buzz on the estate when members of the Anson family returned to it after wintering in their London home. This is no fictional Downton Abbey – it was for real; just about everything people needed for food, warmth and sustenance was grown, made or found within the boundaries of the estate. Beer was made on the estate too; lots of it. An allowance of beer was part of the staff wages; workers would receive eight pints a day. The water came from the estate's own well, barley would have been grown and malted on the estate, and once brewing was finished the spent grains would go to feed the estate's cattle and pigs. However, there is no evidence of hops being grown here, so they would have been bought in from elsewhere, probably from gardens in

Herefordshire and Worcestershire and brought to the estate by canal boat. Once there were two breweries on the estate: one supplied the farmworkers and the other, housed in the servants' quarters, supplied the house. One closed around 1820 and the other kept brewing until the 1880s. The servants' brewhouse was restored at the beginning of the century but no one could be found to take on the big task of running it. Now, thanks to Keith Bott from the nearby Titanic Brewery, beer is made once again on this still-intact estate. The wood-fired, two-and-a-half-barrel brewery is operational on many Sundays throughout the Shugborough Estate's open season.

If a 19th-century farmworker or maid returned to this grand mansion, now a National Trust property, they would find all the significant buildings – the house, servants' quarters, model farm and walled garden – much as they remembered it. Visitors are asked leave the 21st century behind and step into the real 19th-century environment of the of this working estate. You can see, feel, hear and smell history as many costumed characters describe the day-to-day life of a large, dynamic country estate. The estate workers no longer get a daily beer allowance, but it can be bought from the shop. On sale you will find beers with teasing names such as MiLady's Fancy and Butler's Revenge. Other attractions on the estate include a working watermill, kitchens, a dairy, a tea room and rare breeds of farm animals.

If you fancy a pint after all of this, Stafford is not that far away, with several of its hostelries listed in the *Good Beer Guide*. Try the Pie & Ale House in Crabbery Street. The pub's name gives it all away; excellent examples of both can be found. Often on the bar is the excellent Titanic White Star. Sharp and crisp to taste and unlike its namesake ship, this one is meant for sinking.

Visitor information:

Shugborough Estate
  Shugborough, Staffordshire,
  ST17 0XB
  www.shugborough.org.uk
  The estate is open daily March–
  October
Pie & Ale House
  Crabbery Street, Stafford, ST16 2BA
  01785 226108
  9–11; 10–6 Sun

Getting there and away: Stafford rail station is 6 miles from Shugborough. Arriva bus 825 from Stafford passes the estate entrance.

53

Hire a canalboat – ales from the towpath

Taking a canal boat from Sawley Marina to Burton upon Trent is a journey right into the heart of England's brewing heritage. Once, these waterways bustled with commercial vessels; they would have been as busy with boats as the M6 is now with giant, thundering lorries carrying goods from the four corners of the world. Some brought iron made in Sweden and Russia from the port of Hull, others carried groceries from London for consumption in the area. Cargo-carrying canal boats also travelled from the great ports of Bristol and Liverpool to Burton. And on their return trip these boats would have been loaded up with barrels of beer, helping to take the name of Burton not just across England but around the world.

Today the waterways are still busy, but with leisure craft. Sawley is the biggest inland marina in the country. Here you can leave your cares behind you on a hired canal boat, meandering your way through a relaxing world of fabulous pubs – too many to name but a few here – and some great countryside. Moving at a top speed of only four miles an hour, it takes two days to get to Burton and its promise of a pint of Marston's Pedigree. A canal boat is like a good relaxing country walk, but without the physical effort.

Heading west from Sawley, a short river section takes you to Derwent Mouth, and the entrance to the Trent & Mersey canal. After about an hour's cruising the boat arrives at the village of Shardlow, home to a number of good pubs, including the Old Crown inn, a classic 17th-century English pub. It was once a coaching inn and is now decorated with hanging water jugs and brewery and railway memorabilia. It serves up to nine real ales, has a large beer garden to relax in, and twice a year hosts a beer festival. Many choose to moor here for the night and anyone interested in canal life should take time to visit the village's heritage centre, which charts the lives of boaters from the 18th century. Moving on, the village of Swarkestone offers the 17th-century Crewe & Harpur. In Barrow on Trent can be found the Ragley Boat Stop, a spacious pub with a large garden running down to the canal, and by Stenson Lock the Bubble Inn. After about five hours of cruising you come to the village of Willington. The Green Man by the canal bridge is an attractive low-ceilinged two-bar inn, well-liked by locals and boaters and said locally to be the best for ale.

After another two hours' travel the boat arrives in Burton upon Trent. People mooring here can visit Marston's Brewery – home to the Burton union – as well as the National Brewery Centre, or seek out some of the town's finest pubs. In its heyday of the 1790s more than 200 boats and barges were operating from Burton, and another 150 regularly passed through the town. It was only the arrival of better roads and the railways which saw the end of this trade, but by then the name of Burton was known throughout the world as the home of good beer.

CAMRA members booking with Hire a Canalboat are entitled to a five per cent discount on short breaks or trips of up to 13 days. And CAMRA will also benefit from your booking, with a donation made by the company to CAMRA's campaigning funds.

Hire a Canalboat

Ragley Boat Stop
Deepdale Lane, Barrow on Trent, Derby, DE73 7FY
01332 703919
king-henrys-taverns.co.uk/Pubs/The-Ragley-Boat-Stop
🕒 11.30–11

Bubble Inn
Derby Road, Stenson, Derby, DE73 7HL
01283 703113
www.thebubbleinn.com
🕒 12–11.30

Green Man
1 Canal Bridge, Willington, Derbyshire, DE65 6DQ
01283 702377
🕒 11.30–11 (11.30 Wed & Thu; midnight Fri & Sat); 12–11 Sun

Hire a Canalboat
www.hireacanalboat.co.uk

Getting there and away: Long Eaton rail station is 1 mile from Sawley Marina.

Visitor information

Old Crown
Cavendish Bridge, Shardlow, Derby, Derbyshire, DE72 2HL
01332 792392
🕒 11–11.30 (12.30 Fri & Sat); 11–11 Sun

Crewe & Harpur
Swarkestone Road, Swarkestone, Derby, DE73 7JA
01332 700641
www.creweharpurpub.co.uk
🕒 11–11; 11–10.30 Sun

Ragley Boat Stop

54 🛢

Marston's brewery – and three of Burton's greatest pubs

Raise a glass and celebrate one of the greatest brewing centres not just in Britain but in the world. The home of a style of beer that at one time ruled the world, Burton upon Trent's place in the story of beer is equal to that of beer rival Pilsen (Plzen), now in the Czech Republic, whose famous pilsner-style beers have also traversed the globe. At its height, in the 19th century, more than 40 breweries were taking advantage of Burton's supply of water – called liquor by brewers – which is naturally ideal for the brewing of ale-style beer. It was this hard water, high in magnesium and calcium sulphates, which provided ideal conditions for ale yeast to thrive and allowed large quantities of hops to be used, producing a sparkling lighter-coloured beer – the renowned and revered Burton pale ale. Monks first discovered the value of Burton upon Trent's waters; they started brewing in 1002. But it was not for another 700 years, when the canals were first built, that beer from Burton became widely known around the world.

One of the town's greatest brewers is Marston's, which still uses a fermentation system called the Burton Union. In the 1860s brewers from around the world travelled to this brewing mecca to see this new technology. Indeed, stepping inside the Victorian fermentation room with its high-vaulted ceiling is to enter one of the world's great brewing temples. Here can be seen the lines of interlinked wooden barrels and fermenters which give Marston's greatest brew, Pedigree, its pedigree. It is a complex beer with a heady cocktail of sweet malt and dry, citrus-flavoured hops. Like the pipes of a glorious cathedral organ, supported by a double-decked scaffold, iron tubes snake up to take the fermenting beer from the large oak barrels on the bottom up into a trough above. It is the vibrant movement of the fermenting wort passing from the barrel to the trough and back again that helps create the complexity of the Marston's Pedigree. As it dances through the union it gains strength and intensity.

The Elms Inn, which overlooks the river Trent, is a fine place to sup and savour a pint of this fine beer. Built as a house in the 19th century, it is a small parlour pub which has been renovated in Victorian style. When the Pedigree is fresh, breathe it in deeply before taking a sip, and you will experience what is known as the Burton snatch. Before the beer even touches your lips your nose will be assailed by sulphur notes. The smell is like a freshly lit Swan Vesta match, and is the signature mark of a classic Burton pale. This distinctive note derives from the water stored deep underground in gypsum beds, and people either adore it or hate it. It is the beer equivalent of Marmite which, coincidentally, is made from spent yeast left over from the brewing process.

Perhaps Burton's most famous pub

Burton's most famous pub has to be the Coopers Tavern. Close to the railway station, it is a classic, near-unspoilt 19th-century ale house. Once the tap for the Bass brewery, its inside is time-worn and dark. Relaxing leather settles line the walls. Here the beer is served straight from the cask. No longer a brewery tap, it still serves Draught Bass, once the best-known beer in the world, now brewed by Marston's under contract. It is an assertive beer full of glorious fruit notes from the Herefordshire, Worcestershire and Kent hops. And on a good day it too rewards the nose with the Burton signature of a freshly burnt match.

The Burton Bridge Inn is a higgledy-piggledy and friendly pub and home to the Burton Bridge Brewery. Its three rooms are all different but share a quiet, comfortable tranquillity and are the perfect place to try the Burton Bridge's Golden Delicious. Yes, the beer has some crisp, astringent green apple flavours and, of course, hints of the famous Burton snatch.

Visitor information:

Marston's
  Shobnall Road, Burton upon Trent,
  Staffordshire, DE14 2BW
  01283 507391
  www.marstons.co.uk
  Tours by arrangement
  🍺 Shop: 10–5 Mon–Fri; 9.30–12 Sat
Elms Inn
  36 Stapenhill Road, Stapenhill,
  Burton upon Trent, Staffordshire,
  DE15 9AE
  01283 535505
  🍺 12 (1 Mon)–11.30; 12–midnight
  Fri & Sat; 12–11 Sun
Coopers Tavern
  42 Cross Street, Burton upon Trent,
  Staffordshire, DE14 1EG
  01283 532551

🍺 5–11; 12–2.30, 5–11 Wed
& Thu; 12–midnight Fri & Sat;
12–11 Sun
Burton Bridge Inn
  24 Bridge Street, Burton upon Trent,
  Staffordshire, DE14 1SY
  01283 536596
  www.burtonbridgeinn.co.uk
  🍺 11.30–2.30, 5–11; 11.30–11.30
  Fri & Sat; 12–3, 7–11 Sun

Getting there and away: Burton on Trent rail station is 5 minutes walk from the Coopers Tavern.

55 🛢 👪

National Brewery Centre – the UK's premier brewing museum

Burton upon Trent is quite simply one of the greatest brewing towns the world has ever seen. Within it is the National Brewery Centre, the United Kingdom's premier museum dedicated to brewing. It is also home to the

William Worthington's Brewery, famed for producing the legendary White Shield beer – winner of no fewer than seven CAMRA Champion Bottled Beer of Britain awards. The Brewery Centre, formerly known as the Bass Museum, was set up in 1977. Its galleries include an exhibition on how beer is made, a collection of vintage vehicles used for transporting beer, and an interactive display about Burton's history. There is something for everyone – steam enthusiasts can enjoy the No. 9 steam train and Directors' coach, which are featured in mock up of a station platform from the days when the Bass Brewery had its own railway network and was probably the owner of the largest private railway in the country. Among the many road vehicles displayed is the 1920s Daimler bottle car that used to promote beer. In the summer months the gentle giant Bass dray horses are stabled here. It contains a unique collection of Bass artefacts and the history of the Bass brand, with its red triangle logo, which went on to be the first registered trade mark in the world.

The centre also celebrates the people of Burton, whose toil made the town so famous. Its significance as a mecca for brewing can be seen from the model of Burton's town centre and the many breweries which were operating in the 1900s. The story of beer is told from some of its earliest practitioners in ancient Egypt through to the present day, as the tour includes the newly opened William Worthington's Brewery. With care and attention the role of malt and hops are explained. And so too are the unique qualities of the local water for brewing British-style ales. The quality of Burton water was so renowned that up until the 1950s one Bolton brewer, Magee Marshall, transported water from its own Burton well by rail tankers to its brewery in Lancashire.

In the 19th century Burton was one of the wonder towns of the Industrial Revolution and the country's equivalent of a silicon valley. And the name Bass, the King of Brewers, was the best-known firm in the British Empire. The clear beers of Burton were brewed in what came to be known as the Burton Union

The National Brewery Centre, Burton upon Trent

system, mentioned earlier. An example of a redundant union stands on the edge of the centre's car park, a testament to the skill of the brewery engineers and coopers who built it. From Bombay to the Baltic, Burton beers have slaked the thirsts of millions – and the town's name has become a byword for excellence in brewing. And at the end of the tour what could be better than to visit the Brewery Centre's final interactive display, the Brewery Tap. In this bar and restaurant you can appreciate and enjoy a well-earned glass of White Shield.

Worthington's White Shield is probably the world's most authentic India Pale Ale (IPA) and it is a survivor from the 1820s. Worthington was never one of the big Burton brewers and was subsumed within the growing Bass empire in 1927. Somehow the beer survived as a bottled beer, though it is now available on draught here. It was a curiosity as it still contained yeast in the bottle. Drinkers' conversations often focussed on whether the beer should be poured clear or have the yeast tipped into the glass too. It is at its best when it has a swirling fragrant attack of fruity aromatic Kent and Herefordshire hops. There is a hint of spice and banana and some soft toffee. It's history in a glass, and a beer that everyone should try.

Throughout the year numerous exhibitions, lectures, displays of vehicles and other events (many of them with a musical theme) are held at the centre.

56 🚂
Churnet Valley Railway – experience the heights of the Peak District

Trains, boats, (but no aircraft), and some good plain walking or even cycling can all link this stretch of the River Churnet and Caldon Canal. And with large amount of help from the Titanic Brewery, once a year three of the stations on the Churnet Valley Railway also offer a great beer festival.

In an area known as Staffordshire's Rhineland, more than 40 real ales are available from the bars of these three stations and two trains and, if that is not enough, there are a number of fine pubs that hug the sides of this tree-lined and steep-sided valley. So even if the beer festival is not on, a tour of some pubs – with the train taking the strain – is a worthwhile experience. The line is open through the year and, as well as the ale weekend, plays host to many occasions and festivals including 1940s weekends, steam gala gatherings and events for children too. Over the weekend of

Kingsley & Froghall station

Locomotive on the hill – topping Churnet Valley Railway line

the beer festival two trains operate a continuous service from Kingsley & Froghall and Cheddleton stations, stopping at Consall and also taking in the nine miles of the newly-opened track to Cauldon Lowe. Some of the route is of steeply graded railway line offering truly inspiring views of the moorlands, which were virtually unseen for the 75 years the line was closed to passenger trains. The engines struggle as they climb the hills, until they rise, seemingly almost exhausted, to the highest point on the line at Ipstone, more than 320 metres above sea level.

The volunteers who run the line have ambitions to create the biggest heritage network in the country. Plans are in place to eventually restore the line so that it runs all the way to Stoke. Recognising Staffordshire's importance to the world of beer – Burton upon Trent is in the county – many of the beers showcased come from local brewers, and more than 20 are within the county boundary.

At Cheddleton, the picturesque Boat Inn by the canal bridge is only a few moments' walk from the station. The village is worth exploring for its glimpses of the area's industrial past. In the village is the Flint mill. Here narrow boats would moor up and be loaded with ground flint for use by Staffordshire pottery factories. The village's 13th-century St Edward church contains stained glass windows by two leading Pre-Raphaelites – William Morris and Edward Burne-Jones.

The Black Lion at Consall Forge is 100 metres from the station. The pub's attractive garden is seemingly embraced by the tree-clad sides of the valley and is a comfortable place to relax. Nearby are some old lime kilns and a flight of steps known as the Devil's Staircase. With 200 steps to the top of the valley, it is a good way of working up a thirst. And what could be better to slake that thirst than a beer from the local Peakstones Rock Brewery? Its Nemesis, at 3.8% abv, is light and refreshing, with lots of lemon aromas and even a hint of grapefruit.

Visitor information:

Churnet Valley Railway
www.churnet-valley-railway.co.uk
Rail Ale Trail Beer Festival held
Fri–Sun in late July

Boat Inn
Basford Bridge Lane, Cheddleton,
Leek, Staffordshire, ST13 7EQ
01538 360683
www.marstonspubs.co.uk/
boatinnstaffordshire
🕐 12–11 (midnight Fri & Sat)

Black Lion
Consall Forge, Consall, Staffordshire,
ST9 0AJ
01782 550294
www.blacklionpub.co.uk
🕐 12–midnight

The Old Joint Stock, Birmingham

57

Birmingham – UK's second city is a first for many beer drinkers

Britain's second city often seems like a poor relation to some of our other historic cities like Liverpool, Manchester, York, Bristol and Edinburgh. But that is to be unfair on this former industrial hothouse, where the 20,000 swords that Oliver Cromwell's army went to battle with during the Civil War were tempered. Most of our great cities are built on rivers: London has the Thames, Liverpool the Mersey, Bristol the Severn and Cardiff the Taff, all of which offer great walks along their banks. Not so in Birmingham, but the one thing you can bank on is that is has more canals than Venice. Once they were the conduits for industry and the industrial revolution, but today many have been regenerated and offer some great walks snaking through Birmingham's city centre.

For anyone arriving in the city by train all the pubs below are within walking distance of New Street Station. The Old Contemptibles is named in honour of members of the World War I's British Expeditionary Force (BEF) who suffered heavy casualties in 1914 holding up the German advance at Mons. The German Kaiser, Wilhelm II, ordered his men to destroy the "contemptible little army", thereby giving the British force this nickname. The pub adopted the name during the 1950s as a tribute to some of the former Tommies who drank there. The pub's sign is a depiction of the Mons Star, the campaign medal presented to the members of the BEF. Inside, the pub has paintings of soldiers in action and World War I maps displayed in the 'campaign room'. Smart, ornate and marvellously restored, the pub is owned by Nicholsons and has a large and varying range of ales – well worth going over the top for!

The Old Joint Stock was once a bank and stands opposite the cathedral. Built in 1864 by Julius Chatwin, a famed designer of churches, it is now a temple for beer. The large, grand interior sweeps and oozes with Victorian class. If you fancy eating pie then this is the place to be. But beer stars; there is always a choice of local brews, as well as the full range of Fuller's beers. To find London Pride in the Midlands is quite a discovery, as is the Fuller's Discovery, a beer which has turned many lager drinkers on to the delights of ale. A golden beer, it was first brewed in 2005 and is intended to be drunk a little cooler than many ales. Its grist is a mix of malted barley and wheat, to which Liberty and Saaz hops are added in the boil. The result is zesty and full of soft fruit flavours.

Just behind the Old Joint Stock is the Wellington. It has to be one of the jewels in Birmingham's real ale scene. With 16 handpulls on the bar, it claims to hold the record for a pub selling the largest number of real ales in a year – a total of 2,610. In addition it sells a couple of ciders and a perry. Every day feels like a beer festival here, the range is so diverse. No food is served, but if you bring in your own the pub will happily provide a plate and cutlery.

Located on the canalside on Broad Street, the Brasshouse is gaining a reputation for the quality of its ales. Beers from Marston's range normally star along with some guest ales. The pub is widely used by people going to gigs at the nearby Symphony Hall.

The Penny Blacks is another pub with an attractive canalside location. Modern and stylish, it really does show that real ale can be sold in a contemporary environment. Close to the Gas Street canal basin, it is a great place to watch the rippling water, boats, walkers, joggers and cyclists go by. At least five real ales are always on the bar – including Hook Norton's Old Hooky. A full-bodied beer, it has as much character as Birmingham city centre – big, bold and full of pleasant surprises.

Visitor information:

Old Contemptibles
176 Edmund Street, Birmingham, B3 2HB
0121 200 3310
🕙 10–11; 12–6 Sun

Old Joint Stock
4 Temple Row, Birmingham, B2 5NY
0121 200 1892
www.oldjointstocktheatre.co.uk
🕙 11–11; 12–5 Sun

Wellington
37 Bennets Hill, Birmingham, B2 5SN
0121 200 3115
www.wellingtonrealale.co.uk
🕙 10–midnight

Brasshouse
44 Broad Street, Birmingham, B1 2HP
0121 633 3383
www.brasshousebirmingham.co.uk
🕙 10–midnight (1am Thu; 2am Fri & Sat)

Penny Blacks
The Mailbox, Birmingham, B1 1XL
0121 632 1460
www.pennyblacksbar.com
🕙 10–11 (midnight Fri & Sat); 10–10.30 Sun

Getting there and away: Birmingham New Street rail station is 10 minutes walk from the Wellington.

The Wellington boasts up to 16 beers

Purity's reed bed and pond water purification system

58 🛢

Purity – eco brewing in Warwickshire

Most brewers are proud of their green credentials; they start off with simple natural raw materials – cereal and hops – and create drinks of great complexity. Very little goes to waste: used grain goes to feed cattle, spent hops can end up as fertiliser, and excess yeast can become a spread eaten on toast with butter. Energy is managed too, as brewers were early users of heat exchangers, which minimise the amount of energy used for heating and cooling.

Purity has a deeply rural location in the heart of Warwickshire. It was set up with the help of a grant from the Department for the Environment, Food and Rural Affairs. The eco-friendly

brewery, which opened in a converted barn in 2005, goes so far as having its own natural habitat which cleans the brewery's effluent.

Not only does water kick-start the whole brewing process when the malted barley is boiled, it is also used for cleaning brewing equipment and vessels and for heating and cooling. It can take four pints of water to make one pint of beer; some brewers use even more. The Purity brewery was one of the first in the UK to put in a natural system to clean its water effluent, which can be seen by visitors on a brewery tour. A wetland reed bed and pond system naturally breaks down the waste in the brewery's used water as it percolates through it, providing nutrients for the willow and alder trees and creating an idyllic habitat and sanctuary for a host of pond life, before tumbling over a weir and flowing into the nearby river.

Tours of the brewery have to be booked in advance and are normally held on Tuesday and Thursday evenings, for a minimum of 10 people. The tour allows you to see the modern, gleaming brewing equipment and, providing the weather is on your side, the water treatment system. The tour of course includes a tasting of the brewery's award-winning beers. The first beer which flowed out of the brewery's fermenter was Pure UBU. Named after the brewery's dog, it is a modern beer; the cocktail of Challenger and Cascade hops create a fragrant, fruity, almost spicy beer, which is underpinned by the use of Maris Otter malt. Amber in colour, it's a thoroughly green beer.

Visitor information:

Purity
  The Brewery, Upper Spernall Farm,
  Great Alne, Warwickshire,
  B49 6JF
  www.puritybrewing.com
  Tours by arrangement
  🛒 Shop: 8–5 Mon–Fri; 10–1 Sat

Getting there and away: Wootton Wawen rail station is 4 miles from Purity.

59 🛢 👪

Ironbridge – and the story of the Industrial Revolution

There is something quite entrancing about the World Heritage Site which is Ironbridge, with its nine family-friendly visitor attractions and museums set within a steep-sided limestone valley through which the River Severn flows. It is a part of the country where the remains of our industrial heritage and countryside co-exist. The valley's claim to worldwide fame is that it was here the first cast iron bridge was built and designed by Abraham Darby in 1778, with the casting hauled from his foundry in Coalbrookdale. From the riverside its 120-metre span is still a majestic sight. To the 18th-century visitor it must have been a marvel of modern technology. With this iron casting expertise architects were no longer restricted by the limitations of wood and stone, and the Victorians were able to exploit this technology to the full – not least in the building of their breweries.

One of the best museums in the area for a family to visit is the **Blists Hill Victorian Town**. A re-creation of a town in the late-19th century, its attractions include an incline lift, which creaks its way down one of the valley's sides and offers some spectacular views, from the Coalport Canal of the Upper Town to the Green on the Lower Town where you can take a ride on the Clay Mine Railway. There is a bank, where new money can be exchanged for old-fashioned money – pounds, shillings and pence. Children like to spend this in the Victorian sweet shop or at the Victorian fun

WEST MIDLANDS

Blists Hill Victorian Town near Telford

fair. Adults might prefer the New Inn, which is a 19th-century pub, which was transported brick by brick from its original location in Walsall and rebuilt here. The scrubbed wood and sawdust floors look much as they would have done more than 100 years ago. The staff at the pub, which sells Banks's Bitter, are all dressed in period costume.

Opposite the museum is the **All Nations** pub. It was known locally for many years as Mrs Lewis's, after a former landlady. The pub was built more than 200 years ago and then, as now, beer was brewed here. At first it was to satisfy the thirst of workers on the railway line that took the coal from Coalport to various locations. Today, the same historic brewhouse is used as when the brewery opened in 1831. Many drinkers choose the Coalport Mild. A traditional dark mild, it is full of nutty, liquorice flavours from the dark malts used in the grist. Full bodied, it is mild in strength.

Another pub worth seeking out is the **Golden Ball**, which was serving beer 50 years before the iron bridge was built. Hard to find, it is a good place for families as it does food. This pub, too, once brewed its own beer, and the fireplace where the mash was heated and the water source can still be seen.

Visitor information:

Blists Hill Victorian Town
Legges Way, Madeley, Telford,
Shropshire TF7 5DU
www.ironbridge.org.uk
🕙 10–5 (4 winter)

All Nations
20 Coalport Road, Madeley, Telford,
Shropshire, TF7 5DP
01952 585747
🕙 12–midnight

Golden Ball
Newbridge Road, Ironbridge, Telford,
TF8 7BA
01952 432179
www.goldenballinn.com
🕙 11.30–11 (midnight Sat & Sun)

Getting there and away: Ironbridge Gorge is signed from Junction 4 on the M54.

60 🍺 👪

Bromyard Hop Festival

Hops can be seen growing in many of the fields that surround Bromyard. Once upon a time there would have been even more. At one point in the 18th century the land for hops in Herefordshire was the most valuable of any farmland in England, such was the demand for the crop, particularly from the brewers in Burton upon Trent. We tend to think of Herefordshire, Worcestershire and Kent as being the country's main hop-growing areas, but in the late-19th century hops were cultivated in most parts of England, as well as in eight Welsh and five Scottish counties. However, as the volume of beer we drink has declined over the years, so has the acreage of hop farms. An additional factor is that the growth of lager drinking has contributed to the decline of hop growing in this country, as this style of beer generally uses the less aromatic and less bitter hops which are grown on the Continent. Hops

Bromyard hops

were introduced into Bromyard and the Frome Valley in 1577. The annual migration of large groups of workers from London to Kent to harvest the hops is well-known. However, less well-known is that in a similar way during harvest time the town of Bromyard would throng with families from the industrial towns of South Wales, the Midlands and the Black Country.

Once a year, usually on the first Saturday of September, the town celebrates the importance of the hop industry to the area with the Bromyard Hop Festival. The fun includes a parade of vintage and horse-drawn vehicles, a funfair on the Town Green, with craft stalls and a blacksmith, and lots of displays on the theme of hop picking. One of the highlights of the festival is the Hop Pocket World Championship. The event has races for both men and women. A racing pocket is a large sack containing a 70kg measure of hops for the men and 50kg for the women and juniors. At the festival, sweating and perspiring but enthusiastic teams race through the street carrying a pocket. Such is the popularity of the race that the local health centre runs an exercise programme to get locals to a peak level of fitness for it. The event starts in the Market Street, and goes on a circular

Hop Pocket World Championship

route through the town. To make the event even harder, obstacles are placed in the runners' way for them to negotiate.

All the running would make anyone thirsty. The hop pocket run passes the **Queen's Arms** in the High Street. A fine 400-year-old timber-framed building, the pub stocks a good choice of local brews. Also worth seeking out is the **Rose & Lion**, regarded by many as the best pub in town. Known locally as the Rosie, it sells the full range of beers from the Wye Valley brewery. Many choose to drink the Dorothy Goodbody's Golden Ale. A light-coloured beer full of hop bitterness, it is a marvellous example of a modern ale from one of the country's new wave of brewers. And anyone who thinks that stouts are heavy or old-fashioned should be prepared to be surprised if they try the golden ale's big sister, Dorothy Goodbody's Wholesome Stout. Smooth and satisfying, its bitter edge comes from the use of roasted malts, which give mocha and dark toffee flavours followed by a hint of chocolate, and then there's a satisfying fruity and spicy bitter finish from the Northdown hops.

Visitor information:

Bromyard Hop Festival
www.bromyardhopfestival.co.uk
Held on the first Saturday of
September
Queen's Arms
30 High Street, Bromyard,
Herefordshire, HR7 4AE
01885 482281
🍺 11–11 (midnight Thu–Sat;
10.30 Sun)
Rose & Lion
5 New Road, Bromyard,
Herefordshire, HR7 4AJ
01885 482381
🍺 11–11 (midnight Fri & Sat)

61 🍺

Bishop's Castle, Shropshire – home of the country's oldest brewpub

The picturesque and historic small town of Bishop's Castle seems to cling to the side of a steep hill, which is in turn surrounded by even higher hills. The town was once an important sheep market, and its quaint shops are an intriguing mix of farm and country together with arts, crafts and boutiques. For the beer traveller it is also home to one of the most important breweries in the country. The oldest pub in town is the **Three Tuns**, which was built around 1642, when it was given its first brewing licence. Back in the 1970s it was the most handsome-looking of the handful of brewpubs in the country and certainly the one with the longest heritage for continuous brewing. At the time there were just three other pubs left brewing their own beer: the Blue Anchor in Helston (p79), the All Nations, Madeley (p126), and the Old Swan at Netherton, near Dudley. Many critics thought the craft of pub brewing would die out completely, as for the best part of a decade the quartet soldiered on without any others joining their ranks. It seemed only a matter of time before the brewers would retire and no one would want to take their places. How wrong the critics were; pubs brewing their own beer are no longer an endangered species, they are thriving.

The current brewery's building dates from 1888, though the equipment has been replaced in recent years, and is a Lilliputian example of a Victorian tower brewery. The pub and the Three Tuns Brewery have now gone their separate ways, though they happily coexist as the pub serves Three Tuns beers. The beer world has a local retired solicitor, Bill Bainbridge, to thank for saving the brewery. Outraged by plans to turn it into luxury flats, he bought it in 2002 and established it as a brewery once again. Tours of the brewery can be arranged for groups.

Walking down the hill from the Three Tuns, it pays to look up, not only to enjoy the many fine buildings but also for the chance to catch a glimpse of one of the local buzzards circling overhead. The Crown & Anchor Vaults is on the High Street; a no-nonsense pub, regular music sessions are often held here. It serves Ludlow Gold, a well hopped golden ale, the use of the Fuggles and Goldings giving it an aromatic fruitiness which leads to a long, dry aftertaste.

At the foot of the town is the Six Bells pub. the town's other brewery. Run by the indomitable Neville Richards, a.k.a. Big Nev, he started brewing at the pub in 1997, renewing a practice which ceased in the 1900s. The pub runs a famed beer festival in July, which sees the wood-beamed bar's three regular beers augmented by at least 50 more. The pub's house bitter, Big Nev, is pale and somewhat bitter, unlike the man it is named after.

Visitor information:

Three Tuns
Salop Street, Bishop's Castle,
Shropshire, SY9 5BW
01588 638797
www.thethreetunsinn.co.uk
12–11 (10.30 Sun)

Three Tuns Brewery
16 Market Square,
Bishop's Castle,
Shropshire, SYN 5BN
01588 638392
www.threetunsbrewery.co.uk
Shop: 9–5 Mon–Fri
Tours by arrangement

Crown & Anchor Vaults
High Street, Bishop's Castle,
Shropshire, SY9 5BQ
01588 638966
4 (2 Sun)–11

Six Bells
Church Street, Bishop's Castle,
Shropshire, SY9 5AA
01588 638930
www.sixbellsbrewery.co.uk
12–2.30 (not Mon),
5–11; 12–11 Sat; 12–3.30,
7–10.30 Sun

Wales

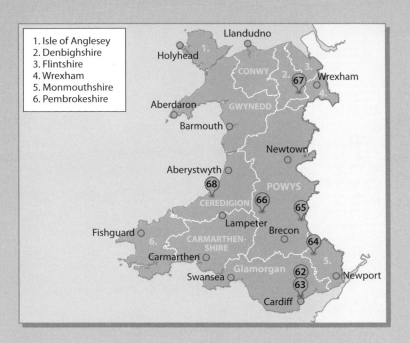

1. Isle of Anglesey
2. Denbighshire
3. Flintshire
4. Wrexham
5. Monmouthshire
6. Pembrokeshire

Contents

Introducing Wales

The low and highs of Wales' valleys and mountains are as dramatic as the fortunes of its pub and brewing industry; life is tough for many of its pubs. Many are deeply rural or in areas where once there was much industry, but which has now been lost, and sadly many have had to close their doors.

Despite that, there is a new vibrancy in the Principality. New brewers proud of their Welsh heritage are starting up on a regular basis, and many of the pubs that are open are working hard to give their customers something different. Underpinning those that are successful is a shared attribute – the quality of their beer. If it is not good enough people will just not use the pub.

For the beer traveller Wales has much to offer. Brains, the country's biggest real ale brewer, is rightly proud of the investment it has put into its pubs in Cardiff. They make ideal stopping off points for anyone on a walking tour of the capital. CAMRA's annual beer festival in the city is testament to the continuing success of brewing in Wales; the number of people attending each year continues to rise, as does the number of indigenous brewers showcasing their beers. No foodie could ever tire of the fabulous Abergavenny food festival – there is nothing like it in the rest of the United Kingdom. For the bibulous, there is a beer-and-book weekend in Hay-on-Wye.

The marvels of country house brewing at Lllanerchaeron are a potent reminder of the importance beer had for the health and vitality of everyone – young or old, rich or poor, people drank beer to stay alive. The steam train out of Llangollen travels through some dramatic countryside, and offers the added attraction of nearby pubs. And then there is bog snorkelling in Llanwrytd Wells – beer can take you to some strange places!

Llangollen railway

62 🍺

Three pubs, three beers – a walk through Cardiff city centre

The City Arms is a permanent beer festival

There is a cosiness and closeness to the centre of Cardiff which seems as friendly as any welcome in the hillsides. Within a short distance are three of the city's finest Brains pubs. Of course the seasoned beer traveller will soon realise there are other fine pubs to catch the eye, but the Old Arcade is as good a place as any to begin. However, before settling down to a pint it is worth

exploring the nearby arcades of shops which twist away from Church Street. Cardiff has several of these retail relics, built in Victorian and Edwardian times. They are a great place for just window shopping and people watching. There is a comfortable intimacy to the Old Arcade. There can be few better places to enjoy a pint of Brains Dark, once described as liquid Wales; it is a classic dark mild. Not too strong, it is malt, chocolate and toffee married to an explosion of hops.

On leaving the pub, turn left and walk down the street until you reach High Street. Turn right and, before you get to Cardiff Castle at the end of the road, you will find the Goat Major. The pub draws its name from a goat taken in the 19th century by the Royal Welsh Regiment as their mascot to the Crimean War. Inside it is comfortable and decorated with warm dark wood. Traditional Welsh food is on the menu. Brains Dark is probably the Cardiff brewer's oldest beer – so it seems appropriate here to try one of its newest, SA Gold. It is a fine example of the trend towards golden beers with a zesty hop finish. Many goldens are marred by their lack of balance and the mediocrity of the mash, leaving the hops to provide all the taste and flavour. SA Gold has the hallmark of a beer made by a brewer who understands that beer requires a joyful harmony between malt and hops. It is zesty and hoppy but underpinned by a glistening veneer of soft toffee flavours. The bitterness of the finish is balanced by its smoothness.

Turn right out of the pub and head back towards Church Street and the Millennium Stadium; opposite, in Quay Street, is the City Arms. Until recently there was not much that made the City Arms stand out from other pubs in the city; it was decent but not distinguished. However, a refurbishment has transformed it into a beer emporium almost unrivalled in the Principality.

Yes, it does sell the full range of Brains beers, including those being tried out in the company's new microbrewery but, more than that, it features a permanent beer festival showcasing many beers from other areas of Wales. There are 35 real ale and cider pumps on the bar, and many beers are served straight from barrels, racked behind the bar. It is not uncommon to find Brains head brewer Bill Dobson drinking here, leading a tutored beer tasting. The pub also features beers from America, Belgium, German and the Czech Republic; step inside into the City Arms and step out into the world of beer!

The Goat Major

Visitor information:

Old Arcade
Church Street, Cardiff, CF10 1BG
029 2021 7999
11.30–11 (12.45am Fri & Sat);
12–11 Sun
Goat Major
33 High Street, Cardiff, CF10 1PU
029 2033 7161
12–midnight (11 Sun)

City Arms
10–12 Quay Street, Cardiff,
CF10 1EA
029 2064 1913
www.thecityarmscardiff.com
11–11.30 (2.30am Fri & Sat;
10.30 Sun)

Getting there and away: Cardiff Central rail station is 10 minutes' walk from the City Arms.

63

The biggest pub in Wales – Great Welsh Beer & Cider Festival

There was a time when all the head brewers in Wales could have fitted into a large family saloon, and included in that number would have been someone from Wales' largest brewer, the AB-InBev-owned Magor brewery, home to Stella lager. Today, you would need a coach to fit them all in, as they number more than 45. Most of these brewers' beers (not Stella) are celebrated at the Great Welsh Beer & Cider Festival, which is held in June for three days. For the festival 150 CAMRA volunteers transform the Motorpoint Arena (formerly the Cardiff International Arena) into the biggest pub in Wales.

It wasn't that long ago that the Welsh brewing industry seemed all but dead and close to the bottom of the glass. The beers, brewed to slake the thirsts of generations of miners and steelworkers, were bought up by national and international giants. Many breweries were closed, losing some of the great names of brewing. Only two managed to survive that time of industrial turmoil – Brains Brewery, now the sponsor of the festival, and Felinfoel. Both are fiercely patriotic and independent. The launch of CAMRA saw the start of a renaissance in the 1970s and '80s and the number of breweries nudged up to towards 20. But still the glass was half empty and not half full; only a brace of the new ones managed to survive to the 1990s – Plassey and Bullmastiff.

Now there is a new wave of brewers with reputations acclaimed far beyond Welsh borders. Names like Otley, Purple

Great Welsh Beer & Cider Festival

Moose and Rhymney are bringing new ideas to the mash tun and fermenting vessel, and once again Wales' brewing glass is bubbling to the top. Each region of Wales now has it own thriving brewing scene. At a time when much of the economy seems bleak, people from Snowdonia to the south Wales valleys are setting up new local breweries and employing local people, part of a wider growing commitment to localism. One of the festival organisers, Arfur Daley, says Welsh brewing hasn't been in such a healthy state for 85 years.

The event also includes the unveiling of the Champion Beer of Wales, the competition for which is held on the Friday of the festival. It is expected that more than 6,000 people will visit, downing over 20,000 pints of ale and 5,000 of cider and perry.

Visitor information:

Great Welsh Beer & Cider Festival
www.gwbcf.org.uk
Held Thu-Sat in early June (check website for dates). Entry fee £6 (free beer tokens for CAMRA members)

Getting there and away: Cardiff Central rail station is 10 minutes' walk from the Motorpoint Arena.

64

Abergavenny – a festival of food and beer

I was brought up just outside Abergavenny in the village Govilon, and was used to foraging for food and was familiar with the area's close links with the land. Eels came from the River Usk; berries were picked on the Blorange hill, which overlooked our house. We would often walk across the field from the now sadly derelict Malt House to the nearest farm to buy fresh faggots and watch Welsh cakes being made on the coal-fired hob. These were for sale in Abergavenny's thriving Saturday market. Tuesday was the big farmers' market in the town. It was not uncommon for a live goose or duck to be bought home from this. The birds provided us with eggs, before being served up on a high day or holy day for lunch.

Abergavenny Food Festival

Food still plays a big part in the life of Abergavenny. The town is renowned for the quality of its butchers and greengrocers, and it is probably for this reason that many pubs in the area, like the Walnut Tree, have an enviable reputation for gastronomy. For one weekend in September, it hosts one of the UK's best-known food and drink festivals. Abergavenny Food Festival has been described as the Cannes or Glastonbury of food festivals. It is a vibrant event for foodies which seems to take over every inch of the town. Stall after stall offers some great epicurean treat or other. Fresh meats, hand-made chocolate, mountains of cheeses and mounds of bread seem everywhere. Chefs give talks, there are numerous tastings and the air is heavy with the, fragrant aromas of food being prepared.

However, the festival is not just for the foodies; the beeries can enjoy themselves too! CAMRA's Gwent Branch always tries to organise a beer festival to coincide with the weekend. The Abergavenny Food Festival Beer & Cider bar normally features 30 different beers – including Otley, Kingstone, Wye Valley and Neath, together with some of the great Welsh ciders which are currently being made.

If you want a beer in a pub, everywhere can seem impossibly crowded, but a good pint can be found in the Angel Hotel it serves beer from Wye Valley, and Dorothy Goodbody's Wholesome Stout is always worth seeking out. A favourite pub is the Hen & Chickens;

Raglan Castle, a few miles from Abergavenny

WALES

draught Bass is normally on sale here. This beer was once the jewel in the Bass brewing empire's star, but has now fallen from grace. It is still a great beer, now owned by AB InBev and brewed by Marston's, full of rich fruit aromas and a marvellous hop bitterness.

Six miles out of town is the Clytha Arms, on the old road to Raglan. This pub is worth a visit in its own right but also hosts a fantastic beer, cheese and music festival over the August bank holiday weekend. Its range of beers and ciders is good. Six real ales are normally on the bars, and the food has won many awards. If castles are your thing, it is only three miles to the impressive ruins of Raglan Castle.

Visitor information:

Abergavenny Food Festival
www.abergavennyfoodfestival.com
Held Fri–Sun in mid September –
check website for details

Angel Hotel
15 Cross Street, Abergavenny, Gwent,
NP7 5EW
01873 857121
www.angelhotelabergavenny.com
🍺 10–3, 6–11 (11.30 Fri & Sat);
12–3, 6–10.30 Sun

Hen & Chickens
Flannel Street, Abergavenny, Gwent,
NP7 5EG
01873 853575
www.sabrain.com/henandchickens
🍺 10.30–midnight; 12–11 Sun

Clytha Arms
Clytha, Gwent, NP7 9BW
01873 840206
www.clytha–arms.com
🍺 12–3 (not Mon), 6–11; 12–11
Sat; 12–10.30 Sun

Getting there and away: Abergavenny rail station is 10 minutes' walk from the Angel Hotel.

---

65 🍺

Hay-on-Wye Ale and Literary Festival

My host, Ed Davies, who runs the town's Ale and Literary Festival, assures me Hay-on-Wye is definitely in Wales. I have my doubts. It always seems like England to me. He says it is Powys. I think it is Herefordshire.

Whatever its address reads, the town is a booklovers' paradise; indeed, most weekends the streets are full of people seeking out the zillions of wallet-emptying secondhand bookshops. It is also is renowned for its famed literary festival in June, when the town bristles and bustles with the glitterati of the publishing world, with guests such as Carol Ann Duffey, Stephen Fry, Dylan Moran, Desmond Tutu and Bill Clinton. However, Ed decided he wanted to run a different festival at another time of the year – one that would bring together his two loves, beer and books. Could one ask for more? Ed's family runs Kilverts, a large, engaging Edwardian pub in the centre of the town. It is one of those places which looks like it has been giving out good cheer for decades. Not so; for many years it was dispensing pills and potions as it was once a doctor's house, and didn't become a hotel and pub until the 1980s.

At the end of August for a weekend the pub becomes a focus for an ale and literature festival. Ed is much more than a fan of beer, he enjoys reading books about beer too. The pub always sells a wide range of ales, but outside in the large garden two marquees are erected. In one a food and beer evening is held. In the other Ed brings together as many beers from north and south Wales as he can fit in. It can be as many as 50.

Kilverts, Hay-on-Wye

CAMRA book authors and contributors to *Beer* magazine have all spoken here, including Zak Avery, Adrian Tierney Jones, Melissa Cole and Pete Brown. And it is not unknown for some of Wales' best brewers to turn up just to have a beer and a chat. They often end up by giving an impromptu tasting in the bar.

The town is a modern-day hippy paradise – organic, sustainable and environmental are all watchwords here. Each Thursday it hosts a great market, which takes in the Memorial Square, the Butter Market and the area around the town clock. The market is close to Kilverts, so a pint of good ale is never far away.

> **Visitor information:**
>
> **Kilverts**
> The Bull Ring, Hay-on-Wye, Powys, HR3 5AG
> 01497 821042
> www.kilverts.co.uk
> 11 – 11 (midnight Fri & Sat)

66

Llanwrtyd Wells – bog snorkelling in Mid-Wales

WALES

You don't have to be mad to live in Llanwrtyd Wells, but it seems to help. Over the course of a year there is a veritable Olympics of alternative sports and beer festivals organised in the town. Events include a man versus horse marathon, mountain bike charriot racing, and a variety of bog snorkelling disciplines including the World Mountain Bike Bog Snorkelling Championship. The **Neuadd Arms Hotel**'s Bells bar features a display of winning boards for some of the town's more unusual championships. For the uninitiated, mountain bike bog snorkelling is exactly what it says; a bit like bog snorkelling, but at a more challenging depth. The competition takes places in one of the bogs on the edge of town at the end of August. Competitors, wearing snorkels, have to cycle two lengths along a specially dug 50-metre trench on a supplied bike. Wetsuits are recommended, I am told. And for anyone who has not had their fill of bog water, a bog snorkelling triathlon is held the same weekend. It comprises a 20-kilometre cross-country run, followed by 50 metres of bog snorkelling, before heading off on a mountain bike for 40 kilometres.

After that, anyone would want a beer. Thank goodness the hotel's beer isn't just any old beer. It is home to the Heart of Wales brewery. Set up in the old stables behind the hotel, it has a six-barrel brew length. Its first brew was produced in a nearby brewery in 2004 for the Mid-Wales Beer Festival, which is held in the town in November. The beer proved so successful that the owners, Lindsay and Catherine Ketteringham, decided they had to have their own brewery. Lindsay now brews twice a week. And what could be better on a championship weekend than a champion beer. Heart of Wales Welsh Black has been voted CAMRA's champion stout for Wales on several occasions. A lot dryer than the water in the bog, it is full of chewy liquorice flavours. The pub also sells Fefinfoel's Double Dragon. Founded in the 1830s, it is the oldest brewery in Wales. Double Dragon is a rich, malty brew, full of fruit flavours and a snatch of aroma hops.

Mountain bike bog snorkelling

Visitor information:

Neuadd Arms Hotel
The Square, Llanwrtyd Wells, Powys, LD5 4RB
01591 610236
www.neuaddarmshotel.co.uk
🕐 9.30–midnight (1am Fri & Sat)

Getting there and away: Llanwyrtd rail station is 10 minutes' walk from the Neuadd Arms Hotel.

67 🚂
Steaming on in Llangollen

If location itself made a perfect pub then the Corn Mill, Llangollen, in north Wales would be one of the best in the world. A former 18th-century corn mill which had fallen on hard times, it has been converted into a fantastic pub, centred around the water wheel which once again relentlessly turns after a quarter of a century of dereliction. Inside it is a flurry of stairs, floors and seating areas. Brave drinkers can stand on a glass floor and watch the River Dee race by beneath their feet. Outside, the

Neuadd Arms Hotel

decks stand proud over the thrusting rapids. Curiosity leads me to try the Boddingtons Bitter, owned by AB-InBev, which is brewed in Manchester by Hydes. The beer is slightly stronger than I remember, at 4.1% abv, and the Golding and Fuggles hops give it a good fruity nose. The beer was once called The Cream of Manchester. Is it still? I don't know, but it was an enjoyable pint.

The pub stands opposite the Llangollen railway station – trains first came to the town in 1861. And, until 1964, they would carry freight and passengers from Wales through to Shrewsbury and Chester in England. Today, following years of hard work by volunteers, trains steam from Llangollen once more.

With the train taking the strain, the line goes up the valley to Berwyn and its 1950s-style restored station, then on to Glyndyfrdwy, through an impossibly narrow tunnel, before arriving in Carrog. Even on a day when the smell of ozone fills the air, the mist clings to the side of the hills and it is impossible to see the sides of the valley rising to the sky, it is a stunning journey to make. And while in Carrog find time

for a pint in the Grouse Inn. A solid unpretentious pub its walls are painted with icing sugar whitewash to protect the thick stone walls from the ravages of wind and rain. Before the train's whistle heralds its journey back, enjoy a pint of Lees Bitter, while looking over the River Dee and the Berwyn mountain range. Like the pub, the Lees Bitter is solid and unpretentious. Like the train which will take me back to Llangollen, the maltiness starts slowly but it gets there, and then comes the bitterness. After a few of these I'll be steaming on as well!

Visitor information:

Corn Mill
Dee Lane, Llangollen, Denbighshire, LL20 8PN
01978 869555
www.brunningandprice.co.uk/cornmill
🕐 12–11 (10.30 Sun)

Grouse Inn
Carrog, Corwen, Denbighshire, LL21 9AT
01490 430272
www.thegrouseinncarrog.co.uk
🕐 12–11 am

The Llangollen railway is a wonderfully scenic way to visit some pubs

68 🍺 👪

Step back in time – country house brewing

Llanerchaeron

There was a time when a country gentleman would always have his own brewery; it would be essential for his survival and the health of his family and the staff. Llanerchaeron is a notable example of an 18th-century Welsh country house, and it would be rare to find a house like this, built before the 19th century, which had no record of the existence of a brewhouse. Whether it be a note in an old handwritten housekeeping book, or a few bricks in an old outbuilding, some record of the craft of brewing can usually be found.

What is notable about the John Nash-designed Llanerchaeron is that the brewery is still in working order. In its heyday it would have provided the staple drink for the household. For hundreds of years men, women and even children depended upon beer for a greater part of their daily fluid intake. In a world that predated the availability of safe tap water, drinking water was not good for people's health. Beer, on the other hand, was made with water that had been boiled, additionally benefiting from the antiseptic properties of hops, and was a virtual liquid bread, given to children from weaning. Often the first drink of the day, it was also taken with the main meal, and at the end of the day it would be drunk for supper.

The house's brewhouse is a time capsule from a different era. Here beer was made as it had been for

Brightly coloured houses at the coastal town of Aberaeron

Llanerchaeron walled garden

hundreds of years – over an open hearth. The skill of the brewer had yet to be augmented by the development of science and technology. On selected days throughout the year brewing days are run, featuring brewing displays and demonstrations. The house also holds apple days, where people can find out more about its orchards and the process of cider making.

This National Trust property also features two walled gardens and a restored salting room. Still a working farm, there are lots of animals to see, including some rare pig breeds.

In the nearby town of Aberaeron can be found the gorgeous, sea-blue Harbourmaster, with its views over the pretty fishing quay. A true Welsh pub, the staff are bilingual and pride themselves on using local ingredients in the food. The seafood is excellent. Purple Moose make the bar's house bitter. It is as gold and refreshing as the sun dappling the water outside. Full of hoppy citrus notes, its finish is as long and as perfect as the day.

Visitor information:

Llanerchaeron
Ciliau Aeron, near Aberaeron, Ceredigion, SA48 8DG
www.nationaltrust.org.uk/llanerchaeron
House: 10.30–5 mid March – October. Garden, farm and shop open year-round.

Harbourmaster

Harbourmaster
2 Quay Parade, Aberaeron, SA46 0BT
01545 570755
www.harbour-master.com
8am–11.30pm

WALES

Yorkshire & the Humber

Pennine Way

Days Out

Introducing Yorkshire & the Humber

Yorkshire and Humberside are at the forefront of a golden era for brewing in the UK. Yorkshire itself has more than 100 breweries – more than any other county in the country – and CAMRA research shows that every pub in Yorkshire has at least 10 breweries within 30 miles of it.

Just a decade ago some were predicting the demise of traditional beers across the region and saying that only a handful of pubs would be left, providing beer for a declining number

The New Inn, Cropton

of dedicated real ale fans. There were some pockets of gritty resistance as redoubtable as Yorkshire's limestone crags, but last orders looked set to be called on real ale to become just a footnote of history, pushed aside by the onward advance of keg beers and international lager brands. Today the real ale sector is in growth across the region, and ever more people are going into pubs to give cask a try; real ale is far from dead, it's thriving. The biggest revelation was to come from the number of people who turned a passion for home-brewing into a thriving business by setting up their own commercial breweries. These people are creating hundreds of different ales of all styles and to suit all tastes. Some were inspired by beers long-gone, others by the new wave of brewers in America.

The region has some great cities, including Leeds, Sheffield and York. Each is a historic place with a burgeoning beer, pub and bar culture. It also offers some epic train journeys which pass through stunning countryside and moorland, or offer a glimpse of the area's industrial heritage. Perhaps the biggest selling tool for local breweries is the name of Yorkshire itself. There is no one type of Yorkshire beer. The range of styles the brewers produce is as big as the region, but the popularity of localism is underpinning the success brewers in the region are having. Yorkshire beer looks like it is definitely here to stay.

Beautiful view from Sutton Bank, North York Moors

69 🏠

Cropton brewery – and the North York Moors

Some people have fairies at the bottom of their garden, the New Inn in Cropton has a brewery. And if that is not enough, it is right on the doorstep of North York Moors National Park and Cropton Forest. It has been quite a year for the brewery; at time when sales of beers from the big national brewers are falling, Cropton's is experiencing double-digit growth. It is good news for the people in this rural area, as a successful pub and brewery means jobs are being created. There is always something special about supping a beer when you have had the chance to chat to the brewer and see where the beer is made. The full range of Cropton's beers are sold in the pub. A favourite is Monkman's Slaughter A strong warming beer, at 6% abv, it really is more suited for drinking at the end

of a walk than before it. Red to the eye, it is a rich-tasting drink that is full of blackberry and other dark fruit flavours, which intertwine with some tangerine citrus notes and chocolate malt flavours.

People staying at the pub should make sure they bring their bikes and walking boots; it is the perfect base for anyone wanting to explore the area. There are numerous walks and trails and the park's bosses are keen to discourage cars from large tracts of the area. A national park for more than 60 years, it is renowned for the purple colour of its heather in the summer. In the autumn, the moors turn dark gold when the bracken changes colour. It is reputed to have some of the loneliest countryside in the UK. The pub holds a music festival in November and another one over the summer

Should you fancy a change of pub, take the four-mile bus ride to Pickering. The Moorsbus runs throughout the summer and stops outside the New Inn. Close to Pickering town's centre is the Sun Inn. The smart little pub has a big garden, which is good news in the warmer months. The pub sells a range of Yorkshire-brewed beer. This includes beers from the Leeds Brewery, which makes the highly drinkable Yorkshire Gold, a zesty, sun-coloured ale, with a bitter and citrus grapefruit finish.

Close to the Sun is Pickering station, a terminus for the North Yorkshire Moors railway. Its steam locomotives travel the 18 miles up to the pretty fishing port of Whitby, through some beautiful moors countryside. Make sure you take your *Good Beer Guide* with you as Whitby has some excellent pubs.

Visitor information:

New Inn
 Woolcroft, Cropton, North
 Yorkshire, YO18 8HH
 01751 417330
 www.newinncropton.co.uk
 11–11; 11.30–10.30 Sun

Sun Inn
 136 Westgate, Pickering,
 North Yorkshire, YO18 8BB
 01751 467080
 www.thesuninn-pickering.co.uk
 4–11, 2.30–midnight Fri;
 12–midnight Sat; 12–11 Sun

Getting there and away: Moorsbus services M6 and M8 run from Pickering to Cropton on Sundays and bank holidays from April to October. See www.northyorkmoors.org.uk/moorsbus

New Inn, Cropton

The Shambles, York

70 [PUB]

Historic York – a pub Shamble

"York this way" says my guide as I get off the train. The city's centre has more than 80 pubs, and even with two days here I am going to need some help. I have three ambitions: to walk as much of the city's famed walls as I can, to visit the Minster – the biggest medieval church in northern Europe – and to find some good pubs. I'm told the walls of York are the best preserved of any in the country and at two miles in length are the longest in the country too. The walls are usually entered through one of the five 'bars', which I discover to my disappointment are not pubs but gates onto the wall.

Thankfully, the homely but sophisticated **Phoenix** is right by Fishergate Bar, meaning I can sit in the pub's garden and watch people walking the wall while I enjoy a pint of Timothy Taylor

YORKSHIRE & THE HUMBER

York city walls and York Minster

Landlord. It is easy to see why this beer has won so many CAMRA awards. It has a maltiness as strong as the city's walls and a floral hoppiness which is almost as high as they are. Jazz is played at the pub on Wednesday and Sunday evenings. I just might come back.

The Brigantes is also close to the city walls and 100 metres from Micklegate Bar. With eight handpumps on the bar, I could be here some time. An unabashed supporter of regional brewers, the pub regularly stocks beers from Yorkshire, Humberside, Lancashire, Lincolnshire, Cumbria and Durham.

Not far from the delightful twists and turns of the mediaeval Shambles is the Blue Bell. The red-bricked pub is a superb two-bar pub, with an Edwardian interior which hasn't changed since 1903. Well, OK, I suspect the toilets are better than they were 100 years ago. The front bar, with its mirrors and wooden ceiling, can get crowded, but so can the cosy panelled Smoke Room at the back, where drinkers get served from a hatch through an engraved glass screen. It is easy to see why it is listed in CAMRA's Inventory of Historic Pub Interiors.

The Maltings is on my way to York Minster, recognisable by the barrel hanging outside. Railway enthusiasts will love it here. There is a fine random collection of bits and pieces which look like they have been taken from skips outside old railway stations and sweetshops. The one-bar pub, with some pretty utilitarian furniture, is real ale heaven. How can one

city have so many good pubs so close together? Three beers from Yorkshire are always on sale, but there are a further four on offer, which could come from anywhere in the country.

The Three-Legged Mare is not the name of the horse I could have bet on but a contemporary bar within touching distance of York Minster. The name comes from a gallows which could take three people in one go! More modern than many of the city's finest, that doesn't stop it having a traditional feel. It is friendly, warm and comfortable. It is as light and airy as a glass of York Brewery's Guzzler. A golden beer, it is a shining example of what British brewers do best – refreshing, satisfying and full of taste and only 3.6% abv.

The York Brewery itself is close to the train station. Check you timetable and make time to fit in a tour of the brewery before catching your train home. The view from the gallery provides an excellent view of the beermaking process. And, after the brewery tour, I celebrated with a final pint of Guzzler in the Tap Room, happy that I'd achieved my three ambitions for the trip.

Visitor information:

Phoenix
74 George Street, York, YO1 9PT
01904 656401
www.thephoenixinnyork.co.uk
6 (4 Fri)–11; 12.30–11 Sat & Sun

Brigantes
114 Mickelgate, York, YO1 6JX
01904 675355
www.markettowntaverns.co.uk
🍺 12–11

Blue Bell
53 Fossgate, York, YO1 9TF
01904 654904
🍺 11–11; 12–10.30 Sun

Maltings
Tanners Moat, York, YO1 6HU
01904 655387
www.maltings.co.uk
🍺 11–11; 12–10.30 Sun

Three–Legged Mare
15 High Petergate, York, YO1 7EN
01904 638246
🍺 11–midnight (11 Sun)

York Brewery
12 Toft Green, York, YO1 6JT
01904 621162
www.york-brewery.co.uk
Tours by arrangement

Getting there and away: York
rail station is 5 minutes' walk from
Brigantes.

71

A tale of two brewers – Theakston and Black Sheep

For a small place, Masham is pretty big when it comes to beer. It is home to two great breweries, owned by members of the same family – Theakston and Black Sheep – the second of which was formed following a family split. Today the commercial rivals are great friends and both have vibrant visitor centres.

Black Sheep Brewery was founded in September 1992 by Paul Theakston, a member of a family that had started brewing in the town of Masham, North Yorkshire in 1827. It had taken five years, some luck and a lot of hard work for his dream to become a reality. Paul left Theakston in 1987 when it was taken over by Matthew Brown and then sold to Scottish & Newcastle. He was something of a brewing visionary, as he opened one of the first purpose-built visitor brewing centres with a shop, bar and restaurant. However, members of the Theakston family remained close to the town's original brewery – indeed, some still worked for the company. It seemed only right in 2003 when four Theakston brothers, whose great-great-grandfather started the firm 176 years before, bought the company back, returning it family ownership. Theakston are one of the few brewers to still use wooden casks, and at the visitor centre you can admire the work of its cooper, who gives displays of the art and skill needed to make a beer barrel.

While in the village, it is a chance to drink the rival brewers' products side by side – the Bay Horse is normally good for this, and Theakston Old Peculier is the brewery's flagship drink. The strange Norman name refers to the

Black Sheep Brewery

relatively low in alpha acid, so the beer is not assertively bitter but has aromatic and floral characteristics, making it an ideal English supping beer with a long, dry finish.

Masham's village square is one of the most elegant and expansive in the country, which gets busy on Wednesday and Saturdays when markets are held. In its heyday 80,000 sheep would have been penned here during the annual sheep sale, which still takes place, though on a much smaller scale, in September. On the third weekend of July the streets fill with the sight, sound and smell of steam and traction engines and fairground organs, which come to the town for a rally of engineering and agricultural heritage.

Peculier of Masham, the town's ancient ecclesiastical court that was established in the 12th century. The beer is a deep ruby-coloured, strong old ale. Luxurious, full-bodied and extremely malty, it has a nose of warming dark berry fruits, which adds sweetness. It is best sipped slowly. This allows the complexity of its lively character to sing on the tongue. Pale and crystal malt, cane sugar, caramel and maize all add to the sweetness and colour of the beer. The aroma and bitterness comes from the Fuggles hops, which are vigorously boiled in the sweet wort and then dry-hopped into every cask.

Underpinning all of Black Sheep's beers is the water from the brewery's own wells, Maris Otter pale ale malt, a little crystal malt, and torrified (heat treated) wheat. These give Black Sheep Bitter its distinctive, full and lasting white head. A full-flavoured premium bitter, with a rich fruity aroma, Best Bitter is boiled with generous handfuls of choice Goldings hops. It is then late-hopped with Fuggles. Fuggles are

Visitor information:

Black Sheep Brewery
Wellgarth, Masham, Ripon, North Yorkshire, HG4 4EN
01765 689227
www.blacksheepbrewery.com
The brewery advises pre–booking tours (£5.95 for adults, £3.95 for children)

Theakston
The Brewery, Masham, Ripon, North Yorkshire, HG4 4YD
www.theakstons.co.uk
01765 680000
Tours daily throughout the year (£6.25 for adults, £3.75 for children)

Theakston brewery

Bay Horse
Silver Street, Masham,
North Yorkshire, HG4 4DX
01765 689236
🕐 11–midnight (1am Fri & Sat;
midnight Sun)

72 🪧

Leeds – five of Yorkshire's finest pubs

When Leeds' imposing town hall was built Queen Victoria turned up to open it. The streets were lined with palm trees and thousands of children sang 'God Save the Queen'. It was a time of huge pride and civic confidence. The city's centre, like the Leeds United football team, has had its up and down since then. The football team might still be in the Championship but many of its pubs are premier class.

The number of beers on sale at **Mr Foley's Cask Ale House** puts it in a league of its own, as there are 10 handpumps on the bar and a large range of bottled beers. The exterior of the pub is not quite as grand as the art gallery opposite or the town hall, but that doesn't stop it from being a listed building. Once it was an office for Pearl Assurance, a company founded by the eponymous Mr Foley. With so many beers on sale, every day feels like a beer festival. Regular brews include beers from Leeds, Elland and York Breweries. A wide range of Belgian brews is stocked, including the fabulous Orval and Rodenbach.

Behind the town hall, and almost as grand, is the 19th-century splendour of the **Victoria Family & Commercial**. Inside there is lots of dark wood and etched glass. There is much evidence of its close links with municipal life in Leeds. And if you like a sausage with a pint, it is the right place to be as more than a dozen different types are on sale. There are not quite as many draught beers on offer, but six should give most people plenty of choice. Beers from

Leeds at night – the city embraces beer old and new

Brewery Tap

floral spiciness to the nose. The beer is another example of how British brewers today often look to their counterparts across the Atlantic for inspiration.

Next to the station is the Leeds brewery's Brewery Tap. On site it brews a lager, which is served straight from a conditioning tank in the cellar. It is a simple, minimalist modern pub. But don't let the simplicity of the décor fool you; the beer list is complex and rewarding, and worth discovering.

Acorn and Leeds breweries are usually on the bar and it is not unusual to see a local politician holding forth while holding a pint. Beer can certainly loosen people's tongues!

I'm not sure if Sir John Betjeman had had a pint when he described the Whitelocks First City Luncheon Bar as 'the very heart of Leeds.' It is certainly a classic pub. Long and narrow, and down an alley, it can be hard to find, but be persistent – it is worth the search. Another well-preserved pub, its atmospheric Victorian interior was installed in 1895. The tiling, collection of mirrors and dominating ceramic bar counter are all worth admiring while drinking a pint.

But Leeds has embraced new beer culture as proudly as it supports the old. The Hop is owned by Ossett Brewery and is underneath the arches of Leeds railway station. Here rock and roll meets real ale. Music memorabilia vies for attention with the large bar which links the two arches. Live music is often played and anyone who thinks that cask ale is an old man's drink should visit this place and have their prejudices disabused. I tried Ossett's Yorkshire Blonde, which uses the American Mount Hood, a hop derived from the German Hallertau hop. Commonly used by America's ale brews, it brings a

Visitor information:

Mr Foley's Cask Ale House
159 The Headrow, Leeds, LS1 5RG
0113 242 9674
🍺 11–11 (1am Fri & Sat)
Victoria Family & Commercial
28 Great George Street, Leeds, LS1 3DL
0113 245 1386
🍺 11–11 (midnight Fri);
10–midnight Sat; 12–8 Sun
Whitelocks First City Luncheon Bar
Turks Head Yard, Briggate, Leeds, LS1 6HB
0113 245 3950
🍺 11–11 (midnight Fri & Sat);
12–6 Sun
Hop
The Dark Arches, Granary Wharfe, Neville Street, Leeds, LS1 4BR
0113 243 9854
www.the-hop.co.uk
🍺 12–midnight
Brewery Tap
18 New Station Street, Leeds, LS1 5DL
0113 2434 414
www.brewerytapleeds.co.uk
🍺 12–11 (midnight Fri & Sat;
10.30 Sun)

Getting there and away: Leeds rail station is two minutes' walk from the Brewery Tap.

73 🛢

Saltaire Brewery – generating brewing excitement

There cannot be many former Victorian power stations which are now a 20-barrel brewery and visitor centre. Once it generated electricity to power Shipley's trams, today it is engendering excitement about beer. Saltaire Brewery makes modern beers using traditional methods and the vessels can be clearly seen behind the glass panels. The brewer, Tony Gartland, is a graduate of BrewLab in Sunderland (see p187). The inspiration for his beers comes from the other side of the Atlantic and his emphasis is on taste and not necessarily an adherence to a brewing style. This has led to the developments of his award-winning flavoured beers, including Triple Chocoholic. It is a stout to which chocolate, chocolate

syrups and chocolate essence has been added. The brewery also makes a porter which is flavoured with fresh ground coffee and hazelnut flavours. The pursuit of interesting tastes to titillate continues with its seasonal beers, with elderflowers, blackberries, cherries, oranges and coriander seeds all finding their way into different brews. The company's best-selling beer is its Blonde, a vibrant straw-coloured beer which gets its large white collar on top by being poured through a sparkler.

The brewery is close to the Leeds-Bradford canal and lies between Shipley and the world heritage site of Saltaire. In mid-September it holds a two-day festival, which coincides with the annual Saltaire festival of music and food. Saltaire was built as a model village to house the workers employed by Sir Titus Salt in his textile mill. It was intended to be paradise on earth – while hell was nearby Bradford. Surrounded by parkland, the village is no museum as it is still lived in. Salt's Mill now contains many shops and an exhibition of David Hockney's artwork. Many people

Saltaire brewery conjours an explosion of flavoured beers

YORKSHIRE & THE HUMBER

choose to walk the 10 minutes along the canalside between the brewery and Saltaire, while others hop on to one of the boats plying the distance between the two.

The brewery holds a winter beer festival in January, while on the last Friday of every month the brewery opens its doors for a beer club. Entrance to the beer festival and beer club is by ticket, which needs to be bought in advance.

Visitor information:

Saltaire Brewery
Unit 6, County Works, Dockfield Road, Shipley, West Yorkshire, BD17 7AR
01274 594959
www.saltairebrewery.co.uk

Getting there and away: Shipley rail station is 15 minutes' walk from Saltaire brewery.

74

Pennine beer – the Keighley & Worth Valley Railway

The **Keighley & Worth Valley Railway** is on the edge of the Pennines in West Yorkshire. It begins in Keighley, the hometown of the Timothy Taylor brewery. It is not the longest line in the country, at just over four miles, but from its start over to Oxenhope the 90-minute round trip is an exhilarating steam journey. It also offers, when the real ale buffet car is running, the chance to drink a proper beer while enjoying a journey that will appeal to film buffs, fans of English literature and people who just appreciate attractive scenery.

The train starts to strain as it pulls out of Keighley and begins the climb up the Worth Valley. It passes some beautiful countryside and silent mills, with stops at Ingrow West, Damems, Oakworth, Haworth and Oxenhope. Travellers buying a full line return can start or end their journey at any of the stations and break their journey wherever they think looks interesting.

The line is famed for being the location of the 1970s classic film *The Railway Children*, one of more than 50 film and television programmes that have used the line as their setting. Travellers getting off at Ingrow West can visit its two transport museums, which are free for anyone with a rover ticket. At Oakworth there is a Railway Children walk, which goes past many of the places used in the film. The single track line also passes through the heart of Brontë country, and the train stops at Haworth, which is only a short walk from the Brontë family museum and home of sisters Charlotte, Emily and Anne. At the

Haworth, the home of the Brontës

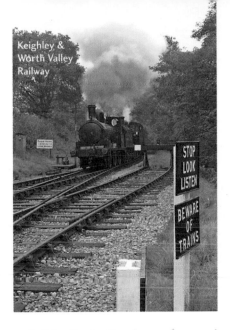

Keighley &
Worth Valley
Railway

75

The train takes the strain – beer across the Pennines

Among rail-alers the Transpennine Real Ale Trail has an almost legendary status. The route traverses the two rose counties of Yorkshire and Lancaster, an iron road linking the two great industrial cities of Leeds and Manchester. When the early ale pioneers made the journey, those travelling from the east would leave Leeds having had a pint of God's gift to Yorkshire – Tetley's Bitter – before heading into the heart of Manchester to seek out a pint of Hydes, J. W. Lees or Holt's. On the way, they would find, within a few moments of each station where the train stops, memorable local pubs of distinction and character. Today, 'God's gift' is still a fine pint, but it is now brewed in Burton upon Trent rather than Leeds. However, anyone making part or all of this journey can experience the blossoming world the rose counties offers to beer fans. Across the region microbrewing is booming and many local pubs are thriving. At weekends the line seems busy with other travellers making this beery pilgrimage, often armed with a copy of CAMRA's *Good Beer Guide* or local CAMRA Branch guides. Many choose to make a whole weekend of the journey – well, there are eight stops on the line as well as fantastic pubs in both Manchester and Leeds to tempt you, and many inducements along the route to stay well past when you'd planned to catch your next train. Luckily there's usually another one soon!

Depending on where you are travelling from, the Cellar Bar in Batley, on the outskirts of Leeds is either

end of the line in Oxenhope a beer and music festival is held in October.

The beer served on the train is usually Timothy Taylor's Golden Best. It is the beer of the Pennines and you can imagine it being drunk by wool mill workers at the end of their shift. Fresh tasting, it is full of malt and fruit flavours. Beers from other local brewers are also sold on the train – Copper Dragon and Naylor's often feature.

On returning to Keighley it is worth checking out the Timothy Taylor brewery tap, the Boltmakers Arms, a small, friendly town-centre pub. It is often used by the volunteers who work on the rail line. The talk on trains and beer can continue well into the night.

Visitor information:

Keighley and Worth Valley Railway
   www.kvvr.co.uk
Boltmakers Arms
   117 East Parade, Keighley,
   West Yorkshire, BD21 5HX
   01535 661936
   🕐 11 –midnight (11 Mon); 12 – 11 Sun

YORKSHIRE & THE HUMBER

Mist over the Pennines, a wonderful setting for a rail-ale journey

the first or last stop on the journey. Adjacent to the station, it is a small, characterful bar which mixes modernity with tradition. Beers from Yorkshire Copper Dragon and Black Sheep are usually on the bar. Copper's Golden Pippin is a fine mix which takes the best of Yorkshire's traditional malty style of ales and matches it to the soaring floral, citrus notes of American cascade hops.

The trains run about every 30 minutes and with Dewsbury only three minutes away, the long, satisfying finish of the Copper Dragon beer seems to make the journey with you. The West Riding Licensed Refreshment Room is on Platform 2 of the station. It's a life-affirming mix of a coal fire, daily newspapers and some locally-brewed ales, including beers from the Church End and Partner breweries. There is even a selection of bottled beers from Belgium and the US and a dedicated foreign beer draught pump. It is a favourite with rail-alers, especially in June, when it holds a famed beer festival. Their website address seems particuarly appropriate: imissedthetrain.com

It seems no time at all before the train pulls into Huddersfield. We passed the canalside Navigation Tavern in Mirfield, which will have to wait for another day.

Serious fans of beer could spend a day in Huddersfield – it has so many good pubs. If you're planning on making a weekend of it then this is the ideal place to break your journey and take full advantage of what Huddersfield has to offer. It is also very hilly, and is located in the beautiful Colne valley on the edge of the Pennines. The town climbs more than 300 metres from east to west. For those who prefer short, flat walks the King's Head is in the station. A *Good Beer Guide* favourite, the building is a curious mixture of grand architectural styles as sweeping romantic flourishes marry with mock-

West Riding Licensed Refreshment Room

Tudor embellishments. The grandeur of the station – yes, it is a station and not a stately home – is matched by the choice of ales. Often on sale are beers from one of south Yorkshire's finest, Bradfield. A glass of Bradfield's Farmer's Blonde is a rewarding pleasure. It is a refreshing beer with a delicate aroma of summer fruits, lychee and peach.

It is almost a crime not to get off at Slaithwaite, the next stop on the line, and try a beer at the Commercial, which has eight handpumps, featuring a mild and a house ale from local brewery Empire, but time is moving on. Instead I chose the Riverhead Brewery Tap in Marsden. The pub has a fine dining room upstairs, where beer is used as an ingredient in many of the recipes, though, from experience, it is worth checking ahead to find out when food is being served. The pub was a grocery shop until about 20 years ago before it was converted. A testament to real ales, there is a baker's dozen of handpumps of the bar. Many come from the pub's own microbrewery, which can be seen through a window at the end of the bar and brews ales with a local connection.

It was hard not to get off at Greenfield – the Railway Inn is just opposite the station and offers a very tempting range of beers, along with highly-regarded pork pies, served with various mustards – but a rich prize lies ahead: the Stalybridge Station Refreshment Rooms. The ebullient barmaid assures me that in Victorian times many stations would have had a bar like this. The Victorians loved varied and ornate architecture, but I doubt if the pubs would have sold such a wide and changing range of ales. Built around 1885, the décor is a time capsule of a different age, when marble was used to top many a bar. There are eight real ales on offer, and you can try the local delicacy: black peas. The atmosphere is so good, I don't mind missing the train. There'll be another one along soon!

Visitor information:

Transpennine Real Ale Trail
www.realaletrail.net
Cellar Bar
51 Station Road, Batley, West Yorkshire, WF17 5SU
01924 423419
4–11; 12–midnight Fri & Sat; 12–11 Sun

West Riding Licensed Refreshment Room
Dewsbury Station, Wellington Road, Dewsbury, West Yorkshire, WF13 1HF
01924 01924
www.imissedthetrain.com
12–11 Mon; 11–11 Tue, Wed & Sun; 11–midnight Thu & Fri; 10–midnight Sat
King's Head
St George's Square, Huddersfield, West Yorkshire, HD1 1JF
01484 511058
www.the-kings-head-huddersfield.co.uk
11.30–11; 12–10.30 Sun
Riverhead Brewery Tap
Argyle Street, Marsden, West Yorkshire, HD7 6BR
01484 841270
12–midnight (1 am Fri); 11–1 am Sat
Stalybridge Station Refreshment Rooms (Buffet Bar)
Rassbottom Street, Stalybridge, Greater Manchester, SK17 1RF
0161 303 0007
www.buffetbar.org
10–11, 12–10.30 Sun

76 🎺

Sheffield's Tramlines – a beer and music festival

Sheffield claims to be England's capital city for the numbers of beers on sale, and it is hard to dispute this, especially on the days when the beer tickers are in town, searching out brews they've never had before. The city should be on every beer travellers' itinerary. There are many beer walks though the city centre and a legendary Valley of Beer trail, which follows tram routes around the city. But more than a boozers' paradise, the former steel city has a vibrant music scene – be it blues, indie, techno or an Arctic Monkeys tribute band, the city has it all. Beer and music come together for one weekend in July with the Tramlines Music Festival. The extravaganza is an

inner-city Glastonbury, without the mud and crush of tents. Regarded as the country's best metropolitan festival, the event gets bigger each year as more venues – including pubs – join in. It is a free festival; all you have to do is turn up. There are even buskers on the buses that take festivalgoers around the city.

A vintage bus usually takes people around the Blues and Ales trail. Beer and blues? What could be better than a pint of Thornbridge's Jaipur and music? The hoppy brew has more notes than a thumping rendition of an energetically played 12-bar blues. Some of the city's best pubs, including the University Arms, Bath Hotel, Harlequin, Kelham Island Tavern, Fat Cat, and Gardeners Rest take part in the blues trail.

For those whose time is limited the city has three pubs which encapsulate the vibrancy of its beer and pubs culture – the Sheffield Tap, Fat Cat and Kelham Island Tavern.

For a first-class drinking experience The Sheffield Tap is hard to beat. Housed in a former waiting room for Sheffield station, it was neglected for many years. It reopened as a bar, gloriously restored, in 2009. It has a fantastic range of ales

Fat Cat – Kelham Island's brewery tap

and it is easy to see why a room which was once used by the railway police as a lock up for prisoners is still an arresting experience. The barman assures me that some drinkers arriving in the city intent on seeing the city's best pubs never leave the Tap until it is time to get the train back home.

All well and good, but they are missing out, and at the very least beer travellers should take the 20-minute walk to Kelham Island. Once a decaying industrial area, it has been rejuvenated in recent years and pubs have helped to lead the way. The Fat Cat, now open for more than 30 years, was in the vanguard of the city's real ale revolution. Its owner, Dave Wickett, remembers the opening day well, as drinkers, starved of real ale by the city's other pubs, queued to get in to try the Timothy Taylor Landlord. In 1990 he opened the Kelham Island Brewery. It has gone on to be one of the most significant breweries in the country, winning CAMRA's Champion Beer of Britain award for its Pale Rider. It is a place where many brewers studied their trade, and its alumni can be found in brewhouses around the world. Sheffield's contribution to the world of beer is indeed global.

Around the corner is the Kelham Island Tavern. Twice CAMRA's National Pub of the Year, it is hard to believe that in 2002 the pub was derelict and in 2007 nearly went under when the nearby River Don burst its banks and

the pub was flooded. It was shuttered, boarded and sadly dilapidated when bought by Trevor Wraith and Lewis Gonda in 2001. But the pair had a vision of running a local pub based on simple virtues – good service, and a wide choice of well-kept beer served by knowledgeable staff – which was a place for people of all ages to sit, chat and sometimes sing or just read newspapers. And now their dream has become a nationally renowned gem, with customers exchanging articulate views on the merits of a Farmers Blonde, a Nutty Black or even a Ludwig Wheat. Outside, the pub has an award-winning subtropical beer garden, the perfect antidote to the area's surrounding post-industrial architecture.

Visitor information:

Tramlines Music Festival
Held Fri–Sun in late July, check the website for details
www.tramlines.org.uk

Sheffield Tap
Platform 1b, Sheffield Station, Sheaf Street, Sheffield, South Yorkshire, S1 2BP
0114 273 7558
www.sheffieldtap.com
🕐 11–11; 10–midnight Fri & Sat

Fat Cat
23 Alma Street, Sheffield, South Yorkshire, S3 8DA
0114 249 4801
🕐 12–11 (midnight Fri & Sat)

Kelham Island Tavern
62 Russell Street, Kelham Island, Sheffield, South Yorkshire, S3 8RW
0114 272 2482
www.kelhamislandtavern.co.uk
🕐 12–midnight

Getting there and away: Sheffield rail station is 1 minutes' walk from the Sheffield Tap.

Kelham Island Tavern

Metropolitan Cathedral Church, Liverpool

North
West

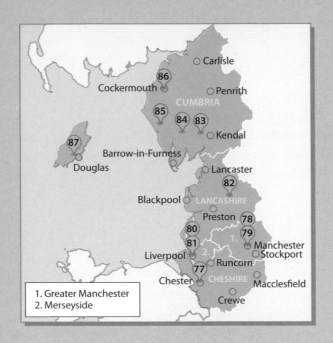

Map legend:
1. Greater Manchester
2. Merseyside

Map labels: Carlisle, Cockermouth, Penrith, CUMBRIA, Kendal, Barrow-in-Furness, Douglas, Lancaster, Blackpool, LANCASHIRE, Preston, Liverpool, Manchester, Stockport, Runcorn, Chester, CHESHIRE, Macclesfield, Crewe

Map numbers: 86, 85, 84, 83, 87, 82, 78, 80, 81, 79, 77

Days Out

Introducing the North West

Hawkshead Beer Hall, Cumbria

The North West is an area of great contrast. From the swagger and brashness of Manchester and Liverpool to the rural joys of the Lake District it is a great place to enjoy some culture, history, breathtaking walks and, of course, beer.

The great cities of Manchester and Liverpool are home to some of the UK's most historic pubs. These preserved gems are no static museum displays, they are vibrant places, bubbling with conversations and people enjoying beer.

The region is also home to some remarkable brewing survivors, with several companies being able to trace their roots back more than 100 years. Manchester in particular still has a fine tradition of breweries which have been owned by the same families for more a century. However, new breweries can also be found in great numbers as the region has embraced with relish the micro brewing revolution. Cumbria has 29 micros, Lancashire and Manchester each have more than 20, Cheshire 27 and Merseyside 10. Many of these breweries have visitor centres and shops and offer the people the chance to learn more about how the beer is brewed.

Chester is one of the country's historic jewels. The city holds a special place in CAMRA's history as it was a pub crawl around its Roman and medieval heritage by four young friends, more than 40 years ago, which lead to the founding of the Campaign.

The Isle of Man lies in the middle of the Irish Sea. Famed for its biker heaven weeks, when the air is filled with the smell of burning oil and the screaming of straining motorcycle engines. However, there is much more to the Island than this. With its three breweries, matchless tranquil walks and some great pubs it is a great place for the beer traveller to explore.

77 🏠

CAMRA's first steps – Chester pub walk

Brewery Tap

CAMRA is more than 40 years old and, with a membership of over 140,000, it's the largest single-issue consumer group in Europe. And it all began with a pub crawl in Chester. The city is renowned for its fine timber-framed buildings and a two-mile near-perfect ancient city wall, but one night four young men, killing time before departing on holiday to Ireland, went out to drink some beer. It was March 1971, and the four founders of CAMRA – Bill Mellor, Graham Lees, Jim Makin and Michael Hardman – were due to fly to the Emerald Isle for seven days of drinking. All of them were under 25 and fond of a few pints. As the quartet traipsed from Chester pub to Chester pub, and finally to the compulsory Indian restaurant, they were all agreed on the lousy quality of much of the beer they had drunk. After their subsequent holiday in Ireland the idea for the Campaign for the Revitalisation of Ale – later the Campaign for Real Ale – was born and the rest, as they say, is history.

As testament to the success of the Campaign – and to how much more enjoyable beer drinking in Chester now is – anyone retracing the original walk around Chester today will find that real ale is alive and well in the city. The Founders' Pub Crawl, devised by the local CAMRA branch to mark the Campaign's 40th anniversary, begins at the Ship in Handbridge. The Ship is a brand new gastro-pub just outside the city walls, close to the old Dee Bridge, the city's oldest bridge and built on the foundations of a Roman predecessor.

Across the bridge and just inside the impressive city walls, the 17th-century

Bear & Billet serves Okells beers, from the Isle of Man. It dates from 1664, having replaced a building destroyed during the Civil War, and is one of the finest black and white half-timbered buildings in the city.

Duke Street, opposite, leads you to the Albion Inn, which has a World War I theme, and is the last remaining classic Victorian street-corner pub within the city walls.

Just outside the Albion you can ascend the city walls, which form a near-unbroken ring around the city centre. Walking anti-clockwise will take you back over the Bridgegate, with its views over the river and the Bear & Billet, below, and round to Castle Drive, from where you ascend the walls again to pass the castle, before dropping down to street level once more to pass the racecourse. As the Watergate appears ahead of you, follow New Crane Street to the right to find the Olde Custom House pub. The Olde Custom House is just five minutes' walk from Chester Cathedral in one of the city's most beautiful streets. It is a genuine 17th century pub, now owned by Marston's, which was originally a town house built in 1637 for Thomas and Anne Weaver.

A few minutes' walk along Watergate Street and you'll find one of Chester's main tourist attractions: the Rows – a network of covered first-floor walkways of medieval origin giving access to shops, and unique to Chester. Tucked away amongst them is the Boot, a 17th-century black and white pub now owned by the Samuel Smith's brewery, where you'll find their Old Brewery Bitter, as well as a range of other beers.

At the time of the founders' pub crawl in 1971 there were no breweries in Chester. Now there are two, one of which – Spitting Feathers – is a microbrewery whose Brewery Tap is located in the Grade II-listed Gamul House, a Jacobean hall located minutes from the Bear & Billet on Lower Bridge Street. The building served time as a boarding school and shops, before becoming derelict. How times have changed: in 2010 the pub won two CAMRA and English Heritage Pub Design Awards for its refurbishment and conversion, and is a great place to round off a day's sightseeing.

Visitor information:

Ship
18 Handbridge, Chester, CH4 7JE
01244 678400
www.theshipchester.com
10–11.30

Bear & Billet
94 Lower Bridge Street, Chester, CH1 1RU
01244 311886
www.bearandbillet.com
12–11 (11.30 Thu; 12.30am Fri & Sat)

Albion Inn
Park Street, Chester, CH1 1RN
01244 340345
www.albioninnchester.co.uk
12–3, 5–11; 12–11 Fri; 12–2.30, 7–10.30 Sun

Olde Custom House
Watergate Street, Chester, CH1 2LB
01244 324435
www.oldecustomhouseinnpub.co.uk
11–11 (1am Fri & Sat); 12–11 Sun

Boot
9 Eastgate Street, Chester, CH1 1LG
01244 314540
11–11; 12–10.30 Sun

Brewery Tap
52–54 Lower Bridge Street, Chester, CH1 1RU
01244 340999
www.thetap.co.uk
12–11 (midnight Sat); 12–10.30 Sun

Getting there and away: Chester rail station is 15 minutes' walk from the Boot.

78 🍺

Premier league pubs – Manchester and the Marble brewery

When it comes to beer, Manchester is in the premier division. There are some outstanding pubs and it still has four thriving independent traditional brewers, each with a history of more than 100 years. Fifty years ago, pretty much every town and city had its own family brewer, but through a combination of ineptness, consolidation and companies just wanting to sell off the family silver, most are long since gone. The area around Manchester bucks this trend, being blessed with Holt, Hydes, Lees and Robinsons. Each is still firmly embedded into the city's beer culture, but to these have been added a wave of new breweries and modern bars which co-exist happily alongside their more traditional counterparts.

One of the new wave of breweries is Marble. Set up in 1997, the company has been pushing at brewing boundaries since it filled its first mash tun. Most of its beers are both organic and vegan, and the brewers are constantly on the search for new tastes for beer which appeal to new audiences and younger people. The upstart's beer can be found in several Manchester pubs, but there can be few better places to seek out these award-winning beers than at the very place where they're brewed: the Marble Arch in Rochdale Road. The brewery has transformed this down-at-heel Victorian street-corner pub and made it buzz again. The decoration includes lots of marble and a curious sloping floor, which seems to become strangely steeper after a few beers. Some might find it rough and ready, but this is pub culture of the highest order and the perfect place to enjoy the brewery's sublime Ginger.

Marble Arch

The Old Wellington, on Cathedral Gates in the city centre, is something of a tourist trap, and it does get crowded on all of its three floors. Built in 1552, this Nicholson's pub is the oldest building of its kind in Manchester, and is situated on Exchange Square, part of an area known as the Shambles. The building has been relocated on several occasions; the last time was after an IRA bomb in the city centre in 1996. The pub was reopened in 1997, but in 1999 was physically moved 100 metres to its current location as part of the city centre's phoenix-like rise from the bomb damage. The large steel rail wheels on which the pub was carried are on display opposite the entrance to the shopping mall.

The Britons Protection on Great Bridgwater Street is a 200-year-old gem. It might be old, but it is still fighting its corner and refuses to be cowed by the fabulous café bar revolution which began in Manchester's Northern Quarter and is now spreading out across the city. The Britons is one of those pubs which don't seem much at first but in reality has rooms and alcoves disappearing off in all directions; it's not to be missed.

Nearby is the Peveril of the Peak. Listed on the CAMRA National Inventory of Historic Pub Interiors, it was named for the stagecoach which once ran from London to Manchester, and much of it remains unchanged since its construction in 1829. It's an old-style boozer in a modern city centre setting.

Visitor information:

A guide to 140 of Manchester's fabulous real ale pubs has been produced by CAMRA's Greater Manchester branch. See www.camragreatermanchester.org.uk for more information.
Marble Arch
  73 Rochdale Road, Manchester, M4 4HY
  0161 832 5914
  12–11.30 (12.30am Sat);
  12–midnight Sun

Old Wellington
 4 Cathedral Gates, Manchester,
 M3 1SW
 0161 839 5179
 www.nicholsonspubs.co.uk/
 theoldwellingtonmanchester
 🍺 10–11; 10–10.30 Sun
Britons Protection
 50 Great Bridgewater Street,
 Manchester, M1 5LE
 0161 236 5895
 www.britonsprotectionpub.co.uk
 🍺 11 (11.30 Sat)–midnight;
 12–midnight Sun
Peveril of the Peak
 127 Great Bridgewater Street,
 Manchester, M1 5JQ
 0161 236 6364
 🍺 12–3 (not Sat), 5–11;
 5 10.30 Sun

Getting there and away: Manchester Victoria rail station is 10 minutes walk from the Old Wellington, and Manchester Oxford Road and Deansgate rail stations are 5 minutes walk from the Britons Protection and Peveril of the Peak.

National Winter Ales Festival 2010

79

Walk on the dark side – CAMRA's festival of winter warmers

Stouts, porters, barley wines and old ales – these are drinks with a long and illustrious past, and they are all celebrated at CAMRA's National Winter Ales Festival. The tradition of brewing heart-warming winter beers is deeply rooted in our psyche. The practice has its roots in pagan celebrations of the winter solstice, when food was in short supply and the nights were long and cold. Later, when monasteries began to be the chief brewers, the tradition continued; the monks would produce holiday beers to celebrate the birth of Christ. In later years, as brewing moved from the spiritual to the secular world, rich winter beers continued to be brewed. Winter beers are as much a state of mind as a singular style. Two hundred years ago, they were often the first brews of the year made by a brewer. The colder days of autumn made it easier for the yeast to thrive and do its work. The magic of fermentation would producer darker, stronger and sweeter beers – ideal for warding off the cold chills of winter and providing people with much-needed nutrients.

Each January, CAMRA celebrates the age-old brewing tradition of warming winter beers with its annual celebration of these styles. The National Winter Ales Festival, which is currently held in Manchester but which will move to Derby from 2014, celebrates the tradition of producing beers for supping on chilly days. Many of these beers are only produced and sold for a few short weeks or months between November and February. They are usually dark in colour and full of rich fruit and spice notes. Some are like liquid Christmas puddings, or akin to having mince pies on draught.

The festival also sees the announcement of the Champion Winter Beer of Britain. This prestigious award, which has been made annually since 1997, is judged by a panel of beer writers, members of the licensed trade, and CAMRA members, with the winner going onto compete for the title of Champion Beer of Britain at the Great British Beer Festival in August (see p52). The 2012 winner was Driftwood Brewery's Alfie's Revenge. The 6.5% abv old ale, named for a stuffed squirrel that once had pride of place in the Cornish brewpub's bar, tickled the tastebuds of the judges by being well-balanced and highly drinkable.

So if the days seem dark and there's a nip of frost in the air, lighten you mood and warm your taste buds with a trip to the festival to see which beer has taken the seasonal crown this year and has been named the best winter supping beer in Britain.

Visitor information:

The National Winter Ales Festival will be held at the Sheridan Suite in Manchester in 2013, and at the Roundhouse in Derby from 2014. Check the website for dates and venue information.
www.alefestival.org.uk/winterales

The extravagant interior of the Philharmonic

80

Liverpool's fab five – a pub tour of Liverpool

There is much more to Liverpool than being the birthplace of the Beatles. The city has some of the finest pubs in the country, all within walking distance of the city centre, and they are renowned for their fine beers and their historical architecture. And with more than 50 fine pubs, choosing a fabulous five is far from easy. Many of the pubs were built while Queen Victoria ruled not just Great Britain but an Empire. The new pubs built reflected the prosperity and pomp of the time. Their grand exteriors were designed to bring the people in and the sumptuous interiors to encourage them to remain.

Unquestionably, the most famous pub in Liverpool is the Philharmonic, built between 1898 and 1900 for brewer Robert Cain. The former Beatle John Lennon once said the price of fame was that he could no longer have a quiet pint in his beloved Philharmonic. It is regarded as England's most ornate pub and is Grade II listed. Its rooms, with stained glass windows, wood panelling and stucco ceilings, drip with decadence. The floors are covered with extravagant mosaics. The skills used to build fine furnishings for luxury liners were used on the pub's interior. The same ornate décor even extends to the pub's marbled gents toilets.

The Dispensary is a Victorian corner pub that has won numerous awards, including a CAMRA/English Heritage one for a superb refurbishment in the 1990s. With seven handpumps, it sells a wide range of beers from local brewers.

The Lion Tavern is another Grade II-listed building, featuring exquisite artwork and etched and stained glass. There is an impressive restored cupola in the rear lounge. The pub is named for the famous 0–4–2 Lion steam locomotive that pulled trains on the Liverpool and Manchester Railway from 1838 onwards.

Near the docks is the Baltic Fleet, also a Grade II-listed building, which doubles as home to the Wapping Brewery. The building comes to a point, like the front of a ship. No doubt that is why there's a snug inside that is simply known as 'the bows'.

The Roscoe Head part of CAMRA history – it is one of only seven pubs which have appeared in every edition

of the *Good Beer Guide* since it was first published in 1974. Inside there are two small rooms, a main bar and a tiny snug; conversation definitely rules, and there is no jukebox or fruit machine. Each September a massive beer festival is held outside the pub.

Visitor information:

Philharmonic
36 Hope Street, Liverpool, L1 9BX
0151 707 2837
🍺 10–11 (midnight Fri & Sat)

Dispensary
87 Renshaw Street, Liverpool, L1 2SP
0151 709 2180
🍺 12–11 (midnight Fri & Sat)

Lion Tavern
67 Moorfields, Liverpool, L2 2BP
0151 236 1734
www.liontavern.com
🍺 11–11; 12–11 Sun

Baltic Fleet
33 Wapping, Liverpool, L1 8DQ
0151 709 3116
www.wappingbeers.co.uk
🍺 12–11 (midnight Sat);
10–10.30 Sun

Baltic Fleet

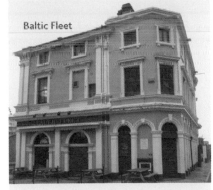

Roscoe Head
24 Roscoe Street, Liverpool, L1 2SX
0151 709 4365
www.roscoehead.co.uk
🍺 11.30 (12 Sun)–midnight

81

A magical mystery tour – two Liverpool beer festivals

With two great football teams – Liverpool and Everton – two majestic cathedrals – Anglican and Catholic – and two celebrated beer festivals, there is much to recommend Liverpool to visitors. The city is also a UNESCO World Heritage Site, which puts it in the same category as the Great Wall of China and the Pyramids of Giza. The home of the Beatles acquired World Heritage status in 2004 because of its impressive waterfront, which is regarded as 'the supreme example of a commercial port at the time of Britain's greatest global significance'.

But in February and autumn every year there's even more reason to visit Liverpool, as the local CAMRA branch demonstrates that Merseyside has both rhythm and booze. For three days in February the branch organises the **Liverpool Beer Festival**, with hundreds of people raising glasses in celebration of ale. Some fans regard it as Britain's best beer festival. It's held in atmospheric Crypt of the Metropolitan Cathedral Church. Visitors enjoying the beers are often temporarily distracted by the venue, looking up to marvel at the skill involved in creating the vaulted beehive brickwork in the crypt's ceiling. The crypt was the only part of the uncompleted cathedral, designed by the great architect Sir Edwin Lutyens in 1930, to be built. The original design was for a structure that would have become the largest cathedral in England, with a dome to rival St Peter's Basilica in Rome. The restrictions imposed by World War II halted construction, and the cathedral is now regarded as one of the greatest

Metropolitan Cathedral Church

buildings never built. More than 200 beers are available at the festival, and it is so successful the entrance is by ticket only, and its popularity is such that the festival is always a sell-out. Tickets go on sale in December of each year, with purchasers limited to four tickets per person. How times have changed! The first CAMRA Beer Exhibition, held in the city, in 1974, had 11 beers. By way of contrast, the 2012 festival had more than 220 beers plus ciders and perries.

If you miss the February beer festival then don't despair. At the beginning of September is the Liverpool Pubs Festival: eight weeks of events celebrating Liverpool pubs and real ale. The celebration includes pub events, pub walks, meet the brewer evenings, beer festivals, student events and live music. The Liverpool & District branch of CAMRA has produced a guide and map to the more than 100 real ale pubs in their area, which can be downloaded from their website. The map also details which pubs are taking part in the branch's LocAle initiative, which promotes the sale of beer produced in breweries within a 30-mile radius of their location. And with more than 10 brewers now in the area, there should be plenty to choose from.

Visitor information:

Liverpool Beer Festival
  Held Thu–Sat in mid Feb.
  See website for dates
  www.liverpoolcamra.org.uk
Liverpool Pubs Festival
  Held Sept–Oct. Free maps are
  available in participating pubs or
  from www.liverpoolcamra.org.uk

Getting there and away: Liverpool Lime Street and Central railway stations are 10 minutes' walk from the Metropolitan Cathedral.

82

Aspinall Arms – and a day's fishing

"And it must have been *this* big." There is something about the conversations of fishing folk, especially after they've had a drink, which leads them to exaggerate the piscine pleasures of the day. A beer helps to lubricate a story and it is always good to catch a Bowland beer.

The Hen Harrier is a rare bird, and the Forest of Bowland in the Ribble Valley is one of the last habitats for it. Several breeding pairs have been recorded in the area and they are an inspiring sight when they perform their extravagant airborne courtships, as the male passes food to the female. It is easy to see why they have the alternative epithet, Skydancer; *Strictly Come Dancing* never flies to these choreographed heights. Less rare but equally inspiring is Bowland Brewery's Hen Harrier, which is served in the Aspinall Arms. The beer's floral aromatic nose soars to a zesty pinnacle with its silky tangerine and peach flavours. The beer is far too easy to drink.

The Aspinall Arms bought back memories of my own childhood, as when I was young my grandmother operated a ferry which ran across the River Usk in South Wales. A ferryboat used to cross the Ribble, which once marked the border between the rose counties of Lancashire and Yorkshire. The boathouse is now long since gone and has been merged into the pub. Today, the river is a popular place to fish. Trout of all kinds and salmon live in the deep whirling pools, which can be found in the 1½ miles of the fishing beat. Day permits for fishing are bought from the pub. I'm not the most avid of fishermen, barely knowing the difference between a nymph and a nobbler (types of fly fishing flies), but there is always something captivating about a day spent by the water eagerly anticipating what will end up in one's keep net and which will be the ones that get away!

For those who prefer to cast a musical net, the pub holds regular music nights and a particularly good three-day Middle Earth Beer Festival, usually some time in April. The valley is known as the centre of England and it is thought the author J. R. R. Tolkien used his experiences walking the area to create the fictional Middle Earth.

Three miles away down Twitter Lane is the Bowland Brewery. It has a visitor centre with a glass wall, through which the brewer can be seen toiling away. On sale in the shop is Artisan Gold, a bottle-conditioned brew which is sold in a champagne-style bottle. If imitation is the sincerest form of flattery the brewing industry should be proud; this style of wired and corked bottle was used by generations of brewers before French winemakers started to put bubbly in them.

Fly fishing on the River Ribble

Visitor information:

Aspinall Arms
Mitton Road, Mitton Whalley,
nr Clitheroe, Lancashire, BB7 9PQ
01254 826223
www.aspinallarms.co.uk
🍴 closed Mon; 12–3; 6–11
(9 Wed); 12–11 Fri & Sat;
12–10.30 Sun
Bowland Brewery
Twitter Lane, Bashall Town, Clitheroe,
Lancashire, BB7 3LQ
01200 443592
www.bowlandbrewery.com

83 🍺

Ings and Staveley – beer at the heart of the Lake District

With the tempting delights of the Lake District on its doorstep, any excuse to turn off the M6 between Lancaster and Carlisle is worth taking. And, frankly speaking, Junction 36 is better than any old excuse. Anyone driving along the A591 from Kendal – the gateway to the Lakes – for about 15 minutes will find there are two great beer attractions.

In the quiet village of Ings is the Watermill Inn. Much more than a beer lover's paradise, more than just a village local, the Watermill has become a local for thousands of visitors to the Lake District from all over the world. If only more pubs could sell beer with such knowledge, style and enthusiasm! Don't be put off by the rough-cut exterior of this former wood mill, which has now been much extended since it became a pub and bed & breakfast establishment 20 years ago. In recent years a brewery has been added to its repertoire. The handpulls for 16 draught beers stand proud in the bars, but that's just the start of the Watermill's beer range, and a long and extensive beer menu is, just like the nearby Lakes, waiting to be explored. The Watermill welcomes all, and you'll see customers happily sipping a Belgian beer from a beautiful glass, or weary walkers sharing a bottled English ale as they devour the pub's Cumberland sausages or crab cakes. And it's not unusual for each member of a group of Lycra-covered cyclists to order a different beer and with delight pass it round to friends for a sip as they discover the variety of mouth caressing tastes that a brewer can create from just hops, malt and yeast. A special welcome is offered to dogs, with free biscuits and water behind the bar, and many of the beers bearing canine-themed names.

On the first Tuesday of each month the Watermill is home to an evening of legends, folklore and music hosted by professional storyteller Taffy Thomas. Many people travel to see this little bit of culture (which itself is probably as old as beer drinking) delighting at the twists and turns of Taffy's many rozzums – the name of the droll little tales of which he says he is the custodian of 2,000 – as they swirl around the bar.

Just two miles away from Ings, and accessible by bus or by a four-mile walk via Hugill Fell and the Kentmere Valley, is the Hawkshead Brewery, which has become a showcase for beer and is a fabulous place to visit. Here owner Alex Brodie brews from the heart. The Hawkshead Beer Hall is a very spacious, modern glass-fronted building that contains a long, smart bar. The space floods with natural light dappling the wooden decor. Two glistening steel fermenting vessels stand at the entrance of the hall and, it is here the

yeast does its daily work, converting sweet malt sugars to beer. There is also a visitor centre, a sampling room, a specialist beer shop and a Beer Kitchen that serves tapas to complement the excellent range of beers. It's the ideal place for a long lunch, and a rural idyll that makes the neighbouring M6 and the prospect of a long trek north or south just a distant memory.

Hawshead Beer Hall

Visitor information:

Watermill Inn
Ings, Cumbria, LA8 9PY
01539 821309
www.lakelandpub.co.uk
🕐 12–11 (10.30 Sun)

Watermill Inn

Hawkshead Brewery
Mill Yard, Staveley, Cumbria, LA8 9LR
01539 825260
www.hawksheadbrewery.co.uk
🌐 12–6 (5 Mon); 12–11 Fri & Sat;
12–8 Sun
Brewery tours for 10 or more by
arrangement

Getting there and away: Staveley rail station is 10 minutes walk from Hawkshead Brewery.

Near Sawrey in Beatrix Potter country

84 🪧

Near and Far Sawrey – a walk through the world of Beatrix Potter

Breakfast is always a good way to start the day, especially before a walk. And the full English – or Cumbrian, as it is called in these parts – is certainly a calorific kick-start to the day. I'm in the Cuckoo Brow Inn, the pub's name inspired by the works of the children's author Beatrix Potter. Today I'd planned a walk over to Near Sawrey, up to the Tarn Eccles and back. Not too strenuous, just a few leisurely miles through some of the prettiest parts of the Lake District.

A footpath follows the road from Far to Near Sawrey. I well remember the first time I went to Near's pub, the Tower Bank Arms. I was on a walking tour of the Lake District, it was February and one of these bright crisp days which often brings out the best of the area. I had been walking for some hours, but was feeling good. The eventual sight of the pub made a good day seem even better. It was beer time. I marched

up to the pub. It was shut! Darn. As I turned away reconciled to walking on, I heard a creaking door bolt drawn. A voice shouted: "Would you like a drink sir? I saw you walking by and thought I'd open a little earlier!" I wish I'd remembered what I drank. It was the perfect beer for that perfect never-to-be-repeated moment, when a beer really hits the spot. Satisfying, soothing and an absolute pleasure. Over the years, the Tower Bank has changed little. It would be a scandal if this gem of a 17th-century pub was ever changed. It still has a slate floor, aged oak beams and a roaring open fire. It now sells beers from local brewers including Hawkshead and Cumbrian Legendary Ales. They say there is gold in the hills; well, Cumbrian's Loweswater Gold should certainly see people rushing to the bar. The beer has a rich seam of tropical fruit notes. This is no fool's drink; it is as rich as the Lakeland scenery.

The pub is set in the heart of Beatrix Potter country. The author's Hill Top house is nearby. The walk up to Moss Eccles Tarn is a stroll through the world of Peter Rabbit, Benjamin Bunny, Squirrel Nutkin, Jemima Puddle-Duck, and Mrs Tiggy-Winkle. The mile up to the lake is both easy on the eye and the foot. It was by this pretty lake that Potter spent many hours fishing and generally mucking about in the water. Some say this was the place which inspired Potter's Jeremy Fisher story. A Site of Special Scientific Interest, it is not uncommon to see walkers washing their muddy boots clean down by the edge of the water.

Retracing my steps to Cuckoo Brow, I'm on a promise with a pint of Ulverston's Celebration Ale. The beer honours of one of Ulverston's most famous residents, Stan Laurel, who went on to be one of Hollywood's earliest comedy film stars, forming a double act with Oliver Hardy. Celebration Ale was created to mark the occasion of a statue of Laurel and Hardy being unveiled in the town. A spicy brew, it is flavoured with coriander and curaçao. If I have too many I'll certainly be, as Oliver Hardy used to say, in "another fine mess".

Visitor information:

Cuckoo Brow Inn
Far Sawrey, Ambleside, Cumbria,
LA22 0LQ
015394 43425
www.cuckoobrow.co.uk
🕐 12–11

Tower Bank Arms
Near Sawrey, Ambleside, Cumbria,
LA22 0LF
www.towerbankarms.co.uk
015394 36334
🕐 11–11 (11–2.30, 5.30–11 Mon–Fri winter); 12–10.30 Sun

85 🍺

Santon Bridge and a whopper of a competition

Archaeologists will tell you that the crags of the Lake District were formed by volcanic activity millions of years ago and the eruption of voluminous ash flows. However, much of the daffodil-covered Lake District, which was immortalised by the poet William Wordsworth in his poem 'I Wandered Lonely as a Cloud', is man-made. Most of the hills and lakes were formed in the 17th and 18th centuries when the area was mined for the hot lava, which was then piped to Manchester and Newcastle to power iron works and heat the houses of the rich. The hills were formed from the spoil left over after the mining. The holes in the ground filled with rainwater to form the lakes themselves. Wordsworth was a founder member of Lakeland Irrigation and Reclamation (LIAR), an early conservation group, which campaigned for the slag heaps to be grassed and then planted with bulbs.

I'm lying of course, but my whopper might be just about good enough to be an entry in the World's Biggest Liar competition. The event is held annually in November at the remote Bridge Inn in Santon Bridge. The competition is the pub's annual celebration of verbal duplicity. Entrants' tall tales are judged on imagination, presentation and sheer brass neck, with the best raconteur judged the world's best liar. The competition started in tribute to a 19th-century landlord of the pub, Will Ritson, who had a reputation for enthralling customers with his tall tales. All can enter the competition, save politicians and lawyers, who are considered too

NORTH WEST

practised in the art of verbal trickery. The Bridge, which was once a coaching inn, is one of the must-visit pubs in the Lakes. It is the quintessential rural hostelry, with low beams, creaking floors and large grates for warming fires. The countryside around the pub is stunning. In summer many people enjoy sitting outside by the river taking in the mountain views while enjoying a pint. So, what to drink? The pub sells a range of Jennings beers including the seasonal World's Biggest Liar. A traditional Lakeland brew, it is fermented inside large hollowed out turnips which grow in Wasdale, similar to the way pumpkin beer is made in some part of America. The beer is then dry-hopped with hops picked from England's most northerly hop garden, which is found nearby on the southern slope of Scafell Pike. I'm lying of course – or am I?

Bridge Inn

86 🛢

Cockermouth – 'water, water, every where', but still plenty to drink

For anyone wanting to explore the many pleasures of the Lake District, there can be few better places to stay than Cockermouth. With its many hotels and bed & breakfasts, it provides an ideal base for the visitor. It also has its own long history and a remarkable story of a brewery's recovery from disaster. The greatest of all Cockermouth residents is the poet William Wordsworth, whose evocative lines paint marvellous word pictures of the beauty of the Lake District. His childhood home in the town is now owned by the National Trust and is popular with visitors.

The town was a strategic fort for the Romans and a thriving market town in the 16th century. Cockermouth also has a ruined Norman castle, which stands high above the town and casts its shadow over the Jennings Brewery. The brewery, below the castle, takes its water from a well used by the castle since it was first built. Jennings often gives its beers humorous names derived from local dialect. One of its most popular is Sneck Lifter, named after a cunning person who tries to quietly lift the latch of a pub's door – the sneck – and to sneak in to spend his last coin on a glass of beer – in the hope he will start a conversation with someone who will buy him a second or even a third.

The confluence of the Rivers Cocker and Derwent, which acted as a defensive line and a conduit for goods, has brought the town of Cockermouth its life and wealth, but in 2009 the two rivers nearly brought its destruction. One rainy afternoon in November the rivers decimated this historic town. Torrents of water swept through scores of homes and businesses in the town centre, as the twin rivers turned on the town after the heaviest rainfall ever recorded in Britain, driving hundreds of people out of their homes. Homes, pubs and the historic Jennings brewery all found themselves deep under water. Some feared that many of the businesses would not survive and that the brewery would never again produce pints of its distinctive beers, brewed from pure Lakeland water. The brewery was shut for three months, with production moving to a sister plant in the Midlands owned by Marston's. Despite rumours that the brewery would shut permanently, Marston's poured money into the renovations, and the brewery, like the town, is thriving again

the only visible legacy of the deluge being the many signs on walls in the town marking the extent of the flood waters. There are regular tours of the brewery, which end with a tasting in the former cooperage, now converted into an atmospheric bar. There is also a shop and tea room on site.

Cockermouth Main Street

Visitor information:

Jennings Brewery
Castle Brewery, Cockermouth,
Cumbria, CA13 9NE
0845 129 7190
www.jenningsbrewery.co.uk
🕐 10–4; closed Sun except in Jul and Aug
Check the website for details of the regular brewery tours

Getting there and away:
Cockermouth is connected by local bus to numerous Lake District towns. See cockermouth.org.uk/bus.htm for bus information.

87 🪧

Biker bliss – the Isle of Man TT, with track side refreshments

They must be mad. There is a harsh, precarious beauty to the screaming sound of a 999cc Honda, throttle full open, hurtling down winding, twisting, rising, falling country roads, at speeds well in excess of 140mph. Astonishingly, the Isle of Man motorcycle races take place on public roads, complete with drain covers, manhole covers, bumps, lumps and uneven surfaces. The moment between the quick and the dead seems infinitesimal as riders flash by, with seemingly only occasional hay bales protecting them from the oblivion of hitting an unremitting stone wall. The Isle of Man mountain circuit is without doubt the greatest challenge any racing motorcyclist can take on. Each year more than 500 riders arrive on the island for the TT races in June or the later Manx Grand Prix races in August and September.

It is a dangerous circuit, 37.37 miles round, which, amazingly, the top riders can lap in 17 minutes at an average speed in excess of 130mph. The riders are the stuff of legend: Geoff Duke, John Surtees, Barry Sheene, Mike Hailwood and Joey Dunlop have all raced here. Today's heroes are multiple winners like Ian Hutchinson and John McGuinness; names adored by their fans.

The mountain circuit begins on the front in Douglas and heads at a breakneck pace west via Ballaugh and Sulby to Ramsey, some 23 miles away. Here the riders, straining every sinew and rivet on their bikes, start the daunting mountain climb from sea level, rising some 430 metres to the highest point at Brandywell. Then it is almost downhill all the way to one of the course's best vantage points, Creg-ny-Baa, and the return to Douglas. The heartstopping adrenalin-wringing circuit has been completed faster than most people can drink a pint. When the day's racing ends, so the seafront in Douglas becomes a focus for impromptu displays of biker machismo. Rolling burnouts leave black rubber marks across the road and over the tram tracks and the air fills with the sound of screaming, howling engines and the sweet smell of burning oil. It's biker heaven. And then there is mad Sunday, when for a couple of hours the course is open for the public to ride bikes around at unrestricted speeds.

Even if the bikes are not racing, the Isle of Man is a beautiful and unspoilt place with a rich history and is well-worth visiting. It has many gentle walks, horse-drawn trams, and three breweries – Bushy's, Okells and Old Laxey. And best of all, many of the pubs offer a view of the TT as it passes. So arrive early, bag a spot, and let the professionals take the risks as you enjoy a pint of the best the island has to offer.

Some pubs which offer a view of the TT circuit are listed below.

Visitor information:

Quarterbridge Hotel
Quarterbridge, Peel Road, Douglas, Isle of Man, IM2 1HB
01624 671008
🍺 3–12 Mon–Thu; 2.30–12 Fri; 12–midnight Sat & Sun

Crosby Hotel
Main Road, Marown, Isle of Man, IM4 2DQ
01624 851293
🍺 12–11 (midnight Fri & Sat); 12.30–11 Sun

Glen Helen Inn
Glen Helen, St John's, Isle of Man, IM4 3NP
01624 801294
www.glenheleninn.com
🍺 11.30–11 (midnight Wed–Sat)

Mitre
Kirk Michael, Isle of Man, IM6 1AJ
01624 801244
🍺 12–2 (not Mon), 5–11 (midnight Fri); 12–midnight Sat

Raven
 The Main Road, Ballaugh, Isle of Man,
 IM7 5EG
 01624 896128
 12–11 (midnight Fri & Sat)

Sulby Glen Hotel
 Main Road, Sulby, Isle of Man,
 IM7 2HR
 01624 897240
 www.sulbyglen.net
 12–midnight (1 am Fri & Sat);
 12–11 Sun

Ginger Hall
 Ballamanagh Road, Sulby,
 Isle of Man, IM7 2HB
 01624 897231
 12–midnight (11 Sun)

Creg–ny–baa
 Mountain Road, Onchan,
 Isle of Man, IM4 5BP
 01624 676948
 12–2 (4.30 Sat & Sun), 6 (5 Fri
 & Sat)–9 (8 Sun)

Getting there and away: The Isle of
Man's Ronaldsway airport is served
by airports throughout the UK, and
ferries to Douglas run from Liverpool,
Heysham and Belfast.

Peel harbour

NORRTH WEST

North East

Newcastle

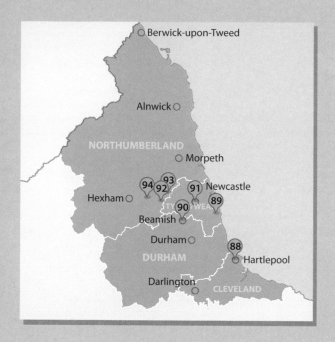

Berwick-upon-Tweed

Alnwick

NORTHUMBERLAND

Morpeth

Hexham

94 93 92 91 Newcastle

90 89

Beamish

TYNE & WEAR

Durham

88

Hartlepool

DURHAM

Darlington

CLEVELAND

Days Out

Introducing the North East

Beer is a passion with people in the North East, perhaps the union was forged when steel workers built giant ocean liners and miners toiled deep underground, digging for the coal necessary to fire the region's furnaces.

Beers and lots of it was the drink of choice for most. People would spend their leisure time in working men's clubs, supping ale. Most of that heavy industry is now long gone, as have the beers and the clubs where they were drunk. The beers of the revered Newcastle and Vaux breweries are distant memories to most people. However, there is a new pride in the area, with an increasing number of local pubs selling locally brewed beer.

Some of the new generation of micro brewers are trying to recreate the beers their fathers drank; traditionally many of the beers were darkish sweet, malty bitter style beers, designed to be easy to drink after a hard day's work. However, others start with a clean slate, they are inspired by the tastes of the world and have discovered hops, lots of them.

But there is much more to the area than its industrial heritage and the inventive skills of its people which gave us the first passenger train. With its breathtaking scenery, hundreds of miles of coastline and the architectural glories of Newcastle upon Tyne some say the North East has it all. It has much history. Castles, fortifications and former battlefields are seemingly around every corner. Within the region are some of the country's most remote dales and moors, which can be experienced by train, cycle or on foot Rest and refreshment can be sought in some fine rural pubs.

Many former industrial sites, like the Beamish Open Air Museum, have been given a new life as tourist attractions and are great places for a family day out. The train lines, which once carried coal into Newcastle, for shipping on to London, offer the traveller a fascinating view of the rugged countryside and are a great way to experience the former Roman frontline, Hadrian's Wall.

Beamish Open Air Museum

Camerons Brewery Visitors Centre

88

PUB

Hartlepool – monkey business, lion brewery and the rat race

There's more to Hartlepool than wind turbines, a golden sandy beach, quayside walks and a sea view to die for – as if that wasn't enough. It has a hidden history, a brewery and one of the country's most curious pubs. Surrounded on three sides by the sea, Old Hartlepool stands on a limestone peninsula. The embrace of the rock helped form a natural harbour, which was used by generations of fishermen. The headland is home to an attractive 12th-century Norman church, St Hilda's. It was named in honour of a nun who arrived on the headland, then wooded, in 648AD.

Other historic attractions include the Heugh Gun Battery and museum. It was from here, just before Christmas 1914, that volunteer gunners fought back against three German battlecruisers attacking the town. The violent exchange

saw the first deaths of British civilians on home soil during World War I, as the bombardment killed 114 men, women and children.

On the headland, soldiers and sailors must have undertaken many brave deeds over the years, but they are best known for the legend of the hanging of the monkey. The story comes from the early 19th century when the country was embroiled in the Napoleonic wars. A French vessel called the *Chasse Maree* was struggling offshore, battling against a gale. When the boat was wrecked, the fisherman rushed to see if they were any survivors, but all they found was the ship's pet monkey, dressed in a military uniform. Fearing invasion, the fisherman are said to have concluded the monkey was a French spy and sentenced it to death by hanging. No one seems to know if the tale of the ape is truth or fable, but the Globe in Northgate on the headland, a fine community pub, is a good place to reflect on all that monkey business.

However, depending on the time of day, many head to the Rat Race Ale House, one of the region's most intriguing pubs. The pint-sized pub is on Platform 1 of the town's railway station. It was founded a few years ago by Peter Morgan, inspired by hearing a speaker at a CAMRA AGM describe how to set up a micropub, and say that all you really needed was a room, beer and a toilet. Using his redundancy money, Peter opened up this quirky pub in a former newsagent's. Inside, there is barely room for 25 people. There is no bar, but there is a choice of four real ales. The pub's opening times coincide with the arrival and departure of the coast trains.

Nearby is Camerons Brewery, founded in 1865. The Lion brewery has a chequered history: it has been taken over and faced closure on several occasions, but it now roars again. Its water is still drawn from a well more than 80 metres deep. The best-known beer here is Strongarm, a warming malty beer, sold in many of the town's pubs. The story of brewing through the ages and the machinations of the brewery from its opening in 1865 to the present day is told in the brewery's visitor centre.

Rat Race Ale House

Visitor information:

Globe
26 Northgate, Hartlepool,
TS24 0LJ
01429 860097
🍺 11–11

Rat Race Ale House
Station Approach, Hartlepool,
TS24 7ED
07889 828648
www.ratracealehouse.co.uk
🍺 12.02–2.15, 4.02–8.15;
12–2.02 Sat; closed Sun

Camerons Brewery
Stockton Street, Hartlepool,
TS24 7NU
01429 868686
www.cameronsbrewery.com
🍺 10–4 (Mon–Sat); Brewery tours:
Mon–Thu (by arrangement)

Getting there and away: Hartlepool rail station is adjacent to the Rat Race Ale House.

89 🛢

Brewlab – learn to brew like a brewer

It is an art, a craft and a skill, and it is a journey which began more than 10,000 years ago. From China to the plains of Africa, from Mesopotamia to the Amazon, there is prehistoric evidence of brewing taking place. In the earliest days of civilisations, when people turned from hunter-gatherers to farmers, people brewed a drink akin to what we call beer. And today many people are still eager to learn the skills of making an alcoholic drink by fermenting a cereal, be it barley, wheat, rice or

NORTH EAST

Students cleaning a brewing vessel

recipe formulation, business start-up advice, brewery visits, marketing and brewery design.

The first day begins with an overview of the brewing process, followed by brewery design and layout, and more details on the ingredients as well as looking at the contribution of water and yeast. The second day includes recipe formulation, fermentation, racking and beer conditioning. Importantly, there are modules on marketing and publicity, tax, and profit and loss. The modules are designed to show the harsh realities of life, and reinforce the message that, just because you can make a good beer, it doesn't mean that people will come to buy it. The final day includes trips to several nearby breweries and talks with brewers who have already completed Brewlab courses. There is an optional fourth day spent at High House Farm brewery where students can observe and assess the brewing process from start to finish. In the evenings, students usually undertake some essential research and development – sometimes over a pint!

The Clarendon pub is a favourite as it has its own 2.5 barrel plant in the cellar and some stunning views across the River Wear from a large rear window. Also popular is Fitzgerald's, which offers Sunderland's largest range of cask ales.

sorghum. At the very least it could make you extremely popular with your friends and, who knows, it could even turn a hobby into a business! Becoming a brewer is many people's dream. Indeed, being your own boss and running your own brewery seems a pretty sexy thing to do. It is a career many people have already decided on. There are now more than 750 people running their own microbrewery in the UK and making the type of beer that they want to drink. For some it is a lifestyle choice; others see it as a pathway to riches.

However, it takes planning and training to turn the dream of wanting to say "I can now host a piss-up in a brewery" into reality, and it is the job of Brewlab in Sunderland to stop it all becoming a nightmare. The organisation's three-day course is ideal for anyone thinking about setting up their own microbrewery. It regularly runs these sessions which, it says, will give people all the information they need to decide whether brewing is the right career choice for them. Normally about 20 students, including many women, attend each course, all of whom could be at different stages of their brewing journey, but who all share a love of beer. The topics covered include beer tasting,

Visitor information:

Brewlab
Unit 1, West Quay Court, Sunderland
Enterprise Park, Sunderland,
Tyne and Wear, SR5 2TE
0191 549 9450
www.brewlab.co.uk

Clarendon
143 High Street East, Sunderland,
SR1 2BL
0191 510 3200
www.bull-lane-brewing.co.uk
🕐 12–midnight (11 Sun)

Fitzgerald's
10–12 Green Terrace, Sunderland,
SP1 3PZ
0191 567 0852
🕐 11–11 (midnight Fri & Sat);
12–10.30 Sun

Getting there and away: Pallion Metro station, with services from Newcastle city centre, is 20 minutes walk from Brewlab.

90 🛢 👥

Beamish Open Air Museum – a journey back in time

Queen Victoria is no longer on the throne, but World War I has yet to cast its dark shadow over a generation of people. The year is 1913, and the Sun Inn, like the rest of Beamish Open Air Museum, is frozen in a moment of time, as a living example of when the North East was at the peak of its industrial pomp. The pub was rebuilt for the museum, having been moved lock stock, spittoon and barrel from its original home in Bishop Auckland in County Durham, where it was known as the Tiger Inn. The small two-bar boozer has a tiny posh lounge with linoleum and leather seats. The public bar has long wooden benches and sawdust on the floor, but thankfully no spit. The bars might be old, but its beers come from the Bull Lane brewery in Sunderland and the prices are bang up to date. However, it is a delight to be served Britain's national drink by someone in period costume.

Outside there are more moments in the time warp: a bank, a sweetshop and even a Masonic hall. There is a terrace of houses, transported from Gateshead, where professional people would have lived. There is a bandstand, a dentist's surgery and a chemist's shop.

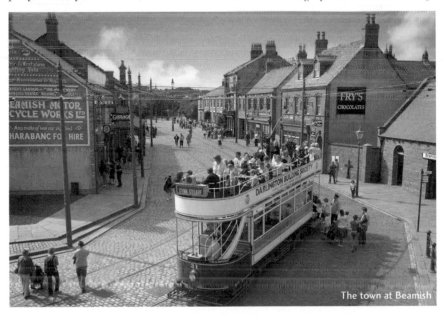

The town at Beamish

This surrealistic tableau is all part of one of the country's most ambitious museums, which covers more than 300 acres. Trams full of visitors arrive from the museum's entrance, and mingle with the costumed townspeople, who are employed to show what life was like in a typical northern town; their role is to reflect and preserve the customs, traditions and dialect of the region. Other visitors arrive on a horse bus or in the museum's replica Daimler bus, and will put questions about the era to the museum's knowledgeable 'locals'.

The 'town' has its own railway, the Pockerley Waggonway, that consists of an engine shed from 1825 and a short track. Three replica steam locomotives, including one of George Stephenson's Locomotion No 1, take visitors for a ride in the unsprung carriages. There are also many artefacts and buildings which reflect the area's mining heritage.

And the museum has now got hands on. It runs a series of courses for people who want to learn the skills of yesteryear, and there is something for everyone. For example, people can learn to cook in a Victorian kitchen using a coal-fired oven, while others might prefer to experience the steam railway's earliest days by driving one of the museum early 1800s replica steam engines, Puffing Billy or the Steam Elephant. There is a course in making the proggy mats, which were a common sight in working-class homes in the northeast of England until the mid-20th century; made from old sacks and recycled fabric, they were an economical option to keep feet warm and toasty in an era before fitted carpets were the norm.

People can also learn how to prepare a heavy horse for a show with one of the museum's expert horsemen; they will have a go at washing and grooming one of Beamish's gentle giants, along with plaiting its mane and tail and harnessing it ready for work.

Sun Inn

Back in the real world, the village of Beamish has some fine pubs. The 300-year-old Black Horse offers great views. Local beers are on offer and the landlord is promising to start his own microbrewery. The Stables Bar is part of the Beamish Hall County House Hotel. It hosts a beer festival every September.

Visitor information:

Beamish Museum
Beamish, Co Durham, DH9 0RG
0191 370 4000
www.beamish.org.uk
🕐 10–5 (summer); Tue–Thu,
Sat–Sun, 10–4 (winter)

Black Horse
Red Row, Beamish,
Co Durham, DH9 0RW
01207 232569
www.blackhorsebeamish.co.uk
🕐 11–11.30 (midnight Sat);
11–11 Sun

Stables Bar
Beamish Hall Country House Hotel,
Beamish, Co Durham, DH9 0YB
01207 288750
www.beamish-hall.co.uk/stables
🕐 11–11 (midnight Fri–Sat);
12–10 Sun

Getting there and away: Buses from Newcastle, Durham and Sunderland. Discounted admission to Beamish Museum for visitors travelling by bus.

91

Newcastle – a hop round the Toon's finest pubs

Seven bridges draw Newcastle and Gateshead together in a tight embrace. Possibly the most famous is the Tyne Bridge which, when it was built in 1928, was the world's longest single-span bridge. These days the bridge is probably most recognised for the Great North Run, as 52,000 runners pass over it on their way to complete a half marathon. Others prefer to cross the river using the sweeping pedestrianised Gateshead Millennium Bridge. For many the south and north side of the river have become one single area to explore. And many visitors cross over from Newcastle to visit the BALTIC art centre, built in an old warehouse. It has no permanent exhibition, but it has quickly won a reputation for the diversity and excitement of its exhibitions of contemporary art.

In June, adrenalin junkies flock to Newcastle's Town Moor, a large green lung of more than 920 acres, which is home to Europe's biggest travelling fair, Newcastle Hoppings, featuring over 100 large rides. Founded in 1882 as a temperance festival, it was supposed to counter the debauchery of Newcastle's horse race meetings. Thankfully, the rest of Newcastle never signed the pledge and the fair's site is close to some of the city's finest pubs.

The Bridge Hotel is next to Robert Stephenson's spectacular rail and road High Level Bridge, which was hurled across the Tyne Gorge in 1849. The rear window and terrace offers some great views of the Tyne and Gateshead quays. The Victorian inside is full of stained glass windows, mosaics and some enticing nooks, crannies and snugs.

The Newcastle Arms is close to the theatre of dreams where the Toon Army gathers to watch football at St James' Park. The single-roomed pub sources its ales from far and wide and has been a multiple winner of the local CAMRA branch's Pub of the Year award. A true mecca for good beer, each year the pub sells more than 650 different real ales.

Newcastle Hoppings

The Duke of Wellington is close to the city centre and Bigg Market, where many hen and stag parties celebrate. The pub's formula is straightforward: good beer, occasional beer festivals and simple home-prepared food.

The Bacchus has rightly won many CAMRA accolades. Close to the Theatre Royal, it is a smart, comfortable bar that holds regular food and beer tastings. Inside there are many photographs which pay homage to Newcastle's industrial and mercantile past.

In the heart of Quayside is the Crown Posada; don't be put off by the unprepossessing exterior, it is inside that counts. The glorious pub is a Grade II-listed building with an

NORTH EAST

elaborately panelled entrance. Inside is a narrow room, with a stunning pre-Raphaelite stained-glass window and a high moulded ceiling. A long, narrow Victorian mahogany bar links the tiny front panelled snug to the larger sitting area at the back. Music is supplied from a small record player by the bar. Enjoy a Mordue Workie Ticket. A former CAMRA champion beer of Britain, its malty resonance and complex hoppy overtones are as rich as the décor. It is a unique pub experience.

River Tyne seen from Hagg Bank Bridge

Visitor information:

Newcastle Hoppings
www.newcastle-hoppings.co.uk
The Hoppings is held annually in the last full week of June.

Bridge Hotel
Castle Garth, Newcastle upon Tyne, NE1 1EQ
01912 326400
11.30–11 (midnight Fri–Sat); 11.30–10.30 Sun

Newcastle Arms
57 St Andrew's Street, Newcastle upon Tyne, NE1 5SE
01912 602490
11–11; 12–10.30 Sun

Duke of Wellington
High Bridge, Newcastle upon Tyne, NE1 1EN
01912 618852
www.thedukeofwellington.info
12–11 (10.30 Sun)

Bacchus
42–48 High Bridge, Newcastle upon Tyne, NE1 6BX
01912 611008
11.30–midnight; 12–10.30 Sun

Crown Posada
31 The Side, Newcastle upon Tyne, NE1 3JE
01912 312169
12 11 (1am Fri & Sat); 7–10.30 Sun

92

The Tyne Valley Line – a cross-country pub crawl

Can there be a better way to travel than on a railway train, especially one that follows one of England's oldest and greatest man-made icons? The Hadrian's Wall or Tyne Valley Line is among England's most scenic railways. It provides a fast and convenient way to travel, in conjunction with the Hadrian's Wall bus, to all the historic sites of the Wall, and it can all begin with a beer in Newcastle. You can use the line for a short trip out of the city, though some prefer to travel all the way across the country from east to west.

All train journeys to and from Newcastle should start or end in the fine Centurion bar in the central station. It is a marvellously restored bar which was once an ornate waiting room for well-heeled first class passengers, before being turned into cells for the railway police. Today, beer rather than bars keeps people in here. Glasses clink but not gaolers keys, and cellmates have mobiles to their ears and are not prisoners. Thankfully, the bar's grandeur has now returned and the full glory of the John Dobson-designed interior can be enjoyed once again.

The station is the starting point for some great train rides along the Tyne Valley Line, which links Newcastle with Carlisle. The 60-mile journey to Carlisle takes travellers through breathtaking hillside-hugging countryside and offers plenty of attractions for walkers and pubgoers. The trains run half-hourly and, with most stations close together, it is easy to break a journey for a walk and a visit to a pub before travelling back to Newcastle or moving on down the line.

One such walk – along the river from Prudhoe to Wylam – happens within the Tyne Riverside Country Park, a popular place for easy walking, cycling or just watching the river go by. Adjacent to Prudhoe station is the Adam & Eve pub. Popular with locals, it has a large garden, which is suitable for children, and an extensive food menu. The walk through the park is about three miles, and it is flat, save for a couple of slopes around the Hagg Bank Bridge. The bridge is an impressive wrought-iron bridge, built to carry coal trains to Newcastle.

In Wylam, close to the station, there is the attractive Boathouse Inn, which holds themed beer festivals on most bank holidays. A winner of many CAMRA awards, it offers 15 handpulls, three of which are dedicated to cider.

There is also a four-mile walk between the two stops, which goes via Horsley, following fields and woodland paths.

People deciding to travel on to Carlisle will not be disappointed; it is a city which is worth a visit in its own right. Cumbria's capital city, it is the western end of Hadrian's Wall. Carlisle Castle is a great medieval fortress which has broodingly watched over the city for 900 years. Inside, visitors can explore ancient chambers, stairways and dungeons to find the legendary licking stones. Here, dehydrated Jacobite prisoners found enough moisture to stay alive, only to be later brutally executed on Gallows Hill.

The imposing red sandstone cathedral dates from 1122, but it was restored in the 1850s after angry Scots had destroyed much of it in the 17th century. Worth seeing is the great East Window, which dominates the choir and timber barrel vault. Close to the cathedral and castle is the King's Head. One of the oldest

Centurion

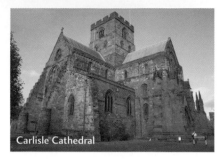

Carlisle Cathedral

pubs in Carlisle, the present building dates from the 17th century, but some claim an inn has been on the site since the 10th century. The friendly pub is an avid supporter of the region's beer.

Visitor information:

Tyne Valley Line
The excellent Whistle Stops guide to the line and the pubs near the many stations can be downloaded for free. See www.cannybevvy.co.uk

Centurion
Central Station,
Newcastle upon Tyne, NE1 5DG
01912 616611
www.centurion-newcastle.com
🍺 10–11 (midnight Fri & Sat)

Adam & Eve
Prudhoe Station, Low Prudhoe,
Northumberland, NE42 6NP
01661 832323
www.adamandeve-pub.co.uk
🍺 12–11 (midnight Fri; 1am Sat)

Boathouse Inn
Station Road, Wylam,
Northumberland, NE41 8HR
01661 853431
🍺 11–11; 12–10.30 Sun

King's Head
Fisher Street, Carlisle, Cumbria,
CA3 8RF
01228 533797
www.kingsheadcarlisle.co.uk
🍺 10–11 (midnight Fri);
11–midnight Sat; 12–11 Sun

93 🍺 PUB
Wylam – a rocket, Hadrian's Wall and a trip underground

The breathtaking beauty of the countryside in rural Northumberland is matched only by the dynamism of the people who have lived here. Each generation has left its fragile mark. From the Romans to the dawn of the railway revolution which swept the world, there is much to see.

One of the best-preserved examples of Hadrian's Wall is found alongside the road just below the hilltop village of Heddon-on-the-Wall. From the high ground above the wall, it is possible to see the full majesty of the defensive line and earth ramparts. Sadly, the wall was not enough to keep foot and mouth out of the village, which is infamously renowned as being the epicentre of a national outbreak of this cattle disease in 2001. The village is where a Roman mile fort once stood, but in an early example of recycling much of the stone was used to build St Andrew's Church, which is of Anglo-Saxon origin, and was consecrated in 630AD.

Heddon is also home to the Wylam Brewery, which has a small visitor centre and shop. Tours of the brewery can be undertaken by arrangement. Wylam is an example of one of the many microbrewery success stories which has swept the country in recent years. From small beginnings in 2000, its beers are now on sale in more than 200 pubs.

Many of the beers have a railway theme. The nearby village of Wylam boasts one of the brewery's unofficial taps, the Black Bull. It is also the birthplace of steam engine pioneer George Stephenson, who designed his first locomotive in 1814. So what should people drink? Wylam's Rocket honours Stephenson's achievement of developing the famed Rocket steam engine in 1829. A strong golden beer, it is as polished as the copper on a Victorian steam engine. A potent aroma of floral hops, swirl like steam in the glass before delivering a wonderful fresh citrus and bitter finish.

Stephenson's Cottage

Nearby is Wylam Waggonway, a popular walk that takes people past the cottage where Stephenson was born. The original waggonway, where horse-drawn carts travelled along wooden track from Wylam colliery to the River Tyne, was built in 1748. In the village's old school, a former classroom has been converted into a small railway museum.

For those heading back to Newcastle, a Wylam beer can be enjoyed at the excellent Tyne Bar, the brewery's second unofficial tap. It is situated at the east end of Newcastle Quayside, under the Glasshouse Road Bridge on Maling Street. This excellent riverside pub sits at the confluence of the Ouseburn and the mighty Tyne. It is a vibrant area, and for anyone who likes going underground one of the highlights (or should that be lowlights?) is a tour of the Victoria Tunnel. Visitors can experience the chilling sounds of a World War II air raid and follow the guides down to discover the tunnel's role as a colliery waggonway. Listen out for the oncoming coal waggons.

Visitor information:

Wylam Brewery
South Houghton Farm,
Heddon-on-the-Wall,
Northumberland, NE15 0EZ
01661 853377
www.wylambrewery.co.uk
Brewery tours run Fri & Sat.
Tours must be pre-booked.

Heddon-on-the-Wall

NORTH EAST

Black Bull
Main Street, Wylam,
Northumberland,
NE41 8AB
01661 853112
www.blackbull-wylam.co.uk
🍺 4 (12 Fri–Sun)–11

Tyne Bar
Maling Street, Newcastle upon Tyne,
NE6 1LP
0191 265 2550
www.thetyne.com
🍺 12–11 (midnight Fri–Sat);
12–10.30 Sun

Victoria Tunnel
www.ouseburntrust.org.uk

Getting there and away: Heddon-on-the-Wall is accessible by bus from Newcastle.

94 🛢 👫

High House Farm brewery – and beautiful Northumberland

Would you like to walk where Roman legions walked, talked and tried to stop the Picts coming further south? Although the address might say Newcastle upon Tyne, High House's location is deeply rural and seemingly far away from the city lights and industrial might of Tyneside. This is former bandit country where, 1,000 years ago, the thin line of rocks and stones which marked one of the northernmost outposts of

Beautiful Northumbrian scenery at High House Farm

the invading Romans was built. And still, today, anyone walking or driving around the area will see tantalising glimpses of Hadrian's Wall, built to keep the northern barbarians away from the sophisticated Romans.

This is marvellous walking country, especially for anyone wanting to explore Hadrian's Wall Path National Trail.

About half a mile from Hadrian's Wall, High House Farm has a gentle three-mile walk through its rolling fields and woodland. It is a haven for wildlife. A stroll over the land gives the possibility of the sight of a fox or hare or even a roe deer. Overhead buzzards, kestrel and sparrowhawks soar over the fields and woodland on the lookout for small mammals or quail. Children will love it. Flowers seen include red campion, bluebells and harebells, meadow cranesbill, pilewort, Welsh poppies, mallow, red deadnettle and flax – not forgetting that the farm grows its own nettles, which are used in one of the brewery's seasonal beers. The brewery's Nettle Ale is a springtime special, which has a floral piquancy but no sting. The top leaves of young nettles are cut and used as a replacement for hops, a technique which would have been widely used before the almost universal adoption of hops.

Brewing began here in 2003. Farmer-turned-brewer Steve Urwin was desperate to find an alternative form of income for his 200-acre farm following the devastation of an outbreak of foot and mouth disease. A fourth generation farmer, he realised that for the farm to be sustainable for future generations he had to come up with something new. As he grew barley on his arable farm, he conceived the idea of emphasising the links between the farm and the glass by making his own beer from the malt made from his harvest.

Once the brewery was established Steve and his wife started to develop a

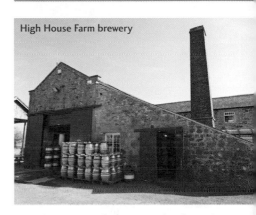

High House Farm brewery

visitor centre and shop on the farm. A coffee shop, a real ale bar and a space for selling local products, arts and crafts, followed. Visitors can see the malt loft and a short exhibition about the process of brewing, as well as the history of the farm. There is also plenty for the kids to do, with an outdoor play area and a children's room with lots of pets and toys to play with. Regular brewery tours are arranged by appointment. And should you fancy getting hitched in a brewery, the site even has a licence for wedding and civil ceremonies.

Visitor information:

Hadrian's Wall Path National Trail
 The website is an excellent resource for anyone wanting to walk all or part of the route.
 www.nationaltrail.co.uk/hadrianswall
High House Farm
 Matfen, Newcastle upon Tyne, Tyne & Wear, NE20 0RG
 01661 886192
 www.highhousefarmbrewery.co.uk
 🕐 Sun–Tue 10.30–5 (9 Thu–Sat); closed Wed
 Tours by arrangement

Getting there and away: High House Farm is off the A69 between Newcastle and Hexham.

Valley of the river Tweed, Peebleshire

Scotland

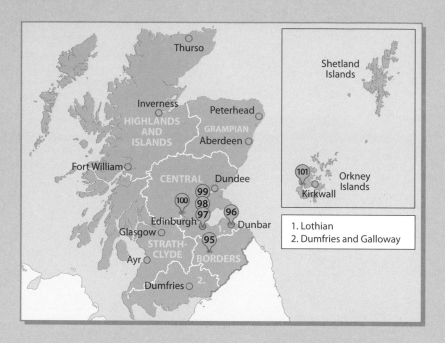

Map labels:
- Thurso
- Inverness
- HIGHLANDS AND ISLANDS
- Peterhead
- GRAMPIAN
- Aberdeen
- Fort William
- CENTRAL
- Dundee
- 100
- 99
- 98
- 97
- 96
- Edinburgh
- Dunbar
- Glasgow
- STRATH-CLYDE
- 95
- BORDERS
- Ayr
- 1.
- Dumfries
- 2.
- Shetland Islands
- 101
- Orkney Islands
- Kirkwall

1. Lothian
2. Dumfries and Galloway

Days Out

Introducing Scotland

Ring of Brodgar, Orkney

Scotland is the land of the thistle and the heather. It is a country of loch and lowland, highland and rolling moors, rich in lore, scenery and culture. It is a rugged place which oozes atmosphere and romance.

Although it has been part of the UK for almost three centuries, it is rightly, fiercely independent, with its own history and culture. It is also home to some of Britain's finest and most historic pubs. Scotland has its own clearly identifiable brewing heritage and a great beer festival, where the nation celebrates the genius of its brewers. The Scottish brewing scene has never been more geographically or stylistically diverse than it is today. Breweries stretch from the Borders up to Shetland. Once the brewers predominated in the south, close to the centres of population, where each day thousands of men worked in shipyards, mines, and hot and noisy factories. Beer was liquid bread, which nourished and rehydrated generations of workers. Over time, brewing became an industrial process on a massive scale, and the art and craft of the brewer were set aside as companies rushed to maximise production.

In the 1950s and 1960s there was a terrible cull of many fine breweries, with some classic beers becoming distant ghostly memories. But in the 1980s a small group of pioneers sought to resurrect Scotland's proud brewing heritage. Today those early pathfinders have become part of a larger movement, perhaps inspired by the Slow Food revolution, with breweries springing up the length and breadth of the country. Many are proud to be using barley grown in Scotland and they are taking brewing to parts of the country where once whisky makers predominated. Today there are more brewers in Scotland than distillers, and some claim that beer in all its styles and colours is now the nation's favourite drink.

There are many more breweries in Scotland than listed here and many more places where they can be enjoyed. Check out CAMRA's *Good Beer Guide* for more on Scotland's booming brewing and pub scene. Be assured that to enjoy a beer in Scotland is to embrace some of the greatest attributes of the Scottish nation – freedom, independence and a desire to enjoy the finer things of life, not least good beers and fine conversation in a well-run bar or pub.

SCOTLAND

95 🛢 👪

Traquair House – Stuart brewery conjures up a modern classic

Dating back to 1107, Traquair House, near the town of Peebles, south of Edinburgh, is the oldest inhabited house in Scotland and is a worthy destination for any visitor. Brewing began here in the early part of the 18th century on a very local scale when it produced beers for the house and the estate's workers. In those days, a brewhouse was as important as a kitchen at a property like this. It fell into disuse some time in the 1800s, however; the vessels remained in place, gathering dust until, in 1965, Peter Maxwell Stuart, 20th Laird of Traquair, decided to revive the tradition and produce a beer, not just for consumption by the household but also for sale to by visitors to the house. He set to work using the equipment

which had lain unused for more than 100 years. Today, the brewery is run by his daughter, Catherine Maxwell Stuart. It is said that, were a brewer from the 18th century to return to the brewhouse, they would be immediately able to get down to work, as so little of the equipment has changed. Indeed, so little of the house is changed that, should Alexander I, the king of Scotland from 1107–1124, return to it, much of it would be recognisable to him.

The house has been in the ownership of the Maxwell Stuarts since 1491, and the family are members of the Stuart clan. They say that the main entrance, the Bear Gates, shut in 1745 after Bonnie Prince Charlie visited the house during the Jacobite uprising, will remain firmly closed until a Stuart returns to the throne. Thankfully, there are other ways of getting into the house than through these gates. Much of the house is on view, including a museum complete with very early wall decorations. In one wing there is a chapel, opened in 1829 after Catholic worship could legally be practiced again in Scotland. There are four craft workshops, and around the back of the house there is an intriguing

The imposing Traquair House, complete with brewery

hedged maze, built in 1981. Covering more than half an acre, it is a ¼ mile walk to reach the centre. At certain times of the year Catherine Maxwell Stuart, the 21st Lady of Traquair, takes people on a personal tour of the house, when there is a chance to sample some of its famous beers. The brewery is best known for its Traquair House Ale, a hearty 7% abv brew. A tawny, dark colour with a sweet sherry flavour, it is fermented in unlined oak vessels before being stored in metal casks for two or three months. Enjoy it, it is a world classic. The beers can by bought in the estate's shop.

Belhaven brewery

96

Dunbar – a brewery tour and a tale from the American War of Independence

About an hour's car ride east of Edinburgh is the historic coastal town of Dunbar. Set on a rocky headland just inside the Scottish border, it is a tranquil resort town of sandstone buildings and broad sandy beaches. It also has a brewing heritage which rivals anything in Britain as, on the southeastern edge of the town is Scotland's oldest continuously-working brewery, Belhaven, now owned by Greene King.

Documents show that commercial brewing began here in 1719, but visitors taking one of the regular tours of the brewery will learn that there was brewing here well before the 18th century. Its ale was supplied to the Franco-Scottish expeditionary force garrisoned at Dunbar Castle in the 1550s, and long before that, brewing activity by monks in the 12th century is recorded.

The two-hour tour of the working brewery ends in traditional brewery tour fashion with a tasting of the beers. Depending on the weather, the tasting could either be outside in the Monks' Garden or inside in the Monks' Retreat. Scotch ales such as Belhaven's are sweet and full-bodied, with malt and roast malt flavours predominating. It is a style which has won Belhaven many plaudits. The 18th-century diarist James Boswell described it as the 'the best small beer I ever had'. In 1837 the Emperor of Austria, Franz Joseph I, selected a

SCOTLAND

Belhaven beer for his cellar, describing it as the Burgundy of Scotland.

About a mile from the brewery is one of the tiny town's harbours. From here walkers can follow part of the John Muir Way, a continuous path which extends for almost 73 kilometres, linking East Lothian with the city of Edinburgh and the Scottish Borders. The path is named after the town's most famous son; Muir migrated to America in the 1830s and is renowned in America as the father of conservation and the founder of the American National Park system. The Dunbar part of the trail, towards Belhaven Bay, is about 3 kilometres long and has spectacular views over the Firth of Forth towards the 100-metre-high Bass Rock, a nature reserve and nesting ground for over 100,000 gannets each summer. At the mouth of the harbour are the ruins of Dunbar Castle, built on a rock which historians say has been fortified for at least 2,000 years. The ruins currently visible are thought to date back to the 15th and 16th centuries, and were built to protect the strategically important harbour. At the east end of the harbour is another fort and battery, this one from the 18th century, built at a time when marauding privateers were particularly active during the American War of Independence. In September 1779 Captain John Paul Jones, Scots-born founder of the American navy, decided to stage a raid. He fired a salvo into the town, but it did little more than rattle a few beer glasses in some bars; returning fire from the town's defences swiftly bought the action to an end.

The reward for a good walk should always be the pint at the end. Close to the harbour is the Volunteer Arms, a cosy, community local. It is decorated with lots of seafaring memorabilia and normally sells a couple of real ales from smaller brewers. Upstairs is a restaurant serving excellent good-value meals with an emphasis on seafood – just what you need after that bracing sea air.

Visitor information:

Belhaven
Spott Road, Dunbar, East Lothian,
EH42 1RS
01368 869200
www.belhaven.co.uk
Brewery tours run Mon–Fri and must be booked in advance. £5.00 (£3.00 concessions)
Volunteer Arms
17 Victoria Street, Dunbar, East Lothian, EH42 1HP
01368 862278
🕐 12–11 (midnight Thu; 1am Fri & Sat); 12.30–midnight Sun

Getting there and away: Dunbar rail station is 15 minutes walk from the Belhaven brewery.

97 🪧

Edinburgh – three of the Scottish capital's finest pubs

There is really only one way to get around the centre of Edinburgh – walking. It is the best way to enjoy the city's fine architecture, real ales and some of the most spectacular pub interiors in Britain. With so many fine pubs, it seems unfair to choose only three, but they are all close to the city's main artery, Princes Street, and they give a taste of what this World Heritage city, with its sense of style, history and elegance, has to offer. Above it all stands the castle, securely built on its own volcanic rock at the top of the Royal Mile. Here can be viewed the Scottish crown jewels and the Stone of Destiny on which Scottish Monarchs are crowned.

The stylish Café Royal

The Café Royal is one of the crowning glories of the city's pub scene. Its interior is as elegant as the city of Edinburgh itself and one of the best in Scotland. Surrounded by original stained-glass windows, Victorian plasterwork, a stunning marble floor and six Doulton ceramic murals featuring famous inventors it is easy to be transported back and imagine the excitement in the city when it first opened on its current site in 1863. Old it might be, but the beers served from the impressive oval island bar, with its ornate brass light fittings are anything but. The beer range reflects the diversity of Scotland's now dynamic brewing scene. Expect to find beers from Caledonian, Harviestoun, Inveralmond and Kelburn.

Almost next door is the Guildford Arms. A large handsome building, it too has architecturally much to recommend it. Built in a golden era of Victorian pub design the opulent, high ceilings and Rococo friezes and cornices are spectacular. Upstairs there is a small modern restaurant and a balcony that offers a fine view of the main bar. But it is the beers that really star, with many from the new wave of Scottish microbrewers. Once Scottish beers were renowned for being dark, malty and sweet, but today's generation of ale creators have discovered hops, and lots of them. One such is Fyne's Avalanche. A golden blond ale, its nose is dominated by citrus lemon flavours which give way to a long, satisfying bittersweet grapefruit finish.

After the dazzling architecture of the first two bars, the Oxford Bar seems almost prosaic. It is a small, plain, no-frills drinking den that has survived from the early 19th century. It is famed for being one of the favourite pubs of Inspector Rebus and his creator, Ian Rankin. Indeed, it has a wide reputation amongst Scottish writers and artists. The front bar has no tables or seats, save a couple of window benches and some stools by the bar. Most people prefer to stand, but some go up the steps to a larger sitting room. You could describe the bar as austere, but that is to be unimaginative; the bar is made rich by the characters that drink here and the vitality of the beer. A regular ale is Cairngorm Trade Winds. Light golden in colour, the high proportion of wheat used in the grist gives it a crisp

SCOTLAND

clean fresh taste. A massive citrus and elderflower nose from the Perle hops gives way to a long, lingering bitter finish. Outside, Princes Street, with its connections to most anywhere in the city, is not far away.

Visitor information:

Café Royal
19 West Register Street, Edinburgh, EH2 2AA
0131 556 1884
www.caferoyal.org.uk
🍺 11 (12.30 Sun)–11 Sun (midnight Thu, 1am Fri & Sat); 12.30–11 Sun

Guildford Arms
1 West Register Street, Edinburgh, EH2 2AA
0131 556 4312
www.guildfordarms.com
🍺 11–11 (midnight Fri & Sat)

Oxford Bar
8 Young Street, Edinburgh, EH2 4JB
0131 539 7119
www.oxfordbar.com
🍺 11–midnight; 12.30–11 Sun

Getting there and away: Edinburgh Waverley rail station is 5 minutes walk from the Café Royal.

98 🛢

A tour of Edinburgh's Caledonian Brewery – a story defined by fire

When the brewery was first opened in 1869, Lorimer & Clark's Caledonian Brewery had more than 40 brewing neighbours in the Edinburgh. Today the Caley, as it is known, is the sole survivor in this city which was renowned for the quality of its water from wells deep underground – wells known as the charmed circle. Edinburgh's alias, Auld Reekie, is said by some to refer to the time when the air would be filled with the smoke from the breweries' chimneys. A tour of the brewery (which needs to be booked in advance) takes about 90 minutes, and begins in the Heritage Centre, before moving on to see the mash tun, coppers and fermenters.

Fire has defined the brewery since it opened. An inferno killed the father of the brewery's founder, George Lorimer, who returned to Edinburgh from London and decided to use his inheritance to build a brewery. In recent times two calamitous blazes nearly saw the brewery closed. And it is flames which contribute to the brewery's distinctively flavoured beers, as the brewery's copper kettles are direct-fired. Caledonian is the only large brewer in Britain to heat the wort in this way, though these days gas is used rather than coal to generate the heat. Brewers at the Caley say this gives the beer a flavour that cannot be achieved with stainless steel and steam heat, as the flames concentrate their energy onto the rolling, boiling wort.

The brewery also still uses whole hops rather than pellets, which are said to add to the intensity of flavours.

The company's best-known brew is Deuchars IPA, the first Scottish beer to be crowned CAMRA's Champion Beer of Britain. A refreshing, crisp beer, it is full of citrus hop flavours which are balanced by some fruit and pleasing butterscotch flavours. Another beer you will be offered to sample is the company's 80/- (80 shilling). In Scotland, beer was categorised by the amount of tax paid on it – the higher the number, the stronger the beer. So the classic Scottish ale is often referred to as an 80/-, while a stronger ale would be known as a 90/- (90 shilling), or Wee Heavy. Sadly, there are few examples of these beers around anymore. Caley's 80/- is a malty brown beer, with hints of dark sugar, while a little touch of hop gives a soft bitterness to the finish.

Visitor information:

Caledonian Brewery
542 Slateford Road, Edinburgh,
EH11 1PH
0131 337 1286
www.caledonianbeer.com
Brewery tours cost from £12 and
must be booked in advance

Getting there and away: Buses 4, 34, 35 and 44/44A connect the city centre and the Caledonian Brewery.

99

Scottish Real Ale Festival – a celebration of Celtic brews

In June, Scotland reels and flings itself into the country's greatest celebration of real ale. The great city of Edinburgh is the location for CAMRA's three-day extravaganza, celebrating the thriving brewing scene in Scotland. The Scottish Real Ale Festival and Champion Beer of Scotland competition bring together under one roof beer fans and lip-smacking brews from most of the country's new wave of brewers.

Micro-brewed real ales packed with flavour are starting to predominate in a country where once bland keg beers and lager ruled. The big brewers have all but pulled out of Scotland, but in their place have sprung up more than 40 microbreweries. Diversity is now the order of the day and IPAs, blond ales, heather beers, stouts and porters with a local twist have taken their place on the bar. Beers have become local, and taste and aroma have moved to the top of the glass. Scotland has an unrivalled reputation for the life-enhancing properties of its water and its whisky; now it is becoming known worldwide by the fans of hops and ales for its tasty aromatic brews. Where once Scotland was renowned for the innovation of its engineers, it is now becoming feted for its creative brewers.

Ten years ago the number of micros in Scotland could be counted on the fingers of two hands. Today, the numbers are increasing and many are expanding. There are organic, environmentally sensitive, peat-flavoured, vegan and vegetarian beers. Some beers are produced using ancient recipes with ingredients foraged from the hedgerows, others are at the cutting edge of a worldwide brewing revolution that is developing new styles, tastes and aromas. And it is this diversity that is portrayed at this Scottish showcase for the nation's dynamic and growing beer scene. From the Hebrides down to the Borders, Scottish beer is booming. The 2011 Champion Beer of Scotland was the Isle of Skye brewery's Cuillin Beast, chosen

Scottish Real Ale Festival

from more than 150 beers present. A 7% abv strong old ale, it is warm, sweet and fruity, and much more drinkable than the strength would suggest. It has plenty of caramel throughout, with a variety of fruit on the nose. No longer do Scottish beers fit into easily assimilated, bland styles. Today, many are hoppy, dry and fulsome; some are refreshing, zesty and full of grapefruit flavours. These are beers worthy of worldwide attention, and once a year they can be found at the Scottish Real Ale Festival.

Visitor information:

Scottish Real Ale Festival
www.sraf.org.uk
Held Thu–Sat in mid June. Check the website for venue information and dates.

100 ≣
Alloa – a historic brewing town

Alloa is in the Central Lowlands of Scotland and lies on the north bank of the Firth of Forth, close to the foot of the Ochil Hills. Once, Alloa was a famed brewing town which rivalled Burton on Trent. With more than nine flourishing breweries, its beers were sent to all four corners of the British Empire. Its good water, supplies of local barley and riverside location made it an ideal port for sending beer far afield. But, by 1999, only one brewery was left, the Forth Brewery, which was saved from certain extinction in 2003 by Scott and Bruce Williams of Williams Brothers Brewing. The Williams brothers' first brewing venture was the Heather Ale Company in 1992, when they began to market their ale, Fraoch, brewed with heather (fraoch being Gaelic for heather). The historic recipe, written in Gaelic, came to Bruce some years earlier when he was running a homebrew shop in Glasgow. According to the story, the recipe was for Leanne Fraoch or Heather Ale. It was given to him by a woman whose goal was to try and recreate a recipe made famous by the old legend of a Pictish king; he supposedly threw himself off a cliff after the Scottish king captured and tortured the Pictish king's son in an attempt to coax the recipe from him. The translated recipe was developed by Bruce Williams, at the time a home brewer, to the recipe that is used today.

The brewery, now called New Alloa Brewery, now produces five historic ales using ingredients from the earliest days of brewing. Ingredients are foraged from the hedges, woods, moors and seashore, while recipes are sourced from old manuscripts. Alba is a strong ale inspired by the Vikings, and its ingredients include sprigs of pine and spruce. Other beers come with even more unusual names. Grozet uses wheat, bog myrtle, hops and meadowsweet, and undergoes a secondary fermentation with Scottish gooseberries. Ebulum is inspired by a 16th-century recipe for elderberry ale. Another intriguing one is Kelpie, a dark ale brewed with organic barley and bladderwrack seaweed, giving a rich roasty, chocolate flavour and a salty finish. But it is Fraoch which has won the brothers the most plaudits, in which the flowering heather used instead of hops gives the beer its floral and peaty aromatic flavours.

The town's second-to-last brewery, Maclay's, is now a pub, the Old Brewery. And anyone with an interest in brewing architecture will soon spot the former brewery courtyard where once casks would have been loaded onto drays. The original well is still there too, along with some of the former brewing rooms.

Outside of brewing, Alloa's greatest attraction is the medieval Alloa Tower, which has the reputation of being the largest surviving keep in Scotland. It belonged to the Erskine family, the Earls of Mar and Kellie, who were supporters of several Stuart monarchs who were unlucky enough to spend part of their early lives in the tower. The tower has been carefully restored and you can go and admire the oak-beamed roof and the tower's dungeon.

Five miles away, in the nearby town of Alva, is the Harviestoun Brewery. Its award-winning brews, which include Bitter & Twisted and Schiehallion, can all bought from its shop.

Alloa Tower

Visitor information:

Williams Brothers Brewing
New Alloa Brewery,
Kelliebank,
Alloa,
Clackmannanshire,
FK10 1NT
01259 725511
www.williamsbros
brew.com
Tours by
arrangement

Old Brewery
East Vennel, Alloa,
Clackmannanshire,
FK10 1ED
01259 722 722
www.oldbrewery.net
🍺 11–midnight (2am Fri & Sat)

Haviestoun Brewery
Alva Industrial Estate, Alva,
Clackmannanshire, FK12 5DQ
01259 769100
www.harviestoun.com
Tours by arrangement

Getting there and away: Alloa rail station is 10 minutes walk from the Old Brewery.

101

Orkney – the mysterious Ring of Brodgar and some fine real ale too

Orkney Brewery

Beyond Britannia, where the infinite ocean opens, lies Orkney. We are off the northern tip of Scotland, where the North Sea and the Atlantic Ocean collide. Here, a group of 70 islands are dotted around the biggest one, known as the mainland – Orkney. The near-treeless islands are peppered with ancient remains, and are nowadays home to many creative craft workers turning clay into pots, bashing silver into jewellery and weaving cloth into fine garments. It is in addition a haven for cyclists, walkers, twitchers and trekkers. The big island is also the home to two of the most northerly of the UK's breweries – Orkney and Highland. For many years Scotland was regarded as place where real ale didn't go. It was said drinkers were wedded to kegged beers often chased by a dram of whisky or a tot of dark rum. But cask ale has taken

hold in Orkney, and the island boasts some well-kept real ale. Kirkwall, the capital, has some fine bars, including the Bothy Bar and the smart, modern Helgi's, which overlooks the harbour. Here drinkers sit in a cosy upstairs room and sip beers from the Orkney Brewery, while watching small ferries scurry to far-flung islands. Orkney is a land of long, light summer days and dark, lengthy winter nights. And the light and dark are reflected in the Orkney brewery's beer range. Northern Light is a light, golden ale, which is full of fruit from the hops and has an aroma that bursts with fresh tangerine vitality. It is countered by Dark Island, a ruby-black beer, which boasts coffee, chocolate and toffee flavours, swirling in harmony with lots of dry dark fruits. It is an old-style Scottish heavy beer, to which handfuls of chocolate malt have been added. Dark Island's label shows one of Orkney's most mysterious ancient sites, the standing stones of the Ring of Brodgar, which is probably more than 4,000 years old. It would be a crime not to visit it. Visitors can arrange a tour of the Orkney Brewery in Quoyloo, which is near the southern shore of the Bay o' Skaill, and also visit Skara Brae, a well-preserved stone village with a complex labyrinth of eight dwellings, complete with stone beds and built-in cupboards from Neolithic times. I bet somewhere they had a brewery too.

Many visitors spend their time on Orkney in Kirkwall, entranced by its cathedral and other attractions. But the atmospheric fishing town of Stromness is not far away. On the harbourside is the Hamnavoe bar in the Stromness Hotel. Here drinkers can try Highland Brewery's Scapa Special. Named after one of Britain's most historic stretches of water, it has been used by ships since prehistory, and is best known for the scuttling of the German battle fleet during World War I. You might be reminded of the scuttling when doing your own sinking of a pint of Scapa Special; the tastebuds are overwhelmed by its full, bitter dryness and the lingering dry aftertaste from the English hops. The hotel hosts several music and beer events and is intimately involved in the Orkney Folk festival in May.

Visitor information:

Bothy Bar (Albert Hotel)
Mounthoolie Lane, Kirkwall,
Orkney, KW15 1HW
01856 876000
www.alberthotel.co.uk
🍺 11 11.30 (midnight Fri & Sat);
12–11.30 Sun

Helgi's
14 Harbour Street, Kirkwall,
Orkney, KW15 1LE
01856 879273
www.helgis.co.uk
🍺 11–midnight (1am Fri & Sat);
12–midnight Sun

Orkney Brewery
Quoyloo, Stromness,
Orkney, KW16 3LT
01667 404555
www.orkneybrewery.co.uk
Tours by arrangement

Stromness Hotel
15 Victoria Street, Stromness,
Orkney, KW16 3AA
01856 850298
www.stromnesshotel.com
🍺 12–midnight
(11–1am Thu–Sat); 12.30–11 Sun

Highland Brewery
Swannay Brewery, Swannay,
Orkney, KW17 2NP
01856 721700
www.highandbrewerycompany.co.uk
Tours by arrangement

Getting there and away: Orkney is accessible by air from Aberdeen, Edinburgh, Glasgow and Inverness, and by sea from Aberdeen and Scrabster.

The Ring of Brodgar, one of many ancient sites on Orkney

Pubs index

General index

Index by theme

Books for beer lovers

CAMRA Books, the publishing arm of the Campaign for Real Ale, is the leading publisher of books on beer and pubs. Key titles include:

CAMPAIGN
FOR
REAL ALE

Good Beer Guide 2012
Editor: Roger Protz

The *Good Beer Guide* is the only guide you will ever need to find the right pint, in the right place, every time. It's the original and best-selling guide to around 4,500 pubs throughout the UK. Now in its 39th year, this annual publication is a comprehensive and informative guide to the best real ale pubs in the UK, researched and written exclusively by CAMRA members and fully updated every year.
£15.99   ISBN 978-1-85249-286-1

Great British Pubs
Adrian Tierney-Jones

Great British Pubs is a celebration of the British pub. This fully illustrated and practical book presents the pub as an ultimate destination – featuring pubs everyone should seek out and make a visit to. It recommends a selection of the very best pubs in various different categories, as chosen by leading beer writer Adrian Tierney-Jones. Every kind of pub is represented, with full-colour photography helping to showcase a host of excellent pubs from the seaside to the city and from the historic to the ultra-modern. Articles on beer brewing, cider making, classic pub food recipes, traditional pub games and various other aspects of pub life are included to help the reader truly appreciate what makes a pub 'great'.
£14.99   ISBN 978-1-85249-265-6

London's Best Beer, Pubs & Bars
Des de Moore

London's Best Beer, Pubs & Bars is the essential guide to beer drinking in London. This practical book is packed with detailed maps and easy-to-use listings to help you find the best places to enjoy perfect pints in the capital. Laid out by area, find the best pubs serving the best British and international beers wherever you are. Features tell you more about London's rich history of brewing and the city's vibrant modern brewing scene. The venue listings include a variety of real ale pubs, bars and other outlets with information on opening hours, local landmarks, and public transport links.
£12.99   ISBN 978-1-85249-285-4

South East Pub Walks
Bob Steel

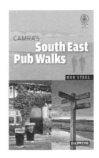

CAMRA's *South East Pub Walks* helps you to explore the beautiful countryside of the South Eastern corner of England, whilst never straying too far from a great pint. A practical, pocket-sized guide to some of the best pubs and best walking in the South East, this guide features 30 walks of varying lengths, all accessible by public transport and aimed at both the casual walker and more serious hiker. Each route has been selected for its unique and varied landscape, and its beer – with the walks taking you on a tour of the best real ale pubs the area has to offer.

£9.99   ISBN 978-1-85249-287-8

Lake District Pub Walks
Bob Steel

A pocket-sized, traveller's guide to some of the best walking and best pubs in the Lake District. The 30 walks are grouped by region around tourist hubs with plenty of accommodation, making the book ideal for a visitor to the Lakes. The book is fully illustrated, with clear Ordnance Survey mapping and written directions to help readers navigate the routes. *Lake District Pub Walks* also explores some of the region's fascinating historical and literary heritage as well as its thriving brewing scene, and has useful information about local transport and accommodation.

£9.99   ISBN 978-1-85249-271-7

300 Beers to Try Before You Die!
Roger Protz

300 beers from around the world, handpicked by award-winning journalist, author and broadcaster Roger Protz to try before you die! A comprehensive portfolio of top beers from the smallest microbreweries in the United States to family-run British breweries and the world's largest brands. This book is indispensible for both beer novices and aficionados.

£12.99   ISBN 978-1-85249-273-1

Order these and other CAMRA books online at www.camra.org.uk/books, ask at your local bookstore, or contact: CAMRA, 230 Hatfield Road, St Albans, AL1 4LW. Telephone 01727 867201

A Campaign of Two Halves

Campaigning for Pub Goers & Beer Drinkers

CAMRA, the Campaign for Real Ale, is an independent not-for-profit, volunteer-led consumer group. We campaign tirelessly for good-quality real ale and pubs, as well as lobbying government to champion drinkers' rights and promote local pubs as centres of community life. As a CAMRA member you will have the opportunity to campaign to save pubs under threat of closure, for pubs to be free to serve a range of real ales at fair prices and for a reduction in beer duty that will help Britain's brewing industry survive.

Enjoying Real Ale & Pubs

CAMRA has over 140,000 members from all ages and backgrounds, brought together by a common belief in the issues that CAMRA deals with and their love of good quality British beer. From just £23 a year – that's less than a pint a month – you can join CAMRA and enjoy the following benefits:

Subscription to *What's Brewing*, our monthly colour newspaper, and *Beer*, our quarterly magazine, informing you about beer and pub news and detailing events and beer festivals around the country.

Free or reduced entry to over 160 national, regional and local beer festivals.

Money off many of our publications including the *Good Beer Guide*, the *Good Bottled Beer Guide* and *CAMRA's Great British Pubs*.

Access to a members-only section of our national website, www.camra.org.uk, which gives up-to-the-minute news stories and includes a special offer section with regular features.

Special discounts with numerous partner organisations and money off real ale in your participating local pubs as part of our Pubs Discount Scheme.

Log onto www.camra.org.uk/join for CAMRA membership information.

Do you feel passionately about your pint? Then why not join CAMRA?

Just fill in the application form (or a photocopy of it) and the Direct Debit form on the next page to receive three months' membership FREE!*

If you wish to join but do not want to pay by Direct Debit, please fill in the application form below and send a cheque, payable to **CAMRA**, to: CAMRA, 230 Hatfield Road, St Albans, Hertfordshire, AL1 4LW. Please note than non Direct Debit payments will incur a £2 surcharge. Prices are given below.

Please tick appropriate box

	Direct Debit	Non Direct Debit
Single membership (UK & EU)	£23 ☐	£25 ☐
Concessionary membership (under 26 or 60 and over)	£15.50 ☐	£17.50 ☐
Joint membership	£28 ☐	£30 ☐
Concessionary joint membership (under 26 or 60 and over)	£18.50 ☐	£20.50 ☐

Life membership information is available on request.

Title _____ Surname _____

Forename(s) _____

Address _____

_____ Postcode _____

Email _____ Date of Birth _____

Signature _____

Partner's details (for Joint Membership)

Title _____ Surname _____

Forename(s) _____

Email _____ Date of Birth _____

CAMRA will occasionally send you e-mails related to your membership. We will also allow your local branch access to your email. If you would like to opt-out of contact from your local branch please tick here ☐ (at no point will your details be released to a third party).

Find out more about CAMRA at **www.camra.org.uk**   Telephone 01727 867201

CAMPAIGN FOR REAL ALE

*Three months free is only available the first time a member pays by Direct Debit

Instruction to your Bank or Building Society to pay by Direct Debit

CAMPAIGN FOR REAL ALE

Please fill in the form and send to: Campaign for Real Ale Ltd. 230 Hatfield Road, St. Albans, Herts. AL1 4LW

Name and full postal address of your Bank or Building Society

To The Manager   Bank or Building Society

Address

Postcode

Name (s) of Account Holder (s)

Bank or Building Society account number

Branch Sort Code

Reference Number

Banks and Building Societies may not accept Direct Debit Instructions for some types of account

Originator's Identification Number

9	2	6	1	2	9

FOR CAMRA OFFICIAL USE ONLY
This is not part of the instruction to your Bank or Building Society

Membership Number

Name

Postcode

Instruction to your Bank or Building Society

Please pay CAMRA Direct Debits from the account detailed on this Instruction subject to the safeguards assured by the Direct Debit Guarantee. I understand that this instruction may remain with CAMRA and, if so, will be passed electronically to my Bank/Building Society

Signature(s)

Date

✂ detached and retained this section

This Guarantee should be detached and retained by the payer.

The Direct Debit Guarantee

- This Guarantee is offered by all Banks and Building Societies that take part in the Direct Debit Scheme. The efficiency and security of the Scheme is monitored and protected by your own Bank or Building Society.

- If the amounts to be paid or the payment dates change CAMRA will notify you 10 working days in advance of your account being debited or as otherwise agreed.

- If an error is made by CAMRA or your Bank or Building Society, you are guaranteed a full and immediate refund from your branch of the amount paid.

- You can cancel a Direct Debit at any time by writing to your Bank or Building Society. Please also send a copy of your letter to us.